THE

Mississippi Quarterly

SERIES IN SOUTHERN LITERATURE

THE

Mississippi Quarterly

SERIES IN SOUTHERN LITERATURE

under the general editorship of

PEYTON W. WILLIAMS

THE FORM DISCOVERED

Essays on the Achievement of Andrew Lytle

M. E. BRADFORD, EDITOR

A FAULKNER MISCELLANY

JAMES B. MERIWETHER, EDITOR

WILLIAM FAULKNER'S *THE WILD PALMS*

THOMAS L. MCHANEY

WILLIAM FAULKNER'S *The Wild Palms*

WILLIAM FAULKNER'S
The Wild Palms

A STUDY

by
Thomas L. McHaney

UNIVERSITY PRESS OF MISSISSIPPI
JACKSON

Grateful acknowledgment is made to the following publishers for permission to quote from the works used in this study:

To Random House, Inc., for permission to quote from the copyrighted works of William Faulkner and from the following copyrighted works: *The Achievement of William Faulkner*, by Michael Millgate, *Lion in the Garden: Interviews with William Faulkner, 1926–1962*, edited by James B. Meriwether and Michael Millgate, *Faulkner—A Biography*, by Joseph Blotner, *The Selected Poetry of Robinson Jeffers* and *The Autobiography of Alice B. Toklas*, by Gertrude Stein.

To Alfred A. Knopf, Inc., for permission to quote from *The Wagner Operas*, by Ernest Newman.

To Pantheon Books, a Division of Random House, Inc., for permission to quote from *Love Declared*, by Denis de Rougemont, translated by Richard Howard.

To Chatto & Windus, Ltd., for permission to quote from *Go Down, Moses, The Hamlet, Intruder in the Dust, The Mansion, Requiem for a Nun, The Unvanquished, The Wild Palms*, and *Faulkner—A Biography*.

To the University of North Carolina Press, for permission to quote from *The Memoirs of Sherwood Anderson, A Critical Edition*, edited by Ray Lewis White.

To Liveright Publishing Co., for permission to quote from Sherwood Anderson's *Dark Laughter*, and from *Mosquitoes*.

To Yale University Press, for permission to quote from *William Faulkner: The Yoknapatawpha Country*, by Cleanth Brooks.

To the University Press of Virginia, for permission to quote from *Faulkner in the University*.

To P. G. Wodehouse for permission to quote from *Company for Henry*, by P. G. Wodehouse.

To Curtis Brown, Ltd., for permission to quote from *Absalom, Absalom!, Light in August*, and *Sanctuary*.

To Mary E. Parkin, executor for the late Ernest Newman, for permission to quote from *The Wagner Operas*.

To Charles Scribner's Sons for permission to quote from Ernest Hemingway's *A Farewell to Arms*.

Chapter One appeared in a slightly different form in *PMLA* and is reprinted by permission of the Modern Language Association of America from that journal, Vol. LXXXVII (May 1972), pp. 465–74.

THIS VOLUME IS AUTHORIZED
AND SPONSORED BY
MISSISSIPPI STATE UNIVERSITY
MISSISSIPPI STATE, MISSISSIPPI

To the memory of
Robert B. Holland
and
Scott C. Osborn

The
Mississippi Quarterly
Series
in Southern Literature

Mississippi Quarterly: The Journal of Southern Culture, as its title implies, is an interdisciplinary journal dealing with all aspects of the life and civilization of the American South; it is now in its twenty-sixth year of publication under the sponsorship of Mississippi State University. For many years, and with increasing distinction, the Quarterly has given major attention to Southern writers of all periods by publishing critical and scholarly articles, bibliographies, edited source materials, letters and reviews; by sponsoring symposia; and by publishing numerous special issues each concerned with the work of a single Southern author. This year, in conjunction with Mississippi State University and the University Press of Mississippi, it is initiating a series of volumes to be designated The *Mississippi Quarterly* Series in Southern Literature. The plan includes a general series, of which *The Form Discovered: Essays on the Achievement of Andrew Lytle* has already appeared; a sub-series on William Faulkner, of which *William Faulkner's The Wild Palms* is the second volume; and a second sub-series of bibliographical studies. The general series is intended to include editions of significant source materials for the study of Southern letters as well as further general critical and scholarly works.

Contents

Acknowledgments

I WISH TO THANK James B. Meriwether for fifteen years of excellent instruction, good example, and friendship; he has created most of my opportunities, and I hope I have made the best of them. Michael Millgate read an early version of this study and provided a number of valuable suggestions for it and for a subsequent version of the first chapter; I am as grateful for his continued help as I am for his excellent book on William Faulkner. Professor Morse Peckham read the manuscript at an early stage and contributed an insight which, I hope, has proved even more valuable through elaboration. I have been helped by the suggestions of Keen Butterworth, George Ellison, Stephen E. Meats, and Noel Polk. The University of South Carolina Department of English and its former chairman, Dr. John C. Guilds, provided generous financial assistance and a stimulating milieu for the original work which has culminated in this book. Georgia State University has aided my research and writing with financial assistance and released time. Students in undergraduate and graduate classes at Georgia State have stimulated and refined the criticism offered in this study, and they have not infrequently pointed the way to new insights. Kathy Cripe was very generous with her time and energy during proofreading.

Mrs. Jill Faulkner Summers, literary executor of the Faulkner estate, has kindly given permission for examination and use of manuscript materials in the Faulkner Collections at the University of Virginia. The staffs of the manuscripts room and the rare books room at the Alderman Library, University of Virginia, have been unfailing in their courtesy and professional help during my visits there. The late Linton Massey, who helped make the great Virginia collection, has also helped me and is due my thanks. My wife, Karen, has participated in all stages of this work; it would not have been done without her.

Introduction

If I forget thee, O Jerusalem, let my right hand forget her cunning.
If I do not remember thee, let my tongue cleave to the roof of my mouth; if I prefer not Jerusalem above my chief joy.
Psalm 137:5–6

WILLIAM FAULKNER'S ELEVENTH NOVEL, *The Wild Palms* (1939), originally had a title paraphrased from the 137th psalm, "If I Forget Thee, Jerusalem." During copy-editing at the publishers, apparently, Faulkner's title was removed by editorial fiat and replaced by what had been the subtitle designating the main plot of the book, the love story "The Wild Palms." [1] This substitution perceptibly altered the immediate effect of the novel; and although it was not the only factor that delayed understanding of one of Faulkner's most important books, the retitling was the first of a series of arbitrary and unnecessary changes that affected the book's reception and directed attention away from Faulkner's artistry. [2] "If I Forget Thee, Jerusalem" comes from a psalm about the Babylonian captivity; it is an admonition to remember freedom and the past. The whole psalm pro-

---

EPIGRAPH: King James Version. The complete psalm has numerous passages which are relevant to *The Wild Palms* and should be read. Isaiah 49:15–16, which Faulkner probably also knew, is applicable to the novel: "Can a woman forget her sucking child, that she should not have compassion on the son of her womb? yea, they may forget, yet will I not forget thee. Behold, I have graven thee upon the palms of my hands; thy walls are continually before me."

[1] In the spring of 1957, Saxe Commins, then Faulkner's editor at Random House, told James B. Meriwether about changing the title and the convict's last speech. It was done, he indicated, very much against Faulkner's wishes.

[2] See the textual appendix to Thomas L. McHaney, "William Faulkner's *The Wild Palms*: A Textual and Critical Study" (Ph.D. dissertation, University of South Carolina, 1968), for a full discussion of the more than 650 changes between typescript and published book.

xiii

Introduction

vides a rich context of imagery and theme, underscoring the importance of hands and cunning and the preciousness of memory; emphasizing captivity; and explicitly bridging the two disparate tales which
make up the novel. Unlike the substituted title, which refers to the
main plot alone, the original title announces the unity of the book. It
also carries an allusion to one of Faulkner's favorite novels, *The
Brothers Karamazov*, in which Psalm 137 is glossed in a manner that
directly parallels Faulkner's own use of the paraphrase.

If the editing and publishing of the book was bad, the subsequent
history of *The Wild Palms* was perhaps worse. The way it was later
published only added to the confusion regarding the novel's integrity.
For all its textual faults, the hard-cover text originally issued by Random House in 1939 presented the novel in the contrapuntal form in
which it had been written, alternating the love story with the subordinate river story. But in 1946 Malcolm Cowley removed "Old
Man" and, with further unauthorized emendation, put it into the
Viking *Portable Faulkner*. Cowley's justification was the belief that
Faulkner was at his best as a writer of "long stories that can be written
in one burst of energy, like 'The Bear' and 'Spotted Horses' and 'Old
Man.' " [3] Critically and biographically incorrect, Cowley's statement
reflects the outdated view of Faulkner as a primitive genius capable
only of inspired creative dashes and *tours de force*. The critic unknow-
ingly gave himself the lie when he picked the texts for his anthology.
He included not "long stories that can be written in one burst of
energy" but episodes from complex novels—*Go Down, Moses* and
The Hamlet and *The Wild Palms*—which had been carefully con-
structed to fit the texture of large fictional schemes.[4]

The unfortunate pattern was established. In 1948, the New American Library issued *The Old Man*, an incorrectly titled cheap edition

[3] *The Faulkner-Cowley File*, ed. Malcolm Cowley (New York: Viking, 1966),
23.
[4] Short story versions of "The Bear" and "Spotted Horses" existed, but
Cowley did not use them; "Old Man" as a separate story could end, Faulkner
wrote Cowley, with Chapter Four and the convict's return to the levee. See
Faulkner in the University, ed. Joseph Blotner and Frederick Gwynn (New
York: Vintage, 1965), 273, and *Faulkner-Cowley File*, 25, 26, 31.

xiv

of the secondary plot. Later the same year they put out a mistitled edition of the main plot alone called *The Wild Palms* (leaving the obvious impression, since Faulkner's original title had been scrapped, that this was the whole book). In 1954 they published a paperback containing both stories, but printed them separately, as if they were two unrelated short novels, instead of alternately, as they had been written.[5] In 1958, "Old Man" was published alone again in that mistitled Modern Library paperback *William Faulkner: Three Famous Short Novels*. The result was that most readers first came to only half of the novel in one of these divided texts, an experience that caused them to ignore altogether the question of Faulkner's meaning and the purpose of the intricately related plots.

It has taken more than three decades for Faulkner's book to be read as it was written. The results are remarkable, no particular thanks to the critic, since the meaning was there all along. It is a profound and moving and significant novel. In two complementary modes of expression, in two complexly related stories, Faulkner explores and dramatizes the ultimate questions of man's fate. What can man do in the face of the inevitable oblivion of death to which he and his kind are irrevocably doomed? What are the results and uses of suffering, freedom, human love? What does it mean to endure? to prevail? "If I Forget Thee, Jerusalem," as it was meant to be called, replies to these questions. Above all it is a work of art, another of Faulkner's perspectives on the human heart in conflict with itself; but it also presents a philosophy which Faulkner had approached gradually in the preceding novels of his most creative decade, a philosophy upon which he drew repeatedly in his fiction and public statements before and after 1939.

This study explores the ten sections of Faulkner's novel as he wrote it, from the original title down to the restoration of the last bowdlerized word. It attempts to preserve the order and suspense of the book,

[5] The physical evidence in Faulkner's manuscripts and typescript and his public statements about the writing of *The Wild Palms* reveal unmistakably that he conceived and executed "Old Man" as chapter-by-chapter counterpoint to the main plot of the novel. See the dissertation cited in note 2 above for elaboration.

Introduction

which is a suspense not merely of plot—after all, the story begins very
near the end of things—but of philosophical import. It follows and
explains Faulkner's strategies and tensions as they emerge and does
not always reveal the full meaning of an event, an image, or a formal
element until the full significance has been spun out. In "Faulkner as
Elegist" (*Hudson Review*, 1954), R. W. Flint wrote that "the novel
has moved toward the condition of poetry" and that Faulkner's fiction
"deserves to be called thoroughly composed, *durchcomponiert*, as the
Germans say of music." Nothing better illustrates the truth of Flint's
observation than the novel we know as *The Wild Palms*. As an illus-
tration and as prelude to the study which follows, I may mention three
major strata of allusion that lie beneath, and give structure and meaning to, the connected plots.

The often noted references to Ernest Hemingway's *A Farewell to
Arms* in *The Wild Palms* are part of a complex personal and biographical context which lies behind the composition of Faulkner's
novel. As Chapter One of this study shows, Faulkner brings in Hemingway, Sherwood Anderson, Anderson's second wife, and possibly
the girl to whom he had dedicated *Mosquitoes* in 1927. There are very
strong echoes of a comic novel which Faulkner attempted while he
was in Paris in 1925; "Elmer" and material associated with it seem to
represent Faulkner's first efforts to deal with the autobiographical
material he more successfully handled in *The Wild Palms*. While its
revelation does not necessarily change the way one reads *The Wild
Palms*, this biographical information does help unravel some of Faulkner's allusions and allows us to explore his techniques and the sources
of his inspiration in a way that has not generally been possible before.

Besides the biographical, another important stratum of allusion in
the book contributes not only to meaning but also to structure. Part
of the underpinning of *The Wild Palms* is the repeated evocation of
Dante's *Divine Comedy*.[6] This is not as thoroughgoing as, say, Joyce's

[6] *Light in August*, however, is the novel to which Carvel Collins refers in
"The Interior Monologues of *The Sound and the Fury*," where he notes that
Faulkner used *The Divine Comedy* for a major episode in a novel. That twenty
years elapsed without further word is perhaps due to the survival of attitudes
toward Faulkner's background and intellect like the one Collins mentions: "A

use of *The Odyssey* in *Ulysses*, but it is more than simple allusion. It, along with one of the philosophical contexts mentioned below, seems to be associated with an essay by Carl Jung which discusses the psychological and visionary modes of writing that Jung found in Dante, in Goethe's *Faust*, and in *Thus Spake Zarathustra*, for example. Whether or not Faulkner had seen Jung's "Psychology and Poetry" —and there is a good possibility that he had—the essay offers a number of insights into a discussion of the two-part structure of *The Wild Palms* and of the different styles of writing that Faulkner employs in "Wild Palms" and "Old Man." At the same time, Faulkner's unfinished "Elmer" also provides a clue to the design of *The Wild Palms*, in this instance a relation to the techniques of the impressionist and post-impressionist painters or to that part of the philosophy of Henri Bergson that was one of the post-impressionists' theoretical justifications. The stark juxtaposition of the two totally different plots of *The Wild Palms* is, in this regard, a natural development in Faulkner's long-term concern with structural innovation, and it can be seen, and better understood, in the context of what he had done in his earliest work—such as *Soldiers' Pay* or "Elmer"—and perfected in such novels as *The Sound and the Fury*, *As I Lay Dying*, and *Light in August*, to name only the most obvious.

The third, and perhaps most significant stratum is the philosophical. It is revealed in the middle of the book when the reporter McCord suggests that Harry Wilbourne has delivered an expression of Schopenhauerian pessimism. McCord is correct, and his profane apostrophe, "sweet Jesus Schopenhauer," draws the reader's eye to repeated allusions to *The World as Will and Idea*. The "tall convict," who finds life outside his open air prison more unbearable than life inside, reminds us that Schopenhauer calls the life of the Will a prison-house. The cyclic adventures of both convict and lovers underscore

---

scholar recently said at an academic convention that Faulkner could not have based a central episode of one of his novels on part of Dante's "Inferno" because Faulkner would never have read *The Divine Comedy* or any other large and difficult work, being a native of Mississippi." *English Institute Essays, 1952*, ed. Alan S. Downer (New York: Columbia University Press, 1954), 30.

Introduction

Schopenhauer's view that life is an endless cycle of pain and boredom to be escaped only by contemplation of the ideal, through art, or by retreat into the oblivion of will-lessness. Charlotte's married name, "Rittenmeyer"—it was originally "Rittlemeyer" in the typescript, but Faulkner altered it—plays on "Maya," the Hindu word which Schopenhauer (and Emerson, in his poem "Maia") borrowed to signify the veil of illusion masking primal reality. The masterpiece of Maya, Schopenhauer asserts, is love. Harry's surname, "Wilbourne," puns too. He has entered medicine because of a provision in his father's *will*; he finds himself *will*-less and at peace on the day he meets Charlotte; he drowns volition and *will* in her yellow eyes, swept away from security and peace, like the convict, by a force of Nature, in his case Love. Harry is a prisoner of love, shackled to Charlotte by her powerful grip on his wrist. Besides the pun on Schopenhauer's *World as Will* ... "Wilbourne" apparently alludes to a source in Hamlet's "to be or not to be" speech, an allusion that is important for the rejection of suicide which ends Harry's part of the novel:

> ... who would fardels bear,
> To grunt and sweat under a weary life,
> But that the dread of something after death,
> The undiscover'd country from whose *bourn*
> No traveller returns, puzzles the *will*
> And makes us rather bear those ills we have
> Than fly to others that we know not of? [italics added]
> *Hamlet*, III, i, 76–82

Harry rejects death, but not out of Hamlet's fear or doubt; Harry has come to understand that death is oblivion, and he decides to live because of the preciousness of his memories.

The reiterated theme of captivity and the premium on life and memory and freedom return attention to the original title from Psalms. There is an alternative to Schopenhauer's pessimism. There are two choices in the novel. But it is neither the psalmist nor Shakespeare who is the justification for the difference between the decisions made at the end by Harry and the tall convict. Their final acts, their final words, can be understood only by comparing the two stories and referring to Schopenhauer and to the philosopher who departed from his pessimism, Friedrich Nietzsche. Nietzsche's *Thus Spake Zarathustra* is reflected at several crucial points in *The Wild Palms* and paraphrased extensively and meaningfully in Harry's last scene. This is no hypothetical context: the passages in Faulkner are too close to the ones in Nietzsche to be accident or coincidence. And though it is possible that Harry's explanation of his relationship to Time in the middle of the book may owe something to the philosophy of Henri Bergson, which Faulkner admitted knowing, the contrast between Schopenhauer, who is invoked in the novel, and Nietzsche, who is paraphrased, provides the key to understanding Faulkner's concept of endurance as it is dramatized in *The Wild Palms*.

The quotations which head the chapters of this study point to important sources or analogues for *The Wild Palms*, but, like the preceding discussion of the main elements of allusion in the novel, they suggest only a little of what went to make Faulkner's novel. This study is not a Road to Xanadu (or Pascagoula) but a careful and thorough critical reading of *The Wild Palms* which has, incidentally, turned up a considerable amount of evidence of Faulkner's intentions, his sources, and even—it is cheerfully granted—the possibly unconscious complexities that resolve themselves into patterns of meaning. Every effort has been made to trust the teller *and* the tale, to use all the evidence available that provides insight into the background, the writing, the meaning of this very complicated and ambitious novel. We are no longer blinded to the Mississippian's intellectual and imaginative capacities by his ironic poses or by certain critical approaches. Aesthetically, Faulkner did not work in either a trance or a vacuum. He was a very conscious artist—conscious of the tradition in which he worked, which his curiosity expanded beyond prose fiction to include the graphic and plastic arts, music, and philosophy as useful sources, and conscious of his own achievement in the struggle to resolve method and meaning. In *The Wild Palms* there are scores of working allusions to the books and writers that Faulkner knew and liked best, as well as references to his previous work and foreshadowing of work to come. The explication of these things is contained within a broad

Introduction

consideration of the total artistry of *The Wild Palms*. There is some
repetition, but none, hopefully, which is unnecessary. *The Wild
Palms* is an intricate structure which can be understood only when
the interplay of form, theme, event, character, image and allusion is
closely observed. Writing on Eliot's *Four Quartets*, Harry Blamires
noted that "allusions, images, and arguments continually throw back
needful further illumination on what has already been said." It follows,
he added, "that the commentator cannot have his say about any given
passage and then mentally tick it off as he moves on to the next. The
guide must occasionally anticipate what has yet to be said . . . and he
must often go back to passages already dealt with, in order to complete their elucidation." [7] The two circular plots of Faulkner's novel
demand a similar attention. Blamires noted that the "throwback of
meaning and the forecasting of meaning are as consistently natural to
the poetic practice of Eliot in *Four Quartets* as they are to that of
Joyce in *Ulysses*." [8] It can be added, without a blush, that the process
is also natural to Faulkner, who learned much from the two older
writers. *The Wild Palms* can stand with the poetry of Eliot and the
fiction of Joyce, and it must be handled with the same critical thor-
oughness and care as their work. To judge from the autobiographical content alone, it is a book which meant a great deal to William
Faulkner at the time he wrote it. To judge from the philosophical development revealed within it, it is a book which is very important for
understanding his "life's work in the agony and sweat of the human
spirit . . . to create out of the materials of the human spirit something
which did not exist before." [9] The year *The Wild Palms* appeared,
Conrad Aiken was not afraid to rank it with *The Sound and the Fury*
as Faulkner's best book. And in a landmark article in appreciation of
Faulkner's seriousness, Warren Beck called it Faulkner's "most ab-

[7] Harry Blamires, *Word Unheard: A Guide Through Eliot's Four Quartets*
(London: Methuen & Co., 1969), 1.
[8] *Ibid.*
[9] William Faulkner, "Address upon Receiving the Nobel Prize for Literature,"
William Faulkner: Essays, Speeches and Public Letters, ed. James B. Meriwether (New York: Random House, 1965), 119.

stractly symbolic" story.[10] Modern criticism has begun to catch up with these two early commentators (both of them, significantly, writers themselves). The following study seeks to establish the complexity and the greatness of *The Wild Palms* unmistakably for everyone.

[10] Conrad Aiken, "William Faulkner: The Novel as Form," *Atlantic Monthly*, 164 (November 1939), 650–54; Warren Beck, "Faulkner's Point of View," *College English*, 2 (May 1941), 747.

WILLIAM FAULKNER'S *The Wild Palms*

Anderson, Hemingway, and the Origins of *The Wild Palms*

[Anderson] had to believe that, if only he kept that style pure, then what the style contained would be pure too, the best. That was why he had to defend the style. That was the reason for his hurt and anger at Hemingway about Hemingway's *The Torrents of Spring*, and at me in a lesser degree since my fault was not full book-length. . . . Neither of us—Hemingway or I—could have touched, ridiculed, his work itself.

WILLIAM FAULKNER
"A Note on Sherwood Anderson" (1953)

WITHOUT DENYING THAT *The Wild Palms* is first and always a complexly wrought, imaginative story of human passion and its consequences, we can see that it is many other things as well. The form of *The Wild Palms* reveals Faulkner's characteristic concern to seek new and effective narrative strategies, although to overemphasize its form as "experimental" is to fail to appreciate that bold formal innovations were a way of life for Faulkner—his writing was "experimental" as getting up in the morning can be experimental: each novel, like each day, brought new challenges and opportunities that Faulkner did not decline to accept. The themes and ideas in the novel demonstrably make up a philosophical substructure that reveals Faulkner's thinking about life and art at an important stage in its development, yet to claim *The Wild Palms* as primarily a philosophical or problem novel

EPIGRAPH: William Faulkner, "A Note on Sherwood Anderson," *Essays, Speeches and Public Letters*, ed. James B. Meriwether (New York: Random House, 1965), 6. [Essay first published in *Atlantic Monthly*, June 1953.]

is to misjudge Faulkner's motives as a novelist and to deny him the remarkably well-integrated artistic intellect he obviously possessed. We illuminate rather than distract attention from what is most important in a Faulkner novel when we uncover the often vast amount of interesting thoughts and subjects which may lie behind it. So it is also with some very personal matters that find their way into *The Wild Palms*.

In writing the novel about the paradox of human freedom and the preciousness of memory and love which he wanted to call "If I Forget Thee, Jerusalem," Faulkner apparently objectified in fictional terms or actually brought to the surface a number of biographical matters, embodying them in his contrapuntal tale not as "facts" of his emotional and physical life but as recurrent allusions, events, characters, and images that play thematic and other roles in the fiction he was spinning. When he began the book, he had endured a long, and recently more acute acquaintance with disappointment and frustration. A recent unsuccessful romantic entanglement apparently recalled an earlier debacle in love; his lack of commercial success made him contrast himself with the booming Ernest Hemingway; and tying these things together because of a number of associations was the memory and the sudden presence of Sherwood Anderson.

Sherwood Anderson's influence on William Faulkner and Ernest Hemingway and the role he played in the publication of their first books of fiction in America are well documented. Anderson's publisher, Boni and Liveright, brought out the expanded *In Our Time* in 1925 and Faulkner's *Soldiers' Pay* the following year. But by the spring of 1926, both young men had insulted Anderson and lost his friendship. In *The Torrents of Spring* (1926) Hemingway parodied Anderson's most recent novel, *Dark Laughter* (1925), and ridiculed his primer-like style; he wrote Anderson a series of high-handed letters to insure that his old benefactor understood that *Torrents*, with its "Red and Black Laughter," was a sock in the jaw and a well-deserved one at that.[1] For his part, Faulkner had prompted Anderson's dislike by mid-April 1926, a month before the Hemingway parody appeared; before the year

---

[1] Ray Lewis White, "Hemingway's Private Explanation of *The Torrents of Spring*," *Modern Fiction Studies*, 13 (1967), 261–63.

was out he too had parodied Anderson's style, in the preface to *Sherwood Anderson & Other Famous Creoles* (pub. New Orleans, 16 Dec. 1926), and used Anderson for the portrait of Dawson Fairchild in *Mosquitoes* (pub. 30 April 1927, but completed by 1 Sept. 1926).[2]

Apparently Hemingway never regretted his break with Anderson, but Faulkner made it plain throughout his career that he had meant Anderson no ill, continuing to express admiration for Anderson's best work and for his standards and vision as an artist.[3] Whatever had caused Anderson to write Horace Liveright in 1926 that Faulkner "was so nasty to me personally that I don't want to write him myself,"[4] he really had little room for complaint about Faulkner's parodies. He had already used Faulkner in his own writing, in the extended portrait of "A Meeting South" (*Dial*, April 1925) and possibly in *Dark Laughter*. Anderson, who knew Faulkner through Elizabeth Prall (for whom Faulkner had worked in a New York bookstore)[5] and who had swapped tales with the young Mississippi poet in New Orleans in 1925 while writing *Dark Laughter*, had not flattered Faulkner in his fictional portraits, but he had not been mean either; what he wrote corresponded to Faulkner's joking self-portraits during the same period: Cadet Lowe of *Soldiers' Pay* and the dirty Mr. Faulkner whom Jenny meets in the park in *Mosquitoes*. On the other side, *Sherwood Anderson & Other Famous Creoles* was recognized as innocent by the New Orleans literati whom the book described,[6] while Faulk-

[2] Publication dates from James B. Meriwether, *William Faulkner: A Checklist* (Princeton, N.J.: Princeton University Library, 1957).

[3] See Faulkner, "A Note on Sherwood Anderson," 3–10.

[4] Sherwood Anderson to Horace Liveright, 19 April 1926, in *Letters of Sherwood Anderson*, ed. Walter B. Rideout and H. M. Jones (Boston: Little, Brown, 1953), 155.

[5] Michael Millgate, *The Achievement of William Faulkner* (New York: Random House, 1966), 13–20. Faulkner apparently knew "Miss Elizabeth" through Stark Young, the native Oxfordian who was drama critic of the *New Republic*. Young, in turn, may have come to know Miss Prall through her brother David, a philosophy professor and aesthetician with whom Young had taught at the University of Texas, 1912–15. It would be worth knowing whether Faulkner ever met David Prall (1886–1940), ever talked philosophy or aesthetics with him, ever read any of Prall's books.

[6] The local reviewer wrote that there was not "a line drawn in malice in the whole collection," New Orleans *Times-Picayune Sunday Magazine*, 2 January 1927, p. 4.

ner's adaptation of Anderson into *Mosquitoes* only returned with interest what Anderson had done using Faulkner. If the characterization of Dawson Fairchild is not especially flattering, it is, like Anderson's sketches of Faulkner, very close to accurate, as Michael Millgate has noted.[7] It is certainly not vindictive. Anderson portrayed himself in his own fiction as a similarly frustrated, groping artist; he had done just such a self-portrait in Bruce Dudley of *Dark Laughter*. Caricature aside, in fact, *Mosquitoes* actually affirmed what Anderson had had to say in *Dark Laughter* about art and love, with several clear allusions to the way Anderson had said it. The similarities are important to themes and images that find their way into *The Wild Palms*, where the Anderson-Hemingway-Faulkner context recurs.

A strong theme in *Dark Laughter* is the inhospitality of American society to real love and to true artistic expression. The hero has abandoned his wife because she is sexually inhibited and an artistic phony, despite her status as a practicing member of Chicago's literary bohemia. Real human love is one of Bruce Dudley's goals, but his wife Bernice flees intimacy; he abandons her and subsequently makes love to a young woman who suffers frustrations like his own. He takes her away from her successful but dull husband, but, because she is pregnant, they must marry and go to live in Chicago, the city he had fled. As the novel closes, she is planning their domestic arrangements, which already resemble what he had had with Bernice, and the abandoned husband finds grim solace in remembering how much his wife had been accustomed to pay for her shoes. The prognosis for the new couple, and for a lasting love affair, is not good. Anderson's hero is never established as an artist. He has aspirations, and he writes a few poems, but as a Chicago newspaperman and as a laborer, he expresses only doubt or cynicism about art. His thoughts and observations on the subject carry the second important theme of *Dark Laughter*: he represents the frustrated American artist trying to find his materials, an approach to them, and a milieu in which to work. Recalling sights along the Mississippi, down which he has come in an open boat, he muses on Mark Twain's failure to write what he must have known, a

7 Millgate, *Achievement*, 72.

failure forced on Twain by America's stifling commercialism and her inhibiting morality,[8] the same forces that thwart real love. The restraints of a puritanical morality and the pressures and temptations of materialism destroy art as well as love. The artist becomes the commercialized dilettante; the lover becomes the conventional spouse.

Two years later in *Mosquitoes* Faulkner makes essentially the same point. His first paragraph introduces the theme of love: " 'The sex instinct,' repeated Mr. Talliaferro . . . 'is quite strong in me. Frankness, without which there can be no friendship, without which two people cannot really ever "get" each other, as you artists say; frankness . . . compels me to admit that the sex instinct is perhaps my most dominating compulsion.' "[9] A Prufrock figure given an ironic speech, Talliaferro is quite impotent and a strong contrast with the young sculptor to whom he is speaking. His speech seems to repeat a catchword of Anderson's and to reflect a passage from *Dark Laughter* where the hero recalls his wife's flights from direct sexual encounters, thinking "Had she stayed [in the room] there was at least a chance he might have *got her*, as it was possible men sometimes *got* their women" (*DL*, 51; italics supplied). The other theme, the problem of the artist in America, is likewise exposed in Faulkner's novel; like Anderson on the Chicago bohemians, Faulkner emphasizes the lack of seriousness among his New Orleans literati and reveals the fate of all who join such communities. In *Dark Laughter*, Bernice's friends had "talked a good deal [and] pretended to despise what they were doing [to make a living] but kept on doing it just the same. 'We have to eat,' they said. What a lot of talk there had been about the necessity of eating" (*DL*, 35). In *Mosquitoes*, Gordon silently pronounces a judgment against the literary people gathered on Mrs. Maurier's yacht: "Talk, talk, talk: the utter and heartbreaking stupidity of words" (*Mosq.*, 186). As Michael Millgate has said, Faulkner's second novel is a round condemnation of all specifically literary milieux.[10]

The Wild Palms shows even more similarity to *Dark Laughter* than

[8] Sherwood Anderson, *Dark Laughter* (New York: Boni & Liveright, 1925), 15–18.
[9] William Faulkner, *Mosquitoes* (New York: Boni & Liveright, 1927), 9.
[10] Millgate, *Achievement*, 68.

Mosquitoes, however, and it places its allusions in the significant context of a broad relation to the writing of Ernest Hemingway, spelling out basic differences between Faulkner and Hemingway and indicating once again, perhaps as a form of homage, essential agreement with Anderson. *The Wild Palms* repeats that the world seems to have no place for art or love. Harry Wilbourne and Charlotte Rittenmeyer, lovers and would-be artists, are forced apart, their love life stifled, by what they must do to earn money to remain together, a tragic paradox that apparently awaited the lovers of *Dark Laughter* as that novel closed. Harry says love "cant last. There is no place for it in the world today"; "respectability" and "money" have beat the lovers (*WP*, 136, 140).[11] Like the crowd in Chicago, Bernice's friends, Harry too is obsessed by the "necessity of eating," measuring out his life in diminishing canned goods. Like Anderson's couple, Harry and Charlotte rent a studio apartment in Chicago, the city to which they have fled from New Orleans (ironically, Anderson's hero had gone the other way, from Chicago to New Orleans); they fill it with Charlotte's dilettante friends and eat the chops which Bruce Dudley had found so symbolic of his dead, middle-class marriage.[12] Charlotte is as false and commercial as Bernice; she meets Harry at a cocktail party where she lies about her artistic abilities (*WP*, 39, 40), and in Chicago she and Harry both build brief careers as commercial artists—she as a sculptress of window dressing figures and he as a writer of adolescent confession stories.

The parallel themes and images between *Dark Laughter* and *The Wild Palms* complement more pointed allusions in Faulkner's novel to Sherwood Anderson's life and work. After their friendship in New Orleans was broken—after Hemingway's *Torrents of Spring* and Faulkner's parodies and whatever else occurred between them—Faulk-

---

[11] The text of *The Wild Palms* (page references noted by *WP*) used throughout this study is the 1939 first edition from Random House. Corrections based on typescript readings are noted where they occur.

[12] Charlotte offers their chops to a cast-iron Saint Bernard on a lawn in a plush Chicago suburb as propitiation to the bourgeois respectability that pursues them; Oak Park, with its Hemingway association, is invoked (*WP*, 89, 98). Cf. Anderson, *Dark Laughter*, 24–25, 36, 48, 51, 54.

ner and Anderson seldom met; both were at the Southern Writers'
Conference in Virginia in 1931 and they met in New York at a party
at least once, Faulkner making at that time a gesture of reconciliation
by reminding Anderson that he was *not* Hemingway.[13] In Faulkner's
words in 1953, Anderson "declined" to see him after 1926.[14] There
came a moment, however, when Anderson did not decline. In the fall
of 1937, when Faulkner was recovering from a bad burn suffered in
an accident in a New York hotel, he told someone that Anderson was
the one person he would like to see, and his old benefactor came to
him.[15]

Faulkner's visit to New York that fall apparently was for the purpose of making final arrangements regarding the publication of his
second Sartoris novel, *The Unvanquished*.[16] Even as he had wound up
that book he had had in mind images which would become important
in the novel to come, *The Wild Palms*—specifically, the linking of sex
and death as ineradicable and related experiences and a thematic emphasis on hands, "those curious appendages ... with which man has
taught himself to do so much, so much more than they were intended
to do or could be forgiven for doing."[17] He was adding to the chronicle of a family whose first appearance in book form, *Sartoris* (1929),
had been dedicated to Sherwood Anderson. Faulkner's description of
Anderson as he had first known him was of a man talking and talking—
"I listening while he talked to me or to people—anyone, anywhere."[18]
In 1925, when he was seeing Faulkner often and composing *Dark*

[13] *Sherwood Anderson's Memoirs: A Critical Edition*, ed. Ray Lewis White
(Chapel Hill: University of North Carolina Press, 1969), 466.

[14] Faulkner, *Essays, Speeches and Public Letters*, 10.

[15] The man who carried the message to Anderson was Faulkner's editor at
the time, Saxe Commins. Carvel Collins, "Faulkner and Anderson: Some Revisions," Talk at the Annual Meeting of the MLA, December 1967, New York.

[16] George Sidney, "Faulkner in Hollywood: A Study of His Career as a
Scenarist" (Ph.D. dissertation, University of New Mexico, 1959), 45; Millgate,
Achievement, 38. Faulkner did not leave Hollywood until August 1937, and he
was back in Oxford talking about the publication of *The Unvanquished* in
November.

[17] William Faulkner, *The Unvanquished* (New York: Random House, 1938),
272.

[18] Faulkner, *Essays, Speeches and Public Letters*, 7.

Laughter, Anderson might have been talking about Tennessee Mitchell, his second wife, whom he had divorced to marry Faulkner's friend Elizabeth Prall and whom he was using partially as a model for Bernice in his new novel.[19] In 1937, when he came to see Faulkner in New York, Anderson had cause to be talking about Tennessee Mitchell once more, because her memory had been raked up meanly by the poet Edgar Lee Masters in his "autobiography," *Across Spoon River* (1936). Anderson's marriage to Tennessee had been brief and not altogether happy, but he had thought a great deal of her, writing in a 1930 letter that she had come closest to meeting his ideal of love. Her death in 1929 had hit him hard.[20] He ought to have resented Masters' thinly disguised portrait of her and his account of an affair they had had before she knew Anderson. Masters whitewashes himself and writes accusingly of "Deirdre's" nymphomania—making sure he unmasks the pseudonym by referring to the famous Claflin sister for whom Tennessee had been named. Whatever the truth of Masters' "fictions"—and Tennessee's unpublished manuscript diary indicates he is not veracious[21]—the poet's words would have interested Anderson and Faulkner in 1937. Masters tells of their visits to an island solitude in Wisconsin and a riverside retreat up in Michigan; "Deirdre" wanted him "to go to another city with her, and there practice law," but he saw the difficulty of reestablishing himself professionally "in a strange place with scandal following" his steps. Always, too, "there were [his] little daughters." "In fact," he writes, "a dull, rubber god guided my steps. Marriage with Deirdre would have been ruin ... I see her now as a cold, uncanny farsighted mind, with a sort of congenital nymphomania." He concludes, "If Nature had no pity in laying this terrible

---

[19] E.g., the passage already quoted reflecting Dudley's belief that "he might have got" his wife if she had stayed in the room instead of fleeing is similar to Anderson's remarks about Tennessee Mitchell in a letter written after her death in 1929: "I used to take her sometimes to the very door, put her hand on the doorknob, but she always ran away like a frightened child" (*Letters of Sherwood Anderson*, 220).

[20] *Ibid.*

[21] William A. Sutton, "Sherwood Anderson's Second Wife," *Ball State University Forum*, 7 (Spring 1966), 39–46. Dale Kramer, *Chicago Renaissance* (New York: Appleton, 1966) covers similar ground less well.

hand upon me for her own blind biological purposes I would have no remorse in fighting Nature with Nature."[22]

The suggestions for both plot and character in *The Wild Palms* are startling. The reluctant young professional man Harry Wilbourne faces resettlement in a strange city with scandal following his steps; his consort is a female love buccaneer whose high regard for what she calls "bitching" approaches an implied nymphomania. They sojourn in a lakeside cabin in the Wisconsin woods. Charlotte fashions a grotesque little papier-mâché god for their fetish. The "terrible hand" of Nature and the "blind biological purposes" both suggest the context of Schopenhauer's World as Will and the imagery of hands and palms in Faulkner's novel. A good bit of Masters' self-portrait points to Harry Wilbourne, while almost everything in his account of "Deirdre" seems to point to Charlotte Rittenmeyer (it is she who leaves her little daughters to go away with Harry). I have seen no evidence that William Faulkner ever met Tennessee Mitchell Anderson, but much written—and it may be assumed spoken—about her indicates that she is the model for a portion of the characterization of the heroine of *The Wild Palms*. She was a dilettante artist who dabbled in several forms. In 1920, during her marriage to Anderson, she joined him at Fairhope, Alabama, on Mobile Bay, and found there multicolored clay which she began working into grotesque, satirical figurines.[23] Seven of Tennessee Mitchell's "Impressions in Clay" were photographed and used as illustrations in the first edition of Anderson's story collection *The Triumph of the Egg* (1921). In *The Wild Palms*, Charlotte, too, is a dabbler; in Chicago she supports Harry by sculpting papier-mâché caricatures and teaming with a photographer who uses them to create illustrations. There are so many similarities between the real and the fictional women, in fact, that one accounts for them only by assuming that Anderson told Faulkner a great deal. Faulkner would have had to know Tennessee very well to fashion such a close portrait. For example, Tennessee recorded her weakness for

[22] Edgar Lee Masters, *Across Spoon River* (New York: Farrar & Rinehart, 1936), 305–307.
[23] *Sherwood Anderson's Memoirs*, 442.

men who had "little interest or aptitude for business, a yearning for the arts" and who lacked "either a decided talent or the courage to pursue" it.[24] Wilbourne qualifies wholly: he is a bungling job-holder who cannot support his lover, a would-be writer and color-blind painter, and, as McCord accuses him, he lacks the "courage of [his] fornications" (*WP*, 101). Anderson and Tennessee vacationed in the Wisconsin woods on Lake Michigan where they lived in a friend's cabin,[25] and Harry and Charlotte do the same. Even Charlotte's attention to Christmas packages for her children (*WP*, 125) may reflect the fact that when Tennessee Mitchell died in December of 1929 there were in her Chicago apartment gift packages for Anderson's children, already wrapped for mailing.[26]

These links to Anderson through his second wife have gone unnoticed, while critics have concentrated on the strong resemblance between Faulkner's novel and Hemingway's *A Farewell to Arms* (1929), a relation tipped off originally by the obvious "hemingwaves" pun in the fifth chapter (*WP*, 97).[27] Parallels between the two novels

[24] Tennessee Mitchell, in Sutton, "Anderson's Second Wife," 41; quoted from her unpublished autobiographical notebook, now in the Newberry Library.

[25] James Schevill, *Sherwood Anderson* (Denver, Colo.: University of Denver Press, 1951), 125. Anderson did some painting, too, and more successfully than Wilbourne (Schevill, *Anderson*, 84; see *WP*, 18).

[26] Kramer, *Renaissance*, 339; Sutton, "Anderson's Second Wife," 44. Sutton says that Anderson's *first* wife had gifts for Tennessee wrapped that Christmas. It is not clear whether Kramer and Sutton are reporting two sets of facts or differently interpreting a single piece of information. Sutton errs, putting Tennessee's death "in 1930" and the editors of Anderson's letters err, placing her death on 29 December 1929. The *New York Times* reported on 27 December 1929 that she had lain dead in her apartment for a week, perhaps from 20 or 21 December.

[27] Similarities of theme and image between *AFTA* and *WP* were noted as early as 1952 by reviewers of the important French translation of the novel. A brief survey of discussions of the similarities is in Thomas L. McHaney, "Anderson, Hemingway, and Faulkner's *The Wild Palms*," *PMLA*, 87, No. 3 (May 1972), 473–74, fn. 29. One omission is Melvin Backman, "Faulkner's *The Wild Palms*: Civilization Against Nature," *University of Kansas City Review*, 29 (Spring 1962), 199–204, where Hemingway's pun on Swift and Armour in "The Snows of Kilimanjaro," apparently picked up by Faulkner, is noted. The story, with a protagonist named Harry who lies dying in a camp chair, appeared in the August 1936 *Esquire*, only a month after *Cosmopolitan* published "The Short Happy Life of Francis Macomber," which Faulkner may have drawn upon for *The Unvanquished*. Beverly Scafidel of the University of South

unquestionably exist, though many important links have been over-looked. The context is larger than hitherto realized, for *A Farewell to Arms*, like *Mosquitoes* and *The Wild Palms*, seems also to owe a debt to Anderson and to *Dark Laughter*; all the novels have in common runaway lovers, the theme of a world antagonistic to love, similar use of escapes by water, and, *Mosquitoes* excluded, apparent allusions to Twain and *Huckleberry Finn*. [28] A minor connection is the similar use of recurring symbolic devices for atmosphere: Anderson's dark laughter, the mosquitoes which harry the lovers in the earlier Faulk-ner novel, the rain of *A Farewell to Arms*, and the rustling wild palm leaves.

Dark Laughter closes with the beginning of a new life for Bruce Dudley and Aline. Aline is pregnant; Bruce is forced to return to Chicago and to a regular job. Looking ahead, he thinks, "Having ex-perimented with life and love they had been caught. Now for them a new chapter would begin. . . . What curious experimental hours ahead for them, Bruce being a laborer perhaps, Aline without money to spend freely, without luxuries. Was what they had done worth the price?" (*DL*, 309) Four years later in *A Farewell to Arms* Heming-way's lovers provide what could very well be his answer to that ques-tion. They carry out the idyll that only begins for Bruce and Aline. Catherine, too, becomes pregnant, but money is not one of the things

Carolina has recently pointed out to me another overlooked correspondence. In Hemingway's "Hills Like White Elephants," which appeared in *transition*, Au-gust 1927, and in *Men Without Women* (New York: Scribner's, 1927), the dis-cussion of abortion is cast in phrases which Faulkner borrowed for *The Wild Palms*. The young man of the story says to the girl, "It's not really an operation at all. . . . It's really not anything. It's just to let the air in and then it's all per-fectly natural."

"Then what will we do afterward?"

"We'll be fine afterward. Just like we were before" (*Men Without Women*, p. 72). In *The Wild Palms*, Charlotte tells Harry, "Just a touch. Then the air gets in and tomorrow it will be all over and I will be all right and it will be us again forever and ever" (*WP*, 220).

[28] Bruce Dudley journeys down the Mississippi in an open boat, musing on Twain; for Hemingway's debt to Twain, see, among other sources, Philip Young's *EH: A Reconsideration* (New York: Harcourt, 1966); for Faulkner's, see Nancy Dew Taylor, "The River of Faulkner and Mark Twain," *Mississippi Quarterly*, 16 (1963), 191–99.

she and Frederick worry about, since it is part of Hemingway's don-née and Frederick can write sight drafts on his family or borrow from a friendly waiter. During her pregnancy Catherine never has a bad time, but she dies in childbirth, and Frederick says of her labor, "this was the price you paid for sleeping together. This was the end of the trap." [29] Coming out of nowhere, like the sudden fact of Cather-ine's death, Frederick's words reply to Bruce Dudley's "Was what they had done worth the price?" What Anderson seemed to want to demonstrate, however, was a different reply. The circular adventures of Bruce Dudley—and the similarly paradoxical affairs of Harry and Charlotte in Faulkner's *The Wild Palms*—are both concerned with the "price" of existence, the cost of loving. Charlotte, in *The Wild Palms*, believes that "the value of love is the sum of what you have to pay for it" (*WP*, 48), a sentiment she says she has learned from books. She sets her price high; Faulkner's lovers go to the extreme of seeking abortion to prevent anything interfering with their love affair. But their paying is done gradually, and all the time, not as a final lump sum extracted by a mysterious cosmic force, and the differences between how Harry and Charlotte pay and how Frederick and Catherine pay reflect an essential difference between Faulkner's view of life and what Faulkner thought was Hemingway's, a difference that underlines beliefs com-mon to Anderson and the protégé who remained loyal.

Faulkner articulated this difference most plainly in his laudatory review of *The Old Man and the Sea* for *Shenandoah*, where he wrote, "this time, he [Hemingway] discovered God, a Creator. Until now, his men and women had made themselves . . . out of their own clay; their victories and defeats were at the hands of each other, just to prove to themselves . . . how tough they could be. But this time, he wrote about pity: about something somewhere that made them all." [30] Faulkner found in *The Old Man and the Sea* what he believed had been lacking in Hemingway's earlier novels, a natural order of which man was both part and combatant. It was absent, for instance, in *A Farewell*

[29] Ernest Hemingway, *A Farewell to Arms* (New York: Scribner's, 1929), 341–42.
[30] Faulkner, *Essays, Speeches and Public Letters*, 193.

to Arms, where Frederick expresses the kind of solipsistic toughness that Faulkner referred to: "You did not know what it was all about. You never had time to learn. They threw you in and told you the rules and the first time they caught you off base they killed you" (*AFTA*, 350).

With purposeful irony, Faulkner has created characters in *The Wild Palms* who adopt the same point of view, for a time, talking like Frederick Henry without any sense of the meaning of their words. Echoing Frederick in the passage above, Harry thinks, "*You are born submerged in anonymous lockstep with the ... myriads of your time ... get out of step once ... and you are trampled to death*" (*WP*, 54). What Frederick says about the cruelty of the world to people with courage—"The world breaks every one ... those that will not break it kills ... you can be sure it will kill you too but there will be no special hurry" (*AFTA*, 267)—is repeated in Harry's words to McCord: "They used money against me. ... They had used respectability ... so They will have to find something else. ... Of course we cant beat Them; we are doomed of course" (*WP*, 140). The same fatalism recurs in Harry's feeling that the black wind of death which comes to cuckold him takes its time (*WP*, 282, 284), as well as in the tall convict's belief that the flood toys with him, biding its time by virtue of a cosmic risibility (*WP*, 147).

Meaningless talk, all of it; what Faulkner's characters say is contrary to their experience and to their actions. Harry's evocation of "They" comes from Charlotte's book-learned romanticism. The tall convict's "cosmic joker" does not exist. Life—like the flood—is a phenomenon of the will in Nature. Harry and Charlotte are a part of that life and as much a part of "They" as anything in the book; they participate in the corruption and commercialization of modern existence and even go against Nature by attempting abortion. The real world is very much with them, and the price for sleeping together is one which they must pay and pay, if they would have it on their own terms. They pay with money, which is accounted in detail and amounts to an obsession for Harry; they pay with freedom, repeatedly forced apart by what they must do in order to eat or fleeing behind

15

doors which create not refuge but prison; they pay with the abortion, a price, Harry cries, which is too great (*WP*, 208). Having driven themselves into increasingly sterile situations, they pay with death and actual imprisonment. The tall convict in the contrapuntal story is pitted against adversaries that are less psychological and more real: the flood and the final stages of his unwanted passenger's labor; he cannot stop either one. When he kicks hawks away from their dead prey to get food or slaughters alligators to earn money, he is clearly as much Nature as the flood. The fact is that one of the functions of "Old Man" is to underscore sharply what is shown more subtly in "Wild Palms" —the life of man is one element in a continuing order of things, without cosmic jokers, the very powerful theme that Hemingway did portray in *The Old Man and the Sea*.

Parallels between *The Wild Palms* and *A Farewell to Arms* show both pairs of lovers as two against the world, but in *A Farewell to Arms* it is as if the world did not really exist, while in *The Wild Palms* there is sufficient and frequent evidence that the world not only exists, it has its own way. At the beginning of each affair the lovers go to sordid hotels where the women feel cheapened, but Catherine overcomes her distaste in a few minutes while Charlotte quarrels with Harry and leaves without allowing them to consummate their love. Both couples have lakeside winter idylls; Frederick and Catherine enjoy the false spring (*AFTA*, 331), but Harry is deceived by the Indian Summer (*WP*, 114) and finds winter upon him before he is ready for it. In the mountains, Frederick and Catherine have a warm wood stove and breakfast in bed; in the Utah mining camp, Harry and Charlotte freeze, despite the crude gasoline stove, and share their quarters with the uninhibited Buckners. Catherine can buy an expensive nightgown whenever she wants it (*AFTA*, 161), but Charlotte never wears a nightgown until near the end when they buy one in order to start her hemorrhaging, the idea being that since they have so little money, with their luck Charlotte will bleed on the expensive gown and ruin it, thus saving her life. Catherine makes all their places into "home" (*AFTA*, 166, 266), but Harry and Charlotte flee through a succession of increasingly barren and unpleasant dwellings. At the end, both women cry out "don't touch me" in their pain (*AFTA*, 353; *WP*, 286); the men see the bodies of their lovers as empty and unreal in death. Frederick Henry walks away in the rain and apparently records his experience in a book that ends with his walking away in the rain. Wilbourne goes to jail for the murder of his lover and there, after much groping, comes to an understanding and an affirmation of the hard nature of man's existence.

There are many verbal echoes of Hemingway in *The Wild Palms*. Charlotte tells Harry that she is pregnant in "short brutal sentences like out of a primer" (*WP*, 205), a probable reference to Hemingway's style and also to the "primer-like" style of Sherwood Anderson, which had been an influence on Hemingway. The deputy asks Harry if "there's as much laying" in hospitals "as you hear about," and Harry's reply, in the flat ironic tone of a Hemingway character, "No . . . there never is any place," seems to allude to the frequent hospital lovemaking of Frederick and Catherine. Like someone following the Hemingway "code," the tall convict accepts the warden's consolatory "You had bad luck" and "It's hard luck" with a laconic "If that's the rule" (*WP*, 331). The cajans who watch the convict's exploits among the alligators wait for him "like the *matador* his *aficianados*" [*sic*] (*WP*, 263).[31] The key reference to Hemingway in *The Wild Palms*, setting parallels with *A Farewell to Arms* aside for a moment, is a more personal touch, however, and like a great deal of its context, it goes back to Sherwood Anderson.

McCord, the tough Chicago newspaperman of Faulkner's novel, has been called a Hemingway figure, either a type of one of his fictional characters or a portrait of the artist himself. But Bradley, the wolfish interloper who brings the lovers a box of food during the lakeside idyll, is the one who is modeled, however roughly, on Hemingway; the scene of his arrival seems to come from a real event recorded by Sherwood Anderson in his 1930 article "They Come Bearing Gifts," a piece which describes both Hemingway and Faulk-

---

[31] Hemingway's interest in bullfighting was already legendary; Faulkner's reference may also acknowledge the numerous allusions to himself in *Death in the Afternoon* (1932).

ner. Anderson recorded Hemingway's visit this way: "I remember him most vividly as coming to my apartment one evening in Chicago. . . . He was leaving for Europe the next morning and had packed into a huge army knapsack all the provisions left over at his place. . . . The big knapsack was filled with canned goods. I remember his coming up the stairs, a magnificent broad-shouldered figure of a man." [32] Faulkner's scene goes as follows: ". . . in the middle of the room stood a stranger carrying balanced on his shoulder a large cardboard box, a man no older than himself, barefoot, in faded khaki slacks and a sleeveless singlet. . . . [Charlotte says,] 'Bradley's the neighbor. He's leaving today. He brought us what grub they had left.' " (*WP*, 106) McCord, instead of a Hemingway figure, is far more likely to be modeled on Sherwood Anderson. The talk between him and Harry often runs to the subject of horses (*WP*, 130, 138): "After ten minutes we sound like *Bit and Spur*," says McCord. That was a topic close to the hearts of both authors. Anderson's father at one time had run a harness shop, and Faulkner's owned a livery stable.[33] Each had a lifelong association with track or field; each wrote fiction on the subject. Anderson's *Horses and Men* (1923), which he put together while he was married to Tennessee Mitchell, was one of Faulkner's favorites;[34] and it apparently figures in *The Wild Palms*, too, where among Charlotte's sculptures are "horses and men" (*WP*, 87). In his two pieces on Anderson (1925 and 1953), Faulkner attributed to Anderson a dream about a horse (a slightly different dream each time) as a metaphor to explain the man.[35]

Why did these references to Anderson and Hemingway fall together the way they did in *The Wild Palms*? They are clearly too consistently interrelated to be accidental or gratuitous. The basis of

[32] Sherwood Anderson, "They Come Bearing Gifts," *American Mercury*, 21 (October 1930), 129. The same anecdote appears, with minor variations, in *Sherwood Anderson's Memoirs*.

[33] See Anderson's obituary in the *New York Times*, 9 March 1941, and Millgate, *Achievement*, 10.

[34] Faulkner, *Essays, Speeches and Public Letters*, 10.

[35] William Faulkner, "Sherwood Anderson," in *Princeton University Library Chronicle*, 18 (1957), 93; Faulkner, "A Note on Sherwood Anderson," *Essays, Speeches and Public Letters*, 3–4.

Anderson, Hemingway, and the Origins of *The Wild Palms*

Anderson's break with Hemingway was the parody of *Dark Laughter* in *The Torrents of Spring* and the accompanying letters. [36] It seems likely that these insults may have complicated Faulkner's relationship with Anderson at a crucial time. Hemingway finished the book by the end of November 1925; he sent it to Horace Liveright on 7 December, long before Anderson's mid-April letter to Liveright about Faulkner's behavior.[37] Faulkner's own parodies were still forthcoming at this time, but probably were not unforeseen in the French Quarter, and he had reviewed Anderson's work rather harshly in April 1925 for the Dallas (Texas) *Morning News*,[38] a piece Anderson probably heard about. Thus the winds which carried news of current and impending attacks by his young protégés may have reached Anderson all at once. He might have found it difficult to distinguish the bumptiousness of one genius from the malice of another. At any rate, Faulkner could hardly have failed to realize that whatever his own feelings and intentions were, he and Hemingway were pretty much in the same boat, as far as Anderson was concerned, and for similar reasons. The fact is borne out by the record Anderson left, in his posthumously published *Memoirs*, of the interim meeting at a New York cocktail party, where Faulkner took hold of the standoffish Anderson's sleeve and said, "Sherwood, what the hell is the matter with you? Do you think that I am also a Hemy?"[39] From this, and from his later writing on Anderson, it is apparent that Faulkner was not happy with his position, that he wanted to mend the break in their friendship.

Also to be considered is what had become of Hemingway since those early days. Faulkner had kept his eye on the competition; he even seems to have parodied *The Torrents of Spring* in his famous preface to the Modern Library *Sanctuary* (pub. 1932). By the mid-thirties the competition had come on strongly; there was an increasingly marked contrast between the success enjoyed by Hemingway and by Faulkner. Faulkner was struggling to make a living by en-

[36] See White, "Hemingway's Explanation."
[37] Carlos Baker, *Ernest Hemingway: A Life Story* (New York: Scribner's, 1969), 159–60.
[38] Rpt. in *Princeton University Library Chronicle*, 18 (1957), 89–94.
[39] *Sherwood Anderson's Memoirs*, 466.

forced labor in Hollywood, buying time to come home and write books that were not selling well. When he was working on *The Unvanquished* and apparently thinking about *The Wild Palms*, Hollywood was the place he had to do it. The chapter of *The Unvanquished* that he wrote at this time to pull together the materials of the novel points ahead, with imagery, to *The Wild Palms* and bears a title that could have come from one of Hemingway's tales. "An Odor of Verbena," which "you could smell alone above the smell of horses" (*Unvan.*, 293),[40] refers to courage; both the phrase and its association seem to come from the white hunter Wilson's regard for the "odor like verbena" in the crushed grass as he and Francis Macomber go on the last buffalo hunt. ("The Short Happy Life of Francis Macomber" appeared in *Cosmopolitan*, September 1936.) During 1937, Hemingway was very much in the public eye, visiting Hollywood to see about *This Spanish Earth* and storming New York in his usual manner. His plans for fighting or covering the war in Spain received wide publicity, his face appeared on the cover, and frequently in the columns, of *Time*. His new novel, *To Have and To Have Not*, coming out at about the time Faulkner was in New York, became a best seller, despite the fact that it was not very good.[41]

Faulkner must have noticed—Michael Millgate has suggested, quite rightly, that *To Have and To Have Not* would have been a proper title for *The Wild Palms* and may help explain the two-part structure of the novel where, as Faulkner once said, the convict had for "free what Charlotte and Harry had given everything for."[42] Coupled with the friendly gesture by Anderson, the result of Faulkner's sense of Hemingway's success may have had a lot to do with the references in *The Wild Palms*. Faulkner had a right to feel a little bitter over his own fate as an American writer, but he was never apt to be vindictive, especially toward a fellow artist whom he could admire. He had a high opinion of what he thought was Hemingway's best work; fre-

40 I am grateful to Professor Stephen E. Meats of the University of Tampa for pointing out this correspondence to me.
41 Baker, *Ernest Hemingway*, 299–324, 619–24.
42 Michael Millgate to Thomas L. McHaney, 31 October 1972. Hemingway's hero is named *Harry* Morgan. *Faulkner in the University*, 180.

quently in his own writing he had alluded to Hemingway and he would do so again after *The Wild Palms*, though never so completely nor with the meanings that seem to be pertinent here.[43] But as an artist, Faulkner had taken a different path from Hemingway; he thought it was the better path, as his well-known and often misunderstood rating of modern writers revealed.[44] His "dispute" with Hemingway was twofold. One aspect of it was Faulkner's high regard for technical experimentation and innovation and the premium he put on tackling extremely difficult artistic problems. The other aspect was the difference in philosophies already discussed, Faulkner's disagreement with the solipsism he saw in Hemingway's early novels.

The Wild Palms affirms life, as we shall see, and it preaches and practices a view of literary art that amounts to a form of homage to Sherwood Anderson. The homage to Anderson, in turn, goes deeper than a mere brushing aside of Hemingway's old attacks, the crossfire that may have caught Faulkner. The source and nature of Faulkner's appreciation of Anderson are also personal; they reveal something of Faulkner's standards as a man.

The final scenes of "Wild Palms" are laid in Pascagoula, Mississippi, the coastal town where Faulkner spent much time during the twenties and where he wrote his second novel, *Mosquitoes*,[45] a novel which has, as we have seen, numerous connections to the life and work of Sherwood Anderson. Faulkner dedicated *Mosquitoes* to "Helen," an apparent reference to Helen Baird of that city. His novel, with the dedication, appeared on 30 April 1927. The following day, 1 May, the New Orleans *Times-Picayune* printed the announcement of her engagement to another man.[46] The evidence, though scant, bears out Michael

---

[43] See William Faulkner, *Pylon* (New York: Smith and Haas, 1935), 50; *Requiem for a Nun* (New York: Random House, 1951), 154, 156, 159–60; Sidney, "Faulkner in Hollywood," 90. Perhaps there is a small joke in the names "Ernest" Talliaferro of *Mosquitoes* and "Ernest V." Trueblood of "Afternoon of a Cow"; both men are milquetoasts.

[44] See *Lion in the Garden: Interviews with William Faulkner, 1926–1962*, ed. James B. Meriwether and Michael Millgate (New York: Random House, 1968), 58.

[45] Millgate, *Achievement*, 23.

[46] New Orleans *Times-Picayune*, 1 May 1927, Sect. 3, p. 4. Helen Baird had gone to a finishing school in Chicago. She married a New Orleanian named Guy Camp-

Millgate's supposition of "some kind of autobiographical or peculiarly personal significance" for *The Wild Palms*.[47] One way or another, Faulkner seems to be memorializing a romantic affair, just as he seems to be memorializing that fated 1 May 1927 when the girl to whom he had dedicated his second novel announced her engagement to someone else (both sections of the novel depict flights that begin on 1 May and there is good evidence that *both* stories were originally set in 1927, though "Wild Palms" was later changed by a decade).[48] The blending of references to a romantic disappointment with references to Anderson's art helps explain one of the most cryptic passages in the novel. When he and Charlotte are leaving Chicago for good, Harry says to McCord, referring to Charlotte and the reporter, "[T]here is something in me you and she parented between you, that you are father

---

bell Lyman (who was the son of citizens of Pascagoula). Faulkner may have known Helen Baird before his bohemian days in New Orleans and Pascagoula. Phil Stone's nephew, William Evans Stone V, writes in *William Faulkner of Oxford*, ed. James W. Webb and A. W. Green (Baton Rouge: Louisiana State University Press, 1965) that his family often rented beach cottages in Pascagoula and that "Bill [Faulkner] went with us several summers." One cottage was the Baird Place. Stone notes that Faulkner dedicated *Mosquitoes* to Helen Baird and that her brother "Pete" was a New Orleans newspaperman (just like Charlotte's brother; *WP*, 88). The announcement of Miss Baird's engagement also noted that she had just returned "last season" from a tour abroad with her mother. It seems possible that Faulkner is drawing on the same experience in *The Wild Palms* that he had used for his abortive early novel "Elmer," where the would-be artist Elmer Hodge pursues his girlfriend Myrtle to Europe after her mother has separated them by taking the grand tour. There are a number of thematic and verbal echoes of "Elmer" in *The Wild Palms*. Elmer Hodge determines to become a painter; when he tells his old girlfriend, however, he must explain that he means a painter of pictures, not houses, the same explanation that Harry Wilbourne makes in the first chapter of *The Wild Palms* to the middle-aged doctor. Elmer, like Harry, has bungling awkward hands. The man who has married Elmer's old girl, Ethel, is described in one respect exactly like the man Bradley whom Harry and Charlotte meet at the Wisconsin lake. Bradley gives Harry "a brief hard violent bone-crushing meaningless grip—the broker's front man two years out of an Eastern college" (*WP*, 106), and Ethel's husband gives Elmer "a soft cruel hand in that automatic celluloid sincerity cultivated by young successful business men" (Elmer TS, unnumbered page). These and other similarities, as well as the general relationship between the "Elmer" papers and Faulkner's later work, are discussed in Thomas L. McHaney, "The Elmer Papers: Faulkner's Comic Portraits of the Artist," *Mississippi Quarterly*, 26, No. 3 (Summer 1973), 281–311.

[47] Millgate, *Achievement*, 179.

[48] See Appendix, "Time and Money in *The Wild Palms*," pp. 195, 200.

of. Give me your blessing." McCord—whose identification with Anderson has been explored—answers in a characteristic phrase, closing the chapter. "Take my curse," he says (*WP*, 141).

In the first place, one is reminded of Gertrude Stein's statement in *The Autobiography of Alice B. Toklas* that she and Sherwood Anderson formed Hemingway.[49] In personal terms, the "curse" which Anderson put on Faulkner—and the term is ironic—has everything to do with the young writer's decision to become a certain kind of artist. As he wrote in the preface to the *Faulkner Reader*, "I wrote a book and discovered that my doom, fate, was to keep on writing books."[50] Or, as he put it in the tongue-in-cheek introduction to *Sanctuary*, "So I told Faulkner, 'You're damned. You'll have to work now and then for the rest of your life.'"[51] The other parent, metaphorically speaking, is the girl he did not marry, for if Faulkner had chanced to settle in New Orleans and had kept on frequenting the literary bohemia there, he would have been a very different writer from the one he became. He would not have been the writer Sherwood Anderson believed he could become. Anderson's *Dark Laughter* and Faulkner's *Mosquitoes* and *The Wild Palms* all warn of the dangers of the consciously bohemian literary life. We can only speculate, but it seems very likely that after his romantic hopes on the coast were frustrated, Faulkner was at last ready to take Anderson's advice and return to Oxford. There he discovered his own little postage stamp of native soil in the writing of his third novel, *Sartoris*. He dedicated that novel to Sherwood Anderson, "through whose kindness I was first published, with the belief that this book will give him no reason to regret that fact." As he tried to tell the reluctant Anderson later, Faulkner was a different man from Ernest Hemingway.

A decade after *Sartoris*, at an even more difficult point in his life—his novels not selling well, himself hurt physically and having just come from his second tour of forced labor in Hollywood, in that

[49] Gertrude Stein, *The Autobiography of Alice B. Toklas* (New York: Vintage, 1960), 216; originally published 1933.
[50] Faulkner, *Essays, Speeches and Public Letters*, 180.
[51] William Faulkner, Introduction, *Sanctuary* (New York: Modern Library, 1932), vi.

period between books which is every novelist's purgatory, watching Hemingway's risen glory and knowing how well he himself had written—Faulkner once again had reason to be grateful to Sherwood Anderson. He put his gratitude into a book. Although he did not dedicate *The Wild Palms* to anyone, it is very likely that he did not need to, for the man most concerned would not have failed to perceive the meaning of the gesture. And for himself the meaning was apparently complex; he would later tell Joan Williams that he wrote the book "to stave off what I thought was heartbreak." [52]

[52] Joseph Blotner, *Faulkner: A Biography*, Vol. II (New York: Random House, 1974), 978. Blotner does not specify, but the context suggests that Faulkner may be referring to Meta Doherty, who figures cryptically in the biography. Blotner, whose book appeared too late for full-scale inclusion in my own work, contributes new information to the background of *The Wild Palms*. Helen Baird, he writes, had a burn scar very much like Charlotte's, and she, too, dabbled in sculpture; the description of Charlotte recalls her own appearance. Blotner, *Faulkner: A Biography*, I, 438; II, 982.

CHAPTER II

Maya:
The World as Illusion

... the sight of the uncultured individual is clouded ... by
the veil of Mâyâ ... he sees not the inner nature of things,
which is one ... and often seeks to escape [from the suffering of his own individuality] by causing the suffering of
another. ...

SCHOPENHAUER
The World as Will and Idea

SINCE THE LATE 1930s, and especially since the Nobel Prize award,
Faulkner's reputation has forced more and more critics to pay close
attention to his work. Careful and multiple readings of his novels reveal that his stylistic peculiarities and structural innovations are not
willful and obscure but functional and carefully planned. Increased
familiarity with the Faulkner canon, or with an individual work, fos-
ters this understanding because his methods—whether instinctive or
planned—are not simply effective conjunctions of matter and method,
they are also generally self-revealing to the attentive reader. The best
way to understand Faulkner is to follow his own advice: read him
more than once, just as to appreciate a painting or a symphony you
must return to the experience of it more than once. The Benjy section
of *The Sound and the Fury* is perhaps the classical example in Faulkner's work of a formal and stylistic difficulty that is resolved by repeated readings of the novel, but any of his more difficult works will
respond to this kind of approach. So it is that the opening of his
eleventh novel (which the typescript at Virginia shows to have been
carefully pared to fit the function it serves) reveals on a second or

EPIGRAPH: Arthur Schopenhauer, *The World as Will and Idea*, trans. R. B.
Haldane and J. Kemp (London: Routledge and Kegan Paul, 1883), I, 454–55.

25

third reading more than the introduction of characters or recurring themes and images. It is, in a sense, also a model for the book as a whole —a model of its physical form and a preview of the process of gradual revelation that occurs as the reader moves through the book.

The opening chapter of *The Wild Palms* is filled with illusions, anomalies, and false information. The "discreet and peremptory" (3) knocking of an unseen hand upon an unknown door,[1] which comes so abruptly, is gradually revealed as filtered through the wakening and reflecting consciousness of a middle-aged doctor. The doctor turns out to be a minor character, while "the man called Harry" at the door and the anonymous woman in the beach chair are the fated principals in this tragic tale of romantic love. Although the final section of "Wild Palms" returns to this beach and the adjacent Mississippi coastal town, only in the first chapter is the middle-aged doctor the center of consciousness; elsewhere the young intern Harry Wilbourne is the center of consciousness, exclusively. The focus upon the doctor is merely one of several surprising turns in a technically unusual novel. On the heels of this chapter comes the first section of "Old Man," a different story altogether. Chapter Three returns to "Wild Palms," but the time shifts from a point near the end of the lovers' flight to the beginning of the love affair in New Orleans. The technical display in Chapter One is in a sense fair warning that *The Wild Palms* is going to be cast in unconventional terms. But it is introductory in a far broader way, too, for what happens here, the images used in this scene, the minor characters, the very structure in which they are presented—all establish patterns which recur throughout the novel.

The doctor's property and his past are described in detail. Stale and barren and dark, the main house is screened from the ill-furnished cabin next door by a hedge of oleander. It is permeated with the smell

[1] Striking similarities to *Macbeth* in *The Wild Palms* suggest that the porter scene is evoked by this opening. Like Macbeth, Harry shares his consort's ambitions, but would achieve them "holily" (I,v,22) when he is faced with using the knife to perform the abortion and seeks other means. In both works, the woman dies and the man comes to his courage in the end. References in *Macbeth* to sparrows and hawks, etc. (I,ii,35; II,iv,12; IV,ii,9–11) may be echoed in Harry's self-characterization as a sparrow (137, 141) and his identification of Charlotte with the hawk (141).

of recent cooking, which in turn suggests the wife's parsimony and her dominance. She is a gorgon, and their marriage bed is childless and loveless. The doctor's choice of a wife and a profession, like his habits and his medical practice and the house he lives in, were willed him by his father, a physician before him. This doctor and his barren wife represent what Harry, a medical student, and Charlotte, stifled in a conventional marriage, might have become. The men were put into the medical profession by their doctor fathers. Each has looked with provincial envy at the swagger and vitality of fellow interns (4, 34–36), and each has only clung unimaginatively to what he has inherited. Both emanate a kind of femininity: the doctor has "soft woman's hands" (4) and submits to his wife's orders, while Harry writes confession stories from the adolescent female point of view and admires his lover for being a better "man" than he is. The doctor had taken his wife to a New Orleans hotel after their marriage, "though they never had a honeymoon," and "though they had slept in the same bed for twenty-three years now they still had no children" (4). The similarities begin to grow ironic, for Charlotte and Harry also visit a New Orleans hotel where they fail to consummate their affair. Though Charlotte wants them to have "all honeymoon," in order to earn money to live together they work opposite shifts and seldom sleep in the same bed. They choose childlessness and desperately struggle to maintain it, but they are confounded by an unwanted pregnancy and by the results of abortion.

The odor of gumbo which says so much about the doctor's marriage points to the "aura of unsanctity and disaster" like a smell which follows the runaway lovers (60). Cofer the realtor can "smell" that they are not married (7). Charlotte fashions a fetish "Bad Smell" for them (95). Harry's jail cell is rank with unsavory odors until a freshening rain coincides with his decision to live (322 ff.). The wind the doctor thinks he knows so well because "he was born here" (3) holds a surprise for him when he leaves the shelter of his innocence to be symbolically reborn; and it will mock and cuckold Harry. The midnight hour of the knocking is one of several pivotal midnights and noons which indicate high and low points on the meridian of the Schopen-

27

hauerian cycle of pain and boredom described in the circular adventures of Harry and the tall convict. The stale cottage where the doctor immures himself and the broken cabin where the lovers attempt to hide are two in a succession of dwellings without fires or hearths which denote the death of inner vitality, the absence of love. The obvious Freudianism of the doctor's flashlight beam "lancing on before him down the brown-stained stairwell and into the brown-stained . . . box of the lower hall" (3) foreshadows Harry's bungling use of the scalpel in the abortion. It also suggests birth. When the doctor leaves the womb-like house and passes through the veil of oleander into the harsh wind, he is born to experience once more. In and out of the water, the convict endures repeated versions of the same act; afterwards, like the doctor, he retreats to his sterile womb as soon as he can. The door, the gap in the hedge, the doorway in the cabin the doctor waits to enter are the first of many portals to experience which carry thematic value. The realtor has observed that the couple wants only "four walls to get inside of and a door to close afterward" (7). Unlike the tight tongue-and-groove cottage, however, the rented cabin lets the wind seep in everywhere. It is another disappointment to lovers who first meet in a decayed garden served by a broken gate. They try to protect their love behind many doors and many walls: in a cheap hotel, a pullman drawing room, a bohemian studio apartment, a screened cabin in the Wisconsin woods, an iron shack at a frozen mine site, and a fleabag San Antonio rooming house. They are divided by the symbolically white door of Charlotte's respectable New Orleans home, by the chromium and glass portal to the department store where she works her upside-down day, and by the rubber-wheeled door of the operating room where she dies. The gate to Harry's jail cell will be the final image. Seeking paradise, Harry and Charlotte enter a personal hell each time, never able to shut reality out of their romantic dream. These images and more receive attention as the stories unfold. Clearly, the opening scene is not gratuitous and does not waste words, a statement that holds true for every scene in the book.

What is learned through the doctor's mind is preliminary to later events, where it continues to illuminate what is learned about Harry.

Maya: The World as Illusion

The tall convict's adventures have the same function on a larger scale. The doctor experiences a gradual demystification, and the reader with him; it does not end until the last word of the novel. Many of the doctor's judgments cannot be trusted, as he himself discovers. His position is already morally equivocal: he rents the cabin to anyone who pays on time (7) and tries to maintain self-imposed ignorance regarding what goes on in it. But Harry has come for him; and we learn that he has been spying on the young couple. He has made a preliminary diagnosis calmly, confidently, clinically. He is aware that the final truth eludes him, "as though he were separated from the truth only by a *veil* just as he was separated from the living woman by the screen of oleander leaves" (6, italics added). The two questions he cannot answer satisfactorily are, 1) What is wrong with the woman? and, 2) What can man as a race have done to her to make her regard all men with the hatred he sees in her eyes? Pursuing this knowledge as he comes down the stairway, he is undisturbed because he does not realize that what he will know when he has found the answers will be awful. He carries the reader with him through the shattering of his innocence, a cataclysm that is directly related to what will happen to Harry and the tall convict.

Like the two other physicians in the novel, he hides behind the identity *Doctor*, except that in his case the veil is torn away. And the veil is Schopenhauer's "veil of Maya," a term the German philosopher borrowed from Hinduism to signify the web of phenomenon which masks primal reality and prevents the individual from recognizing what is common to himself and those he meets in the world. In his essay on Schopenhauer, Thomas Mann describes it this way:

> The universe is . . . a play, a ballet; all your natural, instinctive convictions tell you that it has nothing like the same reality as you . . . is not to be taken with anything like the same seriousness as you yourself are. . . . [S]hrouded in the veil of Maya, the ego sees all other forms of life as masks and phantoms, and is simply incapable of ascribing anything like the same importance or seriousness to them as to itself.[2]

2 Thomas Mann, "Schopenhauer," Introduction to *The Living Thoughts of Schopenhauer* (New York: Longmans, Green, 1939), 19. The essay did not ap-

29

Emerson's poem "Maia" is also apt:

> Illusion works impenetrable,
> Weaving webs innumerable,
> Her gay pictures never fail,
> Crowds each on other, veil on veil,
> Charmer who will be believed
> By man who thirsts to be deceived.[3]

Faulkner's references to Schopenhauer and his philosophy in the novel leave little doubt that the "world as will" is an important context. As noted earlier, McCord accuses Harry Wilbourne of mouthing the German philosopher's brand of pessimism: "For sweet Jesus Schopenhauer. . . . If you're not careful, you'll talk that stuff to some

---

pear in time for Faulkner to see it before completing *The Wild Palms*. Neither was there any Schopenhauer in his library, but he could have gleaned the passages he apparently paraphrases, or the ideas he uses, from several sources. He knew Mann's fiction and greatly admired *Buddenbrooks*, which contains long paraphrases of Schopenhauer as well as extensive direct quotation. For convenience and completeness, I use the full Haldane and Kemp translation which probably was available to Faulkner. It should be recalled that he had access to libraries in Memphis, New Orleans, Los Angeles, New York, and at the University of Mississippi, to mention only the most obvious places where he spent long periods of time during the twenties and thirties, including the period directly prior to the writing and publication of *The Wild Palms*. Short selections from Schopenhauer's philosophy were also available in cheap editions from the Modern Library and Scribner's during the same period.

[3] See also Emerson's essay "Illusions," which begins with a poem in which these lines occur:

> Flow, flow the waves hated,
> Accursed, adored,
> The waves of mutation:
> . . . .
> When thou dost return
> On the wave's circulation,
> Beholding the shimmer,
> The wild dissipation,
> . . . .
> Then first shalt thou know,
> That in the wild turmoil,
> Horsed on the Proteus,
> Thou ridest to power,
> And to endurance.

There is much in the essay that applies to *The Wild Palms*. Faulkner owned two copies of Emerson's *Works* at his death.

guy who will believe it and'll hand you the pistol and see you use it" (100–101). The names Wilbourne and Rittenmeyer both play on the association. Harry is indeed "will borne" and Charlotte, deceived by notions of romantic love and snaring the innocent Wilbourne into her scheme, becomes the masterpiece of illusion. As a representative of the universal delusion of love, which masks the will's urge to reproduction, Charlotte may well have her name "written Maya," as it would be pronounced in Faulkner's South. Further, the convict in his open-air prison—all the imagery of prisons: shackles, bars, doors—emphasizes Schopenhauer's contention that the life of the will is a prison-house. Each character in the novel will in some way rend the veil of Maya and peer beneath the shadow of appearances into primal reality. Each will take a different path when he has the terrible knowledge that such revelation brings. Two of them will be literally in prison. The doctor, specifically, will be outraged several ways. As he begins to understand the nature of the relationship between the people who have rented his wretched cabin, his own moral laxity and his complicity in such affairs is brought home to him. He will confront at last the living embodiment of the "ghosts of a thousand rented days and nights to which he (though not his wife) had closed his eyes" (19). The magnitude of Harry and Charlotte's sin will overwhelm him. But worst of all is the realization that he and Harry are not different at all. Momentarily he will envy the young man who *has proof on the body of love and of passion and of life that he is not dead* (17), the same realization that Harry makes at the end of the novel when he chooses to live with his grief. The doctor will think *I am at the wrong age for this* and lament *why did you have to tell me* (17, 19). If he were young, he could believe that this "bright passion" might also be his; if he were old, it simply would not be possible. But he is middle-aged, and what has happened to Harry will no more happen to him than to Prufrock, though he is not too old. He is less different from Harry than he supposes, for Harry's biography reveals that he too first feels disqualified for love: "because I was too old" (137).

The rending of the veil which brings this insight to the doctor is approached slowly. As he comes down the stairs, he reviews his

31

clinical observations. The woman he has peeped at through the oleander screen is young and apparently fatally ill. She sits staring at the water while the young man gathers needless firewood (9). He is so improvident that he goes hatless "where even young people believed the summer sun to be fatal" (5). The woman's immobility suggests that "abstraction from which even pain and terror are absent, in which a living creature seems to listen to . . . one of its own flagging organs, the heart say" (5). These disclosures are loaded with meaning that unfolds as the story progresses. Harry gathers the useless driftwood as if performing a meaningless ritual. It is summer; they do not need heat and probably are not cooking. Unlike the twigs and limbs which the convict kindles on the Indian mound, Harry's sticks do not go to sustain life, for there will be no birth here and the stove in the cabin is cold. Charlotte is dying in the fatal summer sun, and Harry's act foreshadows her immolation: she dies in burning pain (287), contradictory to her wish for a cool death by water (58). They have a folding beach chair procured in their travels, a residue of the middle-class respectability they have supposedly fled; it is the catafalque of a love that sought every means to escape the fate of the bourgeoisie.[4]

The doctor has decided that whatever organ has failed Charlotte, it is "not the heart" (6), an observation that plays ironically on Charlotte's assertion in the next chapter: "I wanted to make things . . . that you could touch, hold . . . and feel the fine solid weight so when you dropped it it wouldn't be the thing that broke it would be the foot it dropped on except it's the heart that breaks and not the foot, if I have a heart" (47). The veil is going to be torn away soon. His curiosity piqued by the "profound and illimitable" hatred in Charlotte's peculiar yellow eyes, the doctor works down to the realization that it is

[4] Harry says that their life in Chicago is the "stinking catafalque of the dead corpse" of love (139). The convict's finding the pregnant hill woman instead of a living Garbo is the "catafalque of invincible dream" (149). Faulkner liked the image well enough to use it in "Honor" (pub. July 1930); *Pylon*; and *Absalom, Absalom!*, where the quote is most apt for *The Wild Palms*: "Then Ellen died . . . the substanceless shell . . . no body to be buried: just the shape, the recollection, translated on some peaceful afternoon without bell or catafalque into that cedar grove." *Absalom, Absalom!* (New York: Random House, 1936), 126. Cf. *The Wild Palms*, 306: "There was no especial shape beneath the sheet now at all and it came onto the stretcher as if it had no weight either."

not mankind that Charlotte hates, but *"the race of man, the masculine"* (11), and he wonders why. The question he asks is answered partially by his conversation with Harry as they approach the cabin. Three times he has come up to the "veil" (6, 11, 13), and after he has breached the oleander barrier and entered the full sweep of the sea-wind, "the veil was going now, dissolving now, it was about to part now and now he did not want to see what was behind it" (16). But he can no more stop what is coming than the convict can stop the Mississippi River in flood or Harry can stop Charlotte from dying. He "heard his voice ask the question he did not want to ask and get the answer he did not want to hear: 'You say she is bleeding. Where is she bleeding?' 'Where do women bleed?'" (16–17) He does not know everything; he will not until the final chapter of "Wild Palms" when he asks Harry, "Who did this?" But he has the key, not only to what the masculine has done to Charlotte but also to the nature of her hatred.

Harry's "Where do women bleed?" brings home the specifically female nature of Charlotte's suffering. Nothing glosses this scene so well as a passage from Robinson Jeffers' poem "Tamar." Faulkner's regard for the poem is evident in *The Sound and the Fury* and *Absalom, Absalom!*[5], as well as in *The Wild Palms*. It is not likely to have escaped Faulkner's notice that in Hebrew Tamar means "palm tree," a fact recorded in the apparatus to most Bibles. Like Charlotte Rittenmeyer, Tamar Cauldwell loves her brother. Both want an idealized love affair. Both are confounded by their own fecundity, that is, Nature. Both want death by water but get, symbolically in Charlotte's case, death by fire. After an incestuous affair with her brother, Tamar gives herself to another man in order to provide a satisfactory explanation of the pregnancy, but the experience is mortifying and Nature takes a hand in her torment:

> ... daily the insufferable sun
> Rose, naked light, and flaming naked through the pale
> transparent ways of the air drained gray

[5] See Thomas L. McHaney, "Robinson Jeffers' 'Tamar' and *The Sound and the Fury*," *Mississippi Quarterly*, 22, No. 3 (Summer 1969), 261–63. *Absalom, Absalom!* develops its plot out of the same biblical material as "Tamar" does, but there are verbal and other similarities between the two works.

The strengths of nature; all night the eastwind streamed
  out of the valley seaward, and the stars blazed.
The year went up to its annual mountain of death, gilded
  with hateful sunlight, waiting rain.
. . . disgust at herself choked her, and as a fire
  by water
Under the fog-bank of the night lines all the sea
  and sky with fire, so her self-hatred
Reflecting itself abroad burned back against her, all
  the world growing hateful, both her lovers
Hateful, but the intolerably masculine sun hatefullest of all.[6]

A passage from "Old Man" affirms that Faulkner's symbolism is consistent with Jeffers'; the cajan's house is "enclosed and lost within the
furious embrace of flowing mare earth and stallion sun" (255–56).

Like the landscape that Tamar contemplates, this dead beach is a
wasteland. It is also one of the circles of Dante's hell and the first of a
series of allusions to the *Divine Comedy* that will carry Harry Wilbourne symbolically on much the same journey as the Italian poet's.
Charlotte lies on the burning sand while Harry wanders up and down
the beach gathering wood. In Canto XIV Dante journeys to the third
ring of the Seventh Circle where those who have sinned against Nature
and Art are punished: "Some were lying supine upon the ground;
some sitting all crouched up; and others roaming incessantly." Eternal
fire falls on these sufferers and "Ever restless was the dance of miserable hands, now here, now there, shaking off the fresh burning." As
they move on, Dante and Virgil see nearby the statue of "a great Old
Man" from which flow the rivers of hell.[7] As their story progresses,

[6] Robinson Jeffers, *Roan Stallion, Tamar, and Other Poems* (New York:
Boni and Liveright, 1925), 125–26. This collection was brought out by Sherwood Anderson's publisher the same year as *Dark Laughter*. By the next year,
Faulkner was one of the authors on their list too. The phrase "as a fire by
water . . . lines all the sea and sky with fire, so her self-hatred/Reflecting itself
abroad burned back against her" may explain not only Charlotte's hatred but
also the burning plantation house in the second section of "Old Man." It was
"a clear steady pyre-like flame rigidly fleeing its own reflection" (70). The application to Harry and Charlotte's flight is noted later on. Given a number of
images which seem to borrow from Jeffers, this seems another allusion to
"Tamar."

[7] *The Divine Comedy of Dante Alighieri*, The Carlyle-Okey-Wicksteed
Translation (New York: Modern Library, 1932), 76–77, 78–79.

we will see how Harry and Charlotte, too, will sin against Nature and Art; in their travels they will go to a mining camp that is, in Faulkner's words, an "Eisenstein Dante" (187), and the tall convict of the contrapuntal story, "Old Man," will have adventures that reflect those of Dante or his subjects. For now it is enough to say that, like Eliot in his famous poem, Faulkner (who owned two copies of the Carlyle-Wicksteed translation quoted above) found it appropriate to use Dante to describe aspects of the modern wasteland.

This dead beach is brooded over by the middle-aged doctor and his gorgon-headed wife; they are the ultimate cruel extension of the modern successful couple. Respectable people, he in a respectable profession, insulated behind "tongue-and-groove" walls and "closed and locked doors and shutters" (3) on the lee side of the veiling oleander, they rent the cottage that leaks all privacy to whoever can pay the price. Living by the sea, they have "for taste in fish a predilection for the tuna, the salmon, the sardines bought in cans, immolated and embalmed three thousand miles away in the oil of machinery and commerce" (10). This is a wasteland, but that is no consolation to the lovers. It does not excuse, change, or even mitigate their fate. They are not only victims of it, they are part of it, too, having fled here of their own accord after performing the act which has brought barrenness and which will bring death, a price decreed not by a corrupt society but by an indifferent and inexorable Nature. The fact is, Charlotte is deluded in her hateful vision of the masculine. She has been, herself, a better man than Harry. But these sexual differences, like the mask of individuality, are mere illusion, part of the veil of Maya. She has no more justification for her hatred than the tall and plump convicts have for their outrage against the women who have caused them to be in prison. Only Harry will see through the veil of Maya *and* come to a full understanding of what he sees. And that is still a long way off. The chapter ends abruptly, as dramatically as it had begun.

The doctor has been listening to the conversation between Charlotte and Harry, missing the meaning of some of it because he does not understand that what he hears as "rat" is Charlotte's nickname for her

35

husband, "Rat" Rittenmeyer. Even though he knows that Charlotte is hemorrhaging and where, he cannot understand the implication of her other words either. Her voice is "cunning" (21), which keys subtly the verse from Psalms that Faulkner took for his original title: "If I forget thee, O Jerusalem, let my right hand forget her cunning." In her hallucination Charlotte thinks she is persuading Rat to absolve Harry of the abortion. He will not be able to prove anything, she implies, and besides, she says, "I'll plead my ass like they used to plead their bellies" (21). Characterizing herself as a whore—which she does repeatedly in the novel—she refers to the way in which women once could escape the death penalty for a time by pleading pregnancy. But she cannot plead her belly, because she has been made barren by the abortion. The death penalty she is under tolerates no appeal.[8] At this point, what the doctor does not know is also unknown to the reader. Like the entire opening chapter, this brief scene at the chapter's end reveals in a Conradian way the doctor's unreliability as a witness and the ubiquity of illusion. The extreme contrast between the middle-aged couple and the lovers at first works in favor of Charlotte and Harry by putting them into a sympathetic context. But the more one learns about them, the less absolute the difference becomes. Certain so-called "facts" in this chapter will be disputed completely by later revelations. Faulkner is only following a method he used, in various forms, in most of his fiction beginning with *The Sound and the Fury*. He forces the reader to put the story together himself and gives the reader thereby a more immediate involvement in the fictional experience. Much must be discovered before what has happened to these young people can be comprehended. The doctor, and the reader with him, is left at the doorway to that experience as the chapter closes with Harry's words to him, "You can come in now" (22).

[8] Cf. Peachum's reply to Filch in Act I, Scene 2 of Gay's *Beggar's Opera*, where he says Moll "may plead her belly at worst; to my knowledge she hath taken care of that security."

CHAPTER III

Counterpoint:
Captivity and Eternal Return

...I did not write those two stories and then cut one into
the other. I wrote them, as you read it...chapter of the
"Wild Palms," chapter of the river story, another chapter
of the "Wild Palms," and then I used the counterpoint of
another chapter of the river story....
William Faulkner in Japan, 1955

THE NOVEL FAULKNER WANTED to call "If I Forget Thee, Jerusalem" is the love story of Harry Wilbourne and Charlotte Rittenmeyer. The "river story" about the anonymous convict is a thematic
sub-plot that underscores the main story. As early as 1939, Faulkner
was *quoted* as saying "I played them against each other . . . Contra-
puntally."[1] The *paraphrase* of his other remarks in the same interview
makes it seem that he had written all of "Wild Palms" before he wrote
and inserted "Old Man," but that is probably the reporter's mistake;
reporters, and critics, have made a habit of misunderstanding Faulkner.
Whenever he was quoted directly, his statements were essentially the
same, that he wrote the chapters alternately, as the surviving manuscript sheets and the full typescript at the University of Virginia bear
out.[2] But even if Faulkner had never said a word about it, and even if
he had not preserved his early drafts, the result of his writing was
always there, the book itself, and it plainly reveals what he need not

EPIGRAPH: *Lion in the Garden: Interviews with William Faulkner, 1926–
1962*, ed. James B. Meriwether and Michael Millgate (New York: Random
House, 1968), 132.
    [1] *Ibid.*, 36.
    [2] Compare *Lion in the Garden*, 54, with the report by Lavon Rascoe in *West-
ern Review*, 15, No. 4 (Summer 1951), 300–304; and see *Lion in the Garden*,
132, 247–48, and *Faulkner in the University*, ed. Joseph Blotner and Frederick
Gwynn (New York: Vintage, 1965), 171 (corrected version).

have said. These two tales are too closely connected for anyone to assume that they were written at different times and brought together by a casual shuffling.

The main and sub-plots of *The Wild Palms* are in fact so intimately connected that it is simpler to talk first about what was also surely intentional—the way in which they do not touch. For example, the stories are set ten years apart in time. The characters do not ever cross paths or even traverse exactly the same ground, though Harry is sentenced to the penal farm where the tall convict serves his extended term. There is physical evidence that Faulkner once may have intended setting both tales in the same year, 1927, the year of the flood. In the typescript, the date of Harry's birth contains a strikeover: 1900 has been altered to "1910," thus Harry becomes 27 in 1937. Though there are plenty of specific references to 1937 in "Wild Palms," the mood is that of the twenties, not the depression. The New Orleans and Chicago literary bohemias described also belong to the earlier decade. Mention in Chapter Nine of a hulk left over from the war fits a date in 1927 better than one in 1937. And the middle-aged doctor's statement in Chapter One that the building boom "died nine years ago" (18) apparently refers to wartime shipbuilding and economic growth on the Mississippi coast during World War I.[3] Separating the stories by ten years, however, Faulkner put increased emphasis on the role of the second tale as an abstraction, an extended metaphor. He also probably solved a physical problem. If he had used 1927 for the story of Harry and Charlotte, the flood of that year would have proved as much a problem for the lovers' travels as it did for the convict and his pregnant passenger. And besides, writing his novel in 1937 and later, Faulkner merely followed a practice he liked. Whenever he could, he set his novels in the time period during which he was writing them (e.g., see the "present-time" sections of *The Sound and the Fury*, *As I Lay Dying*, and the revisions he made to bring *Sanctuary* up to date, to mention only a few instances).

[3] See *Mississippi: A Guide to the Magnolia State*, compiled and written by the Federal Writers' Project of the Works Progress Administration (New York: Viking, 1938), 287.

Counterpoint: Captivity and Eternal Return

The difference in time points up the secondary role of "Old Man" in yet another way. The first and final chapters of "Wild Palms" occur in the immediate fictional present; Charlotte is dying now. The tale of the tall convict is clearly a story being told, something that occurred "once upon a time," an illustrative fable or parable. Other differences between the stories function in the same way: the anonymity of the characters, the fabulousness of the events, the light irony of the tone in "Old Man" make it a figurative reflection of the main story. "Old Man" is a kind of seriocomic abstraction which illuminates what happens to the fated lovers in "Wild Palms." The body of writing which Faulkner had completed prior to *The Wild Palms* should stand as a reminder that he could and would do whatever he wanted to in the way of structural and language experiments. He was perfectly capable of making "Wild Palms" and "Old Man" cohere any way at all. He chose not to do it by simple physical coincidence of plot. He did it structurally and thematically and by repeating important images and words. One can be almost certain from the manuscript that he began the process of alternating two different plots in his earliest drafts. But it finally does not matter how he wrote the novel, just that he chose to make the parts fit together the way he did. (Chapter 10 of this study offers a possible source, however, for Faulkner's use of the double plot.)

One striking similarity between the plots of *The Wild Palms* is in the way they use the motif of the circular journey. "Wild Palms" begins and ends on the Gulf Coast; "Old Man" begins and ends in the open air penitentiary at Parchman, Mississippi. The opening chapters of the novel, the first installments of "Wild Palms" and "Old Man," both repeat this pattern. Each is a kind of miniature of the larger structure of the novel. For instance, the first chapter of "Wild Palms" begins in a present moment, digresses with strictly limited point of view into the consciousness of a single character whose past unfolds, and then resumes to end precipitously in the present. Because of this beginning *in medias res*, the ninth chapter, which concludes "Wild Palms," is naturally balanced against the first. Similarly, however, Chapter Three (the flight from New Orleans) is paired with Chapter

Seven (the return to New Orleans), while the key chapter, Chapter Five, is itself set in symmetrical form—it begins with the sojourn in Chicago, moves to the interlude in the Wisconsin woods, and ends with another sojourn in Chicago, the whole turning on the Christmas scene with all its implications.

"Old Man" repeats this arrangement. Though brief, the opening section is modeled after the preceding segment of "Wild Palms." It starts off in May, 1927, digresses immediately to unfold the lives of the tall convict and his plump bunkhouse mate, and comes quickly back to May, where it ends precipitously. Chapter Two, where the convicts in the bunkhouse learn about the flood, is balanced by Chapter 10, where they sit and hear the tall convict's adventure. In Chapter Four he is sent out onto the river by a deputy warden; in Chapter Eight he surrenders to a deputy sheriff. In Chapter Six the action turns on the birth of the woman's child.[4] Inherent in this structural device is a cyclic movement that suggests the unceasing round of generation and decay to which all Nature is subject. Birth and death, departure and return, the waxing and waning of the flood come into the novel not only as theme but as form, too—suggesting among other things the image of Ixion's wheel that Schopenhauer uses to portray the futility of the life of the will and Nietzsche's concept of the Eternal Return.

Faulkner's original title, "If I Forget Thee, Jerusalem," paraphrased the psalm that sings of the constancy of the Jews during the Babylonian captivity. Jerusalem in one sense is merely freedom, the real life of the Jews with all its cultural concomitants, forbidden them while they slaved for the wicked and opulent city on the Euphrates. The particular way in which the protagonist of "Old Man" is left unnamed works in the context of this title in an emphatic sense. He is the "tall *convict*." The reader is never allowed to forget—as indeed the convict does not allow himself to forget—that he is a prisoner, a captive of a corrupt society that can give him a ten year extended sentence to keep its books straight. One of the subjects of this novel is

---

[4] Changes in the typescript make it plain that Faulkner reworked the book, however, enlarging it from eight to ten chapters and carefully balancing content and concluding passages to emphasize the pattern of departure and return, the endless cycle of eternal return.

captivity, as Faulkner's title made clear. Harry and Charlotte are captives of a seemingly cruel and loveless civilization. They come to feel trapped by great and opulent and wicked cities. They are also each imprisoned separately in many ways, Charlotte by her marriage to "Rat," by her romantic notions of what a love affair ought to be, and eventually by a biological factor; and Harry by Charlotte, by his own passive habits and inclinations, and eventually by the laws of a vengeful society. The life of the will, Schopenhauer says, is a prison-house.[5]

The convict and his mates toil captive in the open air, a terrible irony. The suits they wear are effective prisons, too, since immediately identifiable: the tall convict will be fired upon when he seeks help downriver because of the suit he wears. Like the "white jackets"[6] of the medical students and doctors, the prison clothes constitute another "veil of Maya," another illusion which keeps people from seeing through the objective individual to a common primal reality. The prisoners have been imprisoned so long they have forgotten what real freedom is like. Harry, in a medical dormitory that is very like the prison bunkhouse, has drifted without freedom or knowledge of freedom. The middle-aged doctor is immured in his tightly closed house, separated from reality by the intervening hedge of oleander, captive to his preconceptions and deadness of spirit. As he says to himself, "*Am I to live forever behind a barricade of perennial innocence like a chicken in a pen?*" (15). Almost all the people in *The Wild Palms* are captives who have forgotten freedom. They get a look at that condition, however, and part of what the novel explores is the contrasting ways in which each reacts to what he sees and learns.

[5] Arthur Schopenhauer, *The World as Will and Idea*, trans. R. B. Haldane and J. Kemp (London: Routledge and Kegan Paul, 1883), I, 254, e.g.: ". . . the penal servitude of willing. . . ."

[6] Cf. Harry's hiding '*behind my white jacket again*' (*WP*, 51) and the middle-aged doctor's attitude toward his classmates in their "drill jackets" (4). The doctors in the book repeatedly hide behind the identity *Doctor*. And there are other masquerades; both the middle-aged doctor and Rat Rittenmeyer have masklike faces (10, 55–56), and Harry is unintentionally deceptive when he wears the tuxedo to the party where he meets Charlotte. Schopenhauer is a fitting analogue for these passages; but so are Carlyle, with his clothes philosophy, and Herman Melville in both *White-Jacket* and *The Confidence-Man*.

The namelessness of the tall convict is also the faceless anonymity of every man to most of his fellow creatures. Likewise, in Chapter One, Harry and Charlotte are only "the man and the woman," the intern is simply "the man called Harry" (20). The meaning, one which will be repeated under various terms, is that most men find it impossible to see beneath the mask of illusion, the veil of Maya, to common humanity, a barrier the tall convict successfully transcends later on in his dealings with the cajan.

The first section of "Old Man" is a short chapter to be set off against the more extensive opening of "Wild Palms" (eight pages against twenty). "Old Man" is demonstrably subordinate. Nevertheless many similarities and ironic contrasts exist between the chapters beyond what has been pointed out already. Like the middle-aged doctor, the convicts go through a gradual process of demystification. They are as ignorant of the river in flood as the doctor is of the *noyades* of passionate and tragic love (see Chapter Four, note 5). Like the doctor they live in sterile and insulated seclusion from such cataclysmic events as they are to witness and share. The doctor was born, raised, educated, and married within a narrow radius of where he lives now. The convicts are similarly confined. They "had but little active interest in the outside world," and some did not "know where the Ohio and Missouri river basins were." Many "had never even seen the Mississippi River" though "they had plowed and planted and eaten and slept beneath the shadow of the levee itself, knowing only that there was water beyond it from hearsay" (28).

The convicts' first contact with the flood and its devastation is the identification they feel with conscripted gangs of laborers "being forced like themselves to do work for which they received no other pay than coarse food and a place in a mudfloored tent to sleep on" (29). This is academic, since the convicts who read about the flood sleep in warm bunkhouses and enjoy good food, free movies, and baseball games. Their vague identification is remote, like the doctor's mild pleasure in being able to diagnose Charlotte. But he is complacently wrong about Charlotte, and they vastly underestimate the awesome character of the flood. In both cases, fuller exposure is coming.

The wasteland atmosphere of the doctor's household is matched by the open-air prison. The land the convicts farmed "and the substance they produced from it belonged neither to them who worked it nor to those who forced them at guns' point to do so . . . it could have been pebbles they put into the ground and papier-mâché cotton- and corn-sprouts which they thinned" (30). In this barren prison-house setting is another strange couple, the sort of bedfellows one supposes prisons make: the tall convict and his plump mate. Like the womanish doctor of "Wild Palms" the second convict is feminized: he goes around the prison farm in a "long apron like a woman" (27), doing household chores. Both he and the tall convict share a somewhat comical and Freudian imputation of impotence based on the inability to handle a gun. The plump convict "would not even have had the synthetic courage of alcohol to pull trigger on anyone" (27), while in his one attempt at crime the other "had shot no one because the pistol which they took away from him was not that kind of a pistol" (24–25).[7]

The convicts share another common trait. The tall convict has "pale, china-colored outraged eyes" (23), while his companion carries a "sense of burning and impotent outrage" (25). In each case, though for somewhat different reasons, the men believe that a corrupt society has conspired unfairly and deceitfully to put them where they are. The tall convict has gotten in trouble with the law because of what he has read. Legalistically, in a phrase he has learned from his brush with Justice, he calls it "using the mails to defraud." He was lured into a ludicrous and unsuccessful crime by trusting information published in mail-order pulp-fiction magazines. He is unaware that the pen-named men whom he cursed were not real men, "not actually men but

[7] Similar comic Freudianism in Faulkner's fragmentary early novel, "Elmer," is discussed in Michael Millgate, *The Achievement of William Faulkner* (New York: Random House, 1966); Quentin Compson is characterized in the same manner in the scene with Dalton Ames in *The Sound and the Fury*. The imagery is handled seriously in "An Odor of Verbena," the last chapter of *The Unvanquished*.

merely the designations of shades who had written about shades"
(25). Illusion, the veil of Maya, beguiles him too. Besides the illusory
Dead-eye Dicks and Jesse Jameses, however, there is "something else
he could not tell them at the trial" about the inspiration for his crime.
It comes out in the final chapter of the novel. But what has happened
to the plump convict foreshadows the information the tall convict has
withheld: "There had been a woman in it and a stolen automobile
transported across a State line, a filling station robbed and the atten-
dant shot to death . . . he and the woman and the stolen car had been
captured while the second man, doubtless the actual murderer, had
escaped" (26–27). Apprehended, the plump convict was made to
choose between two crimes, neither of which he had committed. He
could stand trial for lesser Federal offenses, one of which is violation
of the Mann Act, "by electing to pass through . . . where the woman
raged" (27), or he could accept a sentence for manslaughter and evade
the woman. Rather than face her, whose emotions are imaginable even
without the Mann Act and its imputation of concupiscence, he accepted the greater offense. They sentenced him to one hundred ninety-
nine years; he will have space for several lifetimes in prison. Similarly,
what we learn about the tall convict is that there was a woman in his
crime too. He and his plump mate thus rage quietly against the
feminine. This situation in "Old Man" indicates that the middle-aged
doctor's diagnosis of Charlotte is at least partially correct: she does
show hatred for the *race of man, the masculine.*" And as part of the
burden of "Wild Palms" is to reveal what *"man as a race can have
done to"* her (12), the contrapuntal story will eventually bring out
what the tall convict "could not tell them at the trial, did not know
how to tell them" (25). The two convicts share a comic inversion of
Charlotte's fate. But the meaning is finally serious, even to the last
speech in the novel, where the tall convict sardonically rejects
womankind. And everything applies to Harry Wilbourne, who will
also be brought to jail for a crime which very much has a woman in it.

This chapter of "Old Man" rushes to a climax in a final paragraph
which is carefully balanced against the one that concludes the preceding section of "Wild Palms." Faulkner recast part of the typescript

to make these endings coincide as they do. He rewrote the last two pages of Chapter One and broke what had been a longer section of "Old Man" into two at the point where it now ends. The effect is strong. Hauled out of their beds at the same time of night as the doctor has been hauled out of his, their heads as full of tales of the flood as the doctor's mind is full of his speculations on the couple next door, the convicts hear the deputy: "The levee went out at Mound's Landing an hour ago. Get up out of it!" (30).[8] They are left, like the doctor hearing Harry's "You can come in now," expectantly on the verge of crucial experience.

[8] Mound's Landing is at Scott, Mississippi, in the Delta. The levee break occurred there 22 April 1927 (Memphis, Tennessee, *Commercial Appeal*, 23 April 1927). Faulkner uses the events of the 1927 flood, taking purposeful liberties with dates and making one error. The headline (29) *President Hoover Leaves Washington Tonight* is an anachronism, since Hoover did not take the office until 1929; but Hoover was Secretary of Commerce in 1927 and made the headlines for his visits to the flood area. There is no evidence that Faulkner visited the flooded sections of the Delta in 1927; according to his friend Ben Wasson of Greenville, Miss., it is in fact "highly dubious" that he did so. But Mr. Wasson says "to my personal knowledge, he did visit the penitentiary at Parchman on at least two separate occasions prior to writing" his novel. [Information from an interview with Mr. Wasson by Hodding Carter in a letter to me from Mr. Carter, the well-known Mississippi editor and chronicler of the Mississippi River; 24 November 1967.] It is possible that Faulkner was in Pascagoula, Miss., the setting for the final scenes of *The Wild Palms*, during the period of the flood. The *Times-Picayune Sunday Magazine*, 19 September 1926, p. 4, notes that he "was in New Orleans recently, preparing to return to the city for a winter's stay." He spent much time during "1926, 1927, and 1928" in Pascagoula (Millgate, *Achievement*, 23). If *The Wild Palms* reflects his feelings about the girl to whom he dedicated *Mosquitoes* (written in Pascagoula), perhaps the change of the flood from April to May in the novel reflects, as suggested in Chapter One, the May 1 announcement of her marriage. Harry and Charlotte leave New Orleans on May 1, too (see Appendix).

CHAPTER IV

The World
as Will

The Mâya of the Hindus, whose work and web is the
whole world of illusion, is also symbolised by love.
SCHOPENHAUER
The World as Will and Idea

THE DETAILS OF HARRY'S SIMILARITY to the middle-aged doctor
unfold in the second section of "Wild Palms." Though like the doctor
he has followed his father into a profession, his choice was not forced
upon him by daily precept and admonition, as one may suppose to
have been the older man's case, but by a *will*. His father died when
Harry was two years old. The money bequeathed to him so long before he needs it is now insufficient to meet the changed opportunities
and increased costs of the day. Notwithstanding, Harry unimaginatively plugs away at his studies. Harry has learned to associate everything he has not had with money, assuming that he has *"repudiated
money and hence love"* (34), an equation written large in *The Wild
Palms*. On his twenty-seventh birthday, the day he meets Charlotte
Rittenmeyer, Harry wakes to consider that he has floated "without
volition"—that is, will-lessly—"upon an unreturning stream" (34). He
is not outraged, however. He believes he has a kind of peace, like that
a "middleaged eunuch" might feel. He speculates that in a few years
he will have forgotten entirely what he can still remember but no
longer feel: a longing for the "passionate tragic ephemeral loves of
adolescence" (34). He is at a turning point, but he does not know it
yet. On the verge of completely denying life and achieving Schopenhauer's peaceful will-lessness, he will be plunged into the hopeless

EPIGRAPH: Arthur Schopenhauer, *The World as Will and Idea*, trans. R. B.
Haldane and J. Kemp (London: Routledge and Kegan Paul, 1883), I, 425.

round of willing by Charlotte's love. Like the tall convict, he will get a chance to sample a freedom that he has forgotten.

His life during the two years as an intern in the New Orleans hospital has been as measured as his medical education. He allows himself to smoke once a week, on the week-end. He sends his half-sister, who raised him, small weekly money orders to repay those she mailed him during medical school. He knows his financial situation almost by the minute, thinking of the two thousand dollars that he had eked out with enough left over to buy a train ticket to New Orleans, where he arrived with his "one bag and a dollar and thirty-six cents" (33). No matter how deeply Harry is enmeshed in a tragic and ephemeral love affair, his careful accounting of money against time will not cease. His selfconsciousness and his passivity make him more habituated to watching his money dwindle than to getting more. Such an accounting, as impersonal as an itemized expense account, as dogging as an overdue mortgage, becomes one of the charts of the headlong flight with Charlotte, until they arrive at dead end on the beach, with the same bag and a little less than fifteen dollars. Harry's attitude ought to disqualify him for a love affair of the sort Charlotte envisions. He who can neither get the money they need nor stop worrying about it is hardly the romantic who stakes all for love. The accounting also is one more circle motif: financially, Harry comes back to where he began.

Harry's life is pacific, but the peace is militantly imposed, so that when his fellow intern Flint proposes a party in French Town, Harry feels the "guardian of the old trained peace and resignation" rise to defend: "*You have peace now; you want no more*" (35). To put it in Schopenhauer's language, Harry is in danger of ceasing to deny the will: "the tolerable condition of his own body, the flattery of the moment, the delusion of hope, and the satisfaction of the will ... *i.e.*, lust, is a constant hindrance to the denial of the will."[1] He succumbs to these forces and accepts Flint's offer. He borrows a tuxedo. At the party, he will even look like something he is not. Harry has spoken and thought in innocence; his will is untested, and there is no suffering

[1] *Ibid.*, 507.

47

behind him. At the end, he will have memories to inhabit the old flesh, and that changes everything; he is not going to end as a middle-aged eunuch.

It is Harry who discovers the broken gate in the rotting wall that leads him into a new world of experience. He sees a decayed garden, lush with the smell of jasmine, dominated by the exploding fan of a cabbage palm, set with a stagnant pool ornamented by a terra cotta figure. Similar images recur in the novel. But even in isolation this scene is slightly ominous—static and decayed and filled with exotic opulent aromas. The palm and the water are quiescent; the terra cotta figure is only a statue, not a "tiny terra-cotta colored creature" like the baby on the Indian mound (231). This is another wasteland, but it has more than wasteland significance. The badly played music from the party rides the air "like symbols scrawled by adolescent boys upon an ancient decayed rodent-scavengered tomb" (37). Is the Gershwin that the host, Crowe, plays a song of love? And are the tombs that have been violated the sepulchres of the Romeos and Juliets, the Tristans and Isoldes? The rotting walls of brick lift "a rampart broken and nowhere level against the glare of the city on the low eternally overcast sky" (37). The city is a place of sterility and death, and will be so characterized again. It is also akin to the Babylon that has so much to do with Faulkner's original title, the wicked river-bordered city in the fertile crescent (like New Orleans) and, out of Revelation, akin to Rome as seen by the New Testament prophets. This is the second garden in *The Wild Palms*. The first is in the preceding chapter, where the convicts "watched the approach of the disaster with that same amazed and incredulous hope of the slaves . . . who watched the mounting flames of Rome from Ahenobarbus' [i.e., Nero's] gardens" (29).

In his borrowed formality, Harry receives derisive greetings: "My God, where was the funeral?" (37) His introduction is cruel satire on what is to come. Flint jokingly warns the company that Harry has "a pad of blank checks in his pocket and a scalpel in his sleeve" (37). At the beach, in the first chapter, Harry tells the doctor that he is a painter. The doctor's reaction is provincial. He thinks that Harry means house painter until he is corrected: "I paint pictures ... At least, I think I do" (18). That Harry can even believe himself to be a painter of pictures is a result of his sojourn with Charlotte. At the French Town party he is as provincial as the doctor, and it is Charlotte who apparently lies. He stares bemused at the modern paintings. The objects themselves are completely alien to him; but even more strange, from his impoverished point of view, is the "condition which could supply a man with the obvious leisure and means to spend his days painting" (38). He might have the same view of passionate and tragic and ephemeral love depicted in books.

The gathering is a cocktail party in one of the bohemian purlieus of New Orleans. The guests disregard each other and probably talk a lot about art.[2] Harry must create a strange impression: unknown, standing aloof in evening clothes to regard the paintings "without heat or envy" and lost in his own thoughts. No wonder Charlotte makes the mistake she does. She is either impressed or challenged by his appearance, so she makes a play for his attention. He regards her in one particular just as the older doctor did, clinically, analytically, seeing the inch-long scar on her cheek and recognizing it as a burn "doubtless from childhood" (39). Charlotte's talk is the supersophisticated and meaningless jargon of the arty. When he asks her what she thinks of the painting, " 'Marshmallows with horseradish,' she said, too promptly. 'I paint too,' she added. 'I can afford to say' " (39). Charlotte is lying, as she reveals before the evening is out, probably hoping to impress this impressive-looking figure who appears to be slumming. The challenge she makes is natural to her. Her yellow cat's eyes stare "with a speculative sobriety like a man might" (39). Her grasp on his wrist is "simple, ruthless and firm" (39). She assumes command, taking his wrist, releasing him, taking him up again, giving him orders. There is no mutuality here; her hand, one of the wild palms to which the title peripherally refers, clamps his wrist like a manacle, denying him the opportunity to hold on to her in return. Charlotte's romantic notions and her aggressiveness make her the Byronic lover of the pair.

[2] See the similar condemnation of the bohemian literary life in *Mosquitoes* (New York: Boni and Liveright, 1927), 186.

Harry is the virgin, which she may have recognized when she found him both desirable and necessary to her plans.

Much is made of the "old burn, doubtless from childhood" (39), that Harry perceives on Charlotte's cheek. Later the first evening she tells him the story of how she got it. She was raised in a world of men, a houseful of brothers. Fighting with her favorite brother—the one whom she wanted to marry—she fell into the fireplace and got the scar that is on her shoulder and side and hip (40). Harry questions her further:

> "Do you tell everybody like this? At first?"
> "About the brothers or about the scar?"
> "Both. Maybe the scar."
> "No. That's funny too. I had forgotten. I haven't told anybody in years. Five years."
> "But you told me." [40]

The amount of attention paid to this burn provokes interpretation. The five years is probably the five years she has been married: she is about twenty-five, she has children of two and four. Her life has evidently been conventional up to this time, and Rat has not marked her. The scar dates prior to her marriage. It represents a particular experience with the "race of man, the masculine" (21). It is as if she has been annealed by her accident and become in a manner invulnerable and even masculine herself. Her invulnerability, however, is no more complete than that bestowed on mortals before her; she has a flaw. Although she is a better man than Wilbourne, she is a woman too, and vulnerable like a woman, upon whom children can be fathered and abortions performed. As Harry says bluntly to the doctor, "Where do women bleed?" (17).[3]

Harry does not know it yet, but he has come off the quiet stream of

---

[3] The principal mythic tale of annealing in fire concerns Demeter, one of Faulkner's favorite figures. See *Bulfinch's Mythology* (New York: Modern Library, 1934), 48–49; this is the same edition that Faulkner owned. Demeter is a corn goddess whose followers initiate brides and bridegrooms; she has no husband, but bears a female child to her brother Zeus. Charlotte abandons her husband; initiates Harry into the secrets of the marriage bed; confesses to loving her brother; bears only female children.

life in which he was floating volitionlessly, past the stagnant pool in the rotting garden of love, to be swept away by Charlotte's powerful will. He "seemed to be drowning, volition and will, in the yellow stare" (39). Many associations pertain: the yellow flood that is going to carry off the tall convict, the hawklike omnivorousness to which Harry, like some lesser bird, is prey, the state of satiety and hostility connoted by the word "jaundice," a strong sexuality,[4] the whole complex of figures and ideas that McCord's reference to Schopenhauer (100) helps to unlock, and perhaps more.[5]

The kind of sudden love that occurs between Harry and Charlotte is by no means unique. Thus Cadet Lowe falls for Mrs. Powers in *Soldiers' Pay*; David West for Patricia in *Mosquitoes*; Byron Bunch for Lena Grove in *Light in August*; Laverne for Roger Schumann and the reporter for Laverne in *Pylon*; Judith Sutpen for Charles Bon in *Absalom, Absalom!* and so on. Faulkner used it in his largely original filmscript *Country Lawyer* (completed 27 March 1943), when he was working in Hollywood, and twice called attention to it, as George Sidney has pointed out, by having a voice on the soundtrack say "So it was Romeo and Juliet again, the old, old story of Capulet and Montague."[6] Faulkner was hardly unaware of the tradition of romantic love that tales of Romeo and Juliet and Tristan and Isolde represented. Clearly he seems to be referring to that body of romantic literature in *The Wild Palms*. Professor Cleanth Brooks had drawn attention to this element in Faulkner's work in his discussion of *The*

---

[4] In *Miss Zilphia Gant* (Dallas, Texas: The Book Club of Texas, 1932), 16, the title figure dreams of the itinerant painter: "In the dream his eyes were yellow instead of gray" and he performed "monstrously with his pot and brush." When Charlotte arrives at the hotel, her eyes are "extraordinarily yellow" (45).

[5] A novel Faulkner apparently knew well enough to borrow from in *Sartoris*, Edith Wharton's *The Custom of the Country* (New York: Scribner's, 1913), pits a strong-willed heroine against a weak and dreamy young man who sees them as "fellow victims of the noyade of marriage, but if they ceased to struggle perhaps the drowning would be easier for both" (*Custom*, 224–25). For Faulkner's probable borrowing in *Sartoris*, see Thomas L. McHaney, "Fouqué's *Undine* and Edith Wharton's *Custom of the Country*," *Revue de Littérature Comparée*, 45 (April-June 1971), 180–86.

[6] George Sidney, "Faulkner in Hollywood: A Study of His Career as a Scenarist," Ph.D. dissertation, New Mexico, 1959, p. 181.

Town, a discussion enriched considerably by Brooks' use of the work on the tradition by Denis de Rougemont, *Love in the Western World.*[7] Brooks notes there that the story of Harry and Charlotte belongs in the tradition of "the world well lost for love."[8]

As Brooks says, "passionate and thrilling love, so irresistible that those possessed by it count mere happiness well lost, dominates the stories of the Arthurian cycle; modified and in a different key, it runs through the fiction of the eighteenth and nineteenth centuries; in vulgarized forms it still constitutes the staple of tin-pan alley lyrics and Hollywood movies."[9] Rougement traces the tradition to modern times, but, as Brooks notes, he takes Tristan and Isolde as the archetype and believes Wagner's opera is the best embodiment of the tale. Faulkner did not know Rougemont's work, which did not appear in French until 1939, but he knew the tradition, out of Shakespeare, out of Arthurian romance, and probably even out of Wagner. So the kind of love affair which Charlotte wants—"all honeymoon" and "either heaven or hell"—has its prototypes.[10] Unfortunately for her, Charlotte will not be capable of holding to her own ideal. Charlotte likes "bitching" too much. She is also glib and dishonest with herself, as her lie about painting and her approach to art reveal.

Charlotte's lie about being a painter is eventually corrected. She sculpts. She invites Harry to feel "along the base of her other palm—the broad, blunt, strong, supple-fingered hand" (40–41). What she says about the objects she likes to make—"something with weight... that displaces air and displaces water and when you drop it, it's your foot that breaks and not the shape" (41)—applies to her *chef d'oeuvre,* the love affair, which she also treats as if it were a tangible object: "Not just something to tickle your taste buds... the Might-just-as-

[7] Cleanth Brooks, *William Faulkner: The Yoknapatawpha Country* (New Haven, Conn.: Yale University Press, 1963), 196ff.

[8] See Cleanth Brooks, "The Tradition of Romantic Love and *The Wild Palms,*" *Mississippi Quarterly,* 25, No. 3 (Summer 1972), 265–87.

[9] Brooks, *Yoknapatawpha Country,* 196–97.

[10] Paolo and Francesca, another set of tragic lovers who figure in the tradition, are buffetted by "black air" in Dante's *Inferno,* just as Harry and Charlotte are at the beach. Like Charlotte, they are led to their affair by the books they have read.

well-not-have-been" (41). Like a number of Charlotte's speeches, this
one has some posing in it, though there is also a truth she cannot know.
Harry's final act will be an attempt on his own to salvage from the
wreck of the "object" enough to keep it from being a "Might-just-as-
well-not-have-been." Charlotte is always making speeches, a fault that
Harry eventually picks up from her. They are usually more sound
than meaning, or at least the meaning seems to escape the lovers. After
she has put the rhetorical question "What to do about it?" to Harry,
she makes the cryptic and probably bragging statement that she,
unlike Harry, has been in love before. With whom? Her brother? Or
perhaps she loved her husband once, the conventionally successful
"reasonably insensitive and shrewder than intelligent" (40) bourgeois,
called "Rat" and sometimes behaving like one. The greater likelihood
is that what she says is partially fabrication, like what she first claims
about being an artist. The claim does, however, set the contrast again
between her and Harry—she the experienced lover and he the virgin.

Harry enters the Rittenmeyer house only once, to stand before the
"cold hearth," one of a succession of similar symbols. When he leaves,
self-condemned as the opposite to the successful Rat, a pauper who
cannot even afford taxi fare, the imagery is stark: "Then the door
closed between them. It was painted white. They did not shake hands"
(43). Though Harry and Charlotte may believe later that they are
slipping into the patterns of respectability, Harry is forever after
closed out of the kind of life that this household represents, to the
point that in the penultimate chapter of "Wild Palms" he must
imagine Charlotte's last meeting with Rat in the house. The "rented
door" (46) in the backstreet hotel is at the other end of the spectrum,
but it does not help them either. They move in and out of it unable
to achieve consummation. Charlotte has gotten her notions about love
out of books: "the second time I ever saw you I learned what I had
read in books but I never had actually believed: that love and suffering are the same thing and that the value of love is the sum of what
you have to pay for it" (48). One of the books where she might have
read this, as Chapter One has shown, is *A Farewell to Arms*. Had she
also read Dante's *Inferno*, the story of Paolo and Francesca might have

warned her of the dangers of being enflamed with love by books.[11] Her avowal that "love and suffering are the same thing" fits perfectly into the tradition of romantic courtly love. In fact, as Rougemont points out, "without these myths [of legendary figures like Don Juan or Tristan], Europeans [and, of course, Americans] would not be what they are, would not love as they love, and their passions would be incomprehensible." [12] In one form or another, pure or adulterated in popular entertainment, such tales have become the patterns of love for Charlotte. Her wooden and cliché-ridden dialogue in the hotel scene surely comes from some modern example of the tradition: "Not like this, Harry. Not back alleys. I've always said that: that no matter what happened to me, whatever I did, anything, anything but not back alleys" (46–47). Faulkner undoubtedly composed this dialogue knowing full well how it sounded. He had returned from his second assignment in Hollywood about the time he began *The Wild Palms*.[13] In another place in the novel, he satirizes the impact Hollywood had had on the American landscape and the American girl.[14] He has Harry write "primer-bald moronic fable" that probably contains the same kind of dialogue, since some of the stories begin "I had the body and desires of a woman yet in knowledge and experience of the world I was but a child" (121). Final proof that these words are merely play-acting, although perhaps unconscious, comes in the same scene. At

[11] The analogy to the tall convict is apparent; he curses the writers whose pulp fiction inspired him to commit the crime for which he has been imprisoned, just as Paolo and Francesca curse the one who wrote the tale that plunged them into their affair. Quixotism, which receives specific notice in the form of one of Charlotte's sculptured figures, is also a possibility. Schopenhauer writes about the irony inherent in the tradition, one expressed in *The Wild Palms*: that the attraction which the lovers feel is only Nature, or the will, seeking to renew itself. See Schopenhauer, *The World as Will and Idea*, III, 366–67.

[12] Denis de Rougemont, *Love Declared*, trans. Richard Howard (New York: Pantheon Books, 1963), 20–21.

[13] Sidney, "Faulkner in Hollywood," 45; Michael Millgate, *The Achievement of William Faulkner* (New York: Random House, 1966), 34–35, 37–38.

[14] He describes "the little lost towns, the neon, the lunch rooms with broad strong Western girls got up out of Hollywood magazines (Hollywood which is no longer in Hollywood but is stippled by a billion feet of burning colored gas across the face of the American earth) to resemble Joan Crawford" (*WP*, 209).

first, unable to go through with their planned consummation in the hotel, Charlotte implies with evident sincerity that she has failed and "bitched it" for Harry (47). In the next instant, however, she puts the actual blame on Harry's poverty: "Tell me again you haven't got any money. Say it. So I can have something . . . that I can accept as the strong reason we cant beat even if I cant believe . . . that it could be just . . . money, not anything but just money" (40).[15]

Part of her problem, and Harry's, is the inability to find a way to do what she wants to do. She is willing to give up her home, her husband, her children, but she cannot give up the need for money. "I was thinking about money," (48) she says. So is Harry most of the time. They do not qualify very well as romantic lovers in the ideal. Charlotte's cry, "You damned pauper" (45, 50), is not only an accusation against Harry, but also a frustrated complaint against the world, which seems to deal only in extremes of success or poverty that militate constantly against her. As Schopenhauer puts it, "between desiring and attaining[,] all human life flows on throughout. The wish is, in its nature, pain; the attainment soon begets satiety." [16] As their opportunities increase, this will seem more and more like a truth to the lovers.

They are enabled to embark upon their passionate and tragic and ephemeral affair because Harry finds enough money to carry them from New Orleans to Chicago. He finds it in a trash can, by a kind of minor miracle. In terms of the fiction that Faulkner is constructing, this may seem too convenient (though it is no more convenient than Frederick Henry's sight drafts on the folks back home or his loans from waiters who like him). Faulkner carries it off brazenly: "there was no premonitory buzz or whirr at all, the edges of the papers

---

[15] Cf. Belle Mitchell, in *Sartoris*, who asks Horace Benbow, "Have you plenty of money, Horace?" He is weak like Harry, but he has taken Belle away from her husband (who is not unlike Rat). His answer contains analogies for *The Wild Palms*: "And 'Yes,' he had answered immediately, 'of course I have.' And then Belle again, enveloping him like a rich and fatal drug, like a motionless and cloying sea in which he watched himself drown." William Faulkner, *Sartoris* (New York: Harcourt, Brace, 1929), 257.
[16] Schopenhauer, *The World as Will and Idea*, I, 404–405.

merely tilted and produced from among them, with the magical abruptness with which the little metal torpedo containing change from a sale emerges from its tube in a store, a leather wallet" (51). Faulkner makes this work technically by doing it with a flourish. He is obviously not trying to fool anyone, hence the reference to "premonitory buzz or whirr" (51). He makes it work thematically by virtue of its correspondence to the kinds of things that occur in the love stories Charlotte has probably been reading. There is a particular relation to the love philtre in *Tristan and Isolde*, which is given to the lovers by error and makes their love affair possible. As Ernest Newman says in his discussion of Wagner's operas, the love philtre is never suggested by Wagner to be the *cause* of love between the pair, as it is in the legend, but "having drunk what they imagine to be the draught of Death" the lovers "feel themselves free to confess . . . the love they have so long felt."[17] Intentionally or not, a similar effect occurs in *The Wild Palms*. Charlotte and Harry do not consummate their love until they have the money. Significantly, they perform this ritual as they are departing on the train, a departure cast in terms of a journey by water and thus symbolizing both death (departure) and birth (entering water).[18]

The references to water and departure and death come together explicitly in this scene. Harry marvels at woman's natural affinity for cohabitation, the ability to cast off into "untried and unsupportive

[17] Ernest Newman, *The Wagner Operas* (New York: Alfred A. Knopf, 1949), 208.

[18] A prime fictional analogue is Thomas Mann's *Magic Mountain*, where Hans Castorp's train journey to the sanitarium is cast as travel by water, and for the same reasons that Faulkner has to treat Charlotte and Harry's trip in this manner. For Faulkner, Mann was one of the "two great men in my time" (*Lion in the Garden: Interviews with William Faulkner, 1926–1962*, ed. James B. Meriwether and Michael Millgate [New York: Random House, 1968], 49). A classical definition of these symbols is Freud's *Interpretation of Dreams*, trans. A. A. Brill (New York: Macmillan, 1920), 232, 243–49, etc. Faulkner has said, "Everybody talked about Freud when I lived in New Orleans, but I have never read him" (*Lion in the Garden*, 251). But one of Sherwood Anderson's good friends was a Freudian-oriented psychoanalyst, Trigant Burrow, whom Anderson had met through Tennessee Mitchell. In view of "Old Man," the identification of the imagery in Freudian terms is not so esoteric as it might seem at first glance.

space where no shore is visible" (54). As the train leaves New Orleans across the trestle between Lake Pontchartrain and Lake Maurepas,[19] water is on all sides, "swamp-bound and horizonless, lined with rotting wooden jetties to which small dingy boats were tied" (58). Not a pretty picture, nor a wholesome one, yet Charlotte makes another speech: "I love water . . . That's where to die . . . to cool you quick so you can sleep, to wash out of your brain and out of your eyes and out of your blood all you ever saw and thought and felt and wanted and denied" (58). Nothingness, apparently, is better than grief. Charlotte, the self-styled tragic lover, is already responding to the lure of oblivion, yet this seems only another pose, and in fact when the time comes she will not welcome death. What Charlotte says can be judged false, or at least self-deceived. She may think she is being ultraromantic, and responding to the death-wish, but her next act is to make Harry secure the drawing room where they consummate their love sexually. Most of the passion and intensity and poignance of romantic love was due to the *inability* of the lovers to consummate it. Like Tristan and Isolde, the lovers of the archetype pined for each other as they lay on either side of a naked sword, or its equivalent. Obstacles were a necessity, to the point that many of the lovers, like Tristan with his sword, created them for themselves. In the same regard, as Professor Brooks has pointed out from Rougemont, society is a necessary element when it puts barriers in the lovers' way: a permissive society is no good to those who desire to be passionate and tragic lovers.[20] Schopenhauer

---

[19] Faulkner probably made this train trip himself, traveling between New Orleans and Oxford. He makes an unaccountable slip. Rittenmeyer plans to stay on until the train reaches Hammond (La.), and Charlotte goes to the smoking car (the "men's room," as Harry says; typically, Charlotte is not deterred) to say goodbye. Harry suspects she will not return, and when she does it is without being firm in her resolution to carry on the affair: "If he were to get back on the train, with a ticket to Slidell—" (59). Hammond is the first medium-sized town on a more eastward route out of New Orleans, one that would send them through Hattiesburg, Mississippi. If the train were going from Hammond to Slidell, it would have to go in a circle back toward New Orleans. Or perhaps Faulkner has not made an error at all, given all the other circle motifs in the novel.
[20] Brooks, "Romantic Love and *The Wild Palms*," 272.

expresses the idea very simply: "possession takes away the charm."[21] But the sexual union of the lovers has another element to it, too, practical and primary: the procreative. The sexual act by its very basic biological nature is the prime affirmation of life and the will to live.[22]

Harry's reflections seem to take into account this latter association. He feels "embattled and doomed and lost, before the entire female principle" (57). When she addresses him strongly about "cutting it" —that is, severing her last tie to Rittenmeyer by consummating her affair with Harry—he thinks *"She doesn't love me now . . . She doesn't love anything now"* (59). It is as if he is only a pawn of Nature—like the tall convict swept on by the flood—a mere necessity to "the female principle" in its function of generation. Charlotte talks like the conventional romantic heroine, less in love with her lover than she is in love with love; but "bitching" is one of her chief and favorite occupations. And "bitching" is what eventually brings her doom.

Charlotte inverts another literary tradition in the prelude to the consummation scene. She tells Harry "It's not finished. It will have to be cut" (words which apply ironically to the abortion). When Harry fails to understand, she paraphrases scripture, and then puns on it: " 'If thine eye offend thee, pluck it out, lad, and be whole.' That's it. Whole. Wholly lost—something. I've got to cut it" (59). The quotation is from Matthew 5:29. The next verse is a balanced phrase: "And if thy right hand offend thee, cut it off, and cast it from thee. . . ." Matthew 5:27–31 is an admonition against adultery—either through covetousness or divorce. Charlotte has turned the meaning of it upside-down, using it to justify adultery. The connection to Faulkner's original title is also plain. Later, when she has conceived a child that will "offend" the continuation of the idealized love affair which she has never actually created, she will want to pluck that out too, by cutting.

Harry is merely naive, following in her wake. One index of his naiveté, and of the care Faulkner has taken to be sympathetic to many characters in this book, is the intern's marvelling at Rittenmeyer's

21 Schopenhauer, *The World as Will and Idea*, I, 405.
22 *Ibid.*, 421–27.

emotions. Like Charlotte, Harry accepts the stereotype of Rittenmeyer, but seeing the dull and conventional businessman on the train, handing over his wife as if he were giving away the bride, Harry thinks *"Why, he's suffering, he's actually suffering,* thinking how perhaps it is not the heart at all, not even the sensibilities, with which we suffer, but our capacity for grief or vanity or self-delusion or perhaps even merely masochism" (55). The phrase "it is not the heart" has accrued weight by repetition (6, 11, 47). The remainder of the sentence applies pointedly to Harry's final scene. He is going to learn a lot about grief.[23]

More images from the preceding chapters are picked up at the close of Chapter Three. Harry's first reaction to booking the drawing room is a characteristic exclamation, "But that will cost—", which Charlotte stifles equally characteristically: "You fool!" (59). Similar scenes, over taxicabs (43, 45, 50), approach the force of a leitmotif or a symbol in the book. As he follows Charlotte down the aisle of the day coach, he is painfully self-conscious, believing that their intentions are obvious and that "they must have disseminated an aura of unsanctity and disaster like a smell" (60).[24] In the drawing room—he has never been in one before—it is he who must close and lock the door between them and the rest of the world: he fumbles at the lock skillessly (60). The scene fades out as Charlotte begins undressing

[23] Compare William Faulkner's *Intruder in the Dust*, where Chick Mallison's coming of age is expressed in the recognition of Lucas Beauchamp's grief through his understanding of Nub Gowrie's. He first sees them as "an old nigger who had just happened to outlive his old nigger wife" and a "violent foulmouthed godless old man who had happened to lose one of the six lazy idle violent ... worthless sons." Seeing Gowrie's grief, he understands Lucas's in words very much like Harry's: *"Why, he's grieving"* (New York: Random House, 1948, pp. 25, 161).
[24] Here Charlotte speaks favorably of death by water; in Chapter Five she will affirm that love is "like the ocean: if you're no good, if you begin to make a bad smell in it, it just spews you up somewhere to die" (*WP*, 83). She has not fashioned the "Bad Smell" yet, but the importance of the image has been announced. In Faulkner's original version of *Sartoris*, "Flags in the Dust," Benbow's sister reacts to his statement that one should not pity people since they are just chemicals by saying, "Maybe that's the reason so many of the things people do smell bad" (typescript, 485–86). I am indebted to Professor Noel E. Polk of the University of Texas at Arlington for calling this to my attention.

him, "pushing aside his own suddenly clumsy fingers" (60). Faulkner's title should have been retained: Harry is captive, forgetful of freedom, and his hands have become inept.[25]

---

[25] Harry and Charlotte go to the hotel on a Saturday (51). Working backward from the Labor Day weekend, 1937, on which they drive to the Wisconsin woods, one arrives with reasonable certainty at the date of May 1, the first Saturday in May that year. The convict's flight begins in May, too, though the actual flood occurred in April. See Appendix.

CHAPTER V

Counterpoint:
The Prison of Willing

So he went to Parchman. . . .
"This here's all swamp," he said. "It dont look healthy."
"It aint healthy," the deputy said. "It aint intended to
be. This is the penitentiary. I cant imagine no more un-
health a man can have than to be locked up inside a bob-
wire pen for twenty or twenty-five years."

WILLIAM FAULKNER
The Mansion

THE TRIP WHICH THE TALL CONVICT TAKES at the beginning of
his adventure conforms to the one begun by Charlotte and Harry in
the preceding chapter and underscores particularly the fact that
Harry's flight is more a captivity than a run to freedom. The setting
emphasizes Schopenhauer's claim that all life is a prison. Once they are
out of the open-air penitentiary, the convicts see water ravelled out in
plow furrows "like the bars of a prone and enormous grating" (61),
and when the furrows disappear, only a "flat and motionless steel-
colored sheet" remains (62). Repeated departures by water—whether
in a truck, a train, or a boat—emphasize the symbolism of death and
birth of the previous chapter.

Neither the convict nor Harry has lived a particularly pleasant life
prior to the adventures he is forced to undertake. Held by Charlotte's
grasp and obeying her commands, Harry locks the metal door of the
compartment where they seal their love and their fate, and immediately he is caught in an affair that will circumscribe his life more than
his own inactivity did before. Removed by command from the com-

EPIGRAPH: William Faulkner, *The Mansion* (New York: Random House,
1959), 47–48.

fortable prison farm, shackled in the open truck to the brutish men, moving into a chaotic environment, the convict will have to struggle for existence as he has never had to before. Despite the unwholesome, rotten, swamp-bound landscape on the outskirts of New Orleans, Charlotte spoke romantically of death by water. Waterbound themselves, the convicts watch the struggles of a stranded Negro family to save their possessions and themselves from the rising flood, a scene more typical of the real nature of things. The convicts do not register the seriousness of what they see any more than Charlotte does. The water looks "not innocent, but bland," but they soon realize that it has motion, terrific speed, "as if once they had become aware of movement . . . the water seemed to have given over deception" (62–63). As the road disappears under the flood, Faulkner's image is shaped to apply to the lovers: it enters the water "like a flat thin blade slipped obliquely into flesh by a delicate hand" (64). It has been "cut" for the convicts, too; they have cast off irrevocably.

As Carolyn Reeves has shown, Faulkner spells out the outrageous and inharmonious qualities of the worlds through which the characters travel, using "Old Man" for physical effect.[1] Time is even out of joint, the dawn "belated" (61) and the rains like those of November rather than May (67). The truck moves south from Parchman, the convicts looking west toward the flood (61–62); apparently they are headed to Mound's Landing, where the levee broke. They have been travelling for several hours, from after midnight through the belated dawn (30, 61) and on to noon the next day (65). When they reach the rail line upon which their journey will continue, they are probably at Moorhead, Mississippi, that famous spot where "the Southern cross the Yellow Dog," as it goes in W. C. Handy's song "The Yellow Dog Blues."[2] The convicts act less than human. The only one who ques-

[1] Carolyn Reeves, "*The Wild Palms*: Faulkner's Chaotic Cosmos," *Mississippi Quarterly*, 20, No. 3 (Summer 1967), 148–57.

[2] This would be at a point some twenty miles east and ten miles south of Scott, Mississippi, where Mound's Landing was located, and a rail junction from which they could proceed in the direction of the main Mississippi levee. Moorhead always suffered inundation during flood time. *Mississippi: A Guide to the Magnolia State*, compiled and written by the Federal Writer's Project of the Works Progress Administration (New York: Viking, 1938), 405. The passenger

tions the truck's proceeding on a road they cannot see is ironically a kind of Quixote-figure, or perhaps modeled on Dante: "a middle-aged man with a wild thatch of iron-gray hair and a slightly mad face" (64).[3] "They're going to drown us! Unlock the chain!" he cries, but "for all the answer he got the men within radius of his voice might have been dead" (65). They react to him as they did to the struggling family in the flood, unable or unwilling to sympathize or to recognize their common plight. Later, assembled at the cotton warehouse where furniture and refugees from the flood are being housed, the convicts—"twinned by their clanking and clashing umbilicals" (67)—are "shackled in braces like dogs at a field trial" (67). Like Harry with his Charlotte, the tall convict evidently has his "partner" too, the plump pallid hairless woman-like lifer who goes out in the boat with him and for whom Nature, or fate, exchanges the pregnant woman.

The convicts have been conditioned by their servitude to act like beasts; besides being dog-like, they stand "almost ruminant, their backs turned to the rain as sheep and cattle do" (67), knowing they will not be given shelter because they are not as valuable as the furniture stored in the warehouse. To their captors they are as if inanimate, a view they practically acquiesce in themselves. When they smell food they make no instinctive move towards it, but wait until they are "herded" (68) into lines.

Paradox is the chief quality of the chaos which the flood has produced, which is fitting, since out of this destruction and flood will come plenty, just as out of death once again comes life, the Eternal Return. The bridge they had crossed earlier was only "two delicate and paradoxical iron railings slanting out of the water" (65). The railroad embankment rises out of the flood "in a kind of paradoxical denial and repudiation of change and portent" (66). The train departs 'running backward now though with the engine in front where

---

car has a cast iron stove "hovered about by the ghosts of a thousand Sunday excursions to Memphis or Moorhead and return" (69).

[3] The often hysterical middle-aged poet of the *Inferno* seems to be evoked elsewhere in "Old Man,' too. Compare also Charlotte's statue of the knight of La Mancha: "a Quixote with a gaunt mad dreamy unco-ordinated face" (*WP*, 91).

before it had moved forward but with the engine behind" (69). Two
of the important sets of recurring allusion in *The Wild Palms* come
together significantly in this scene. The picture of the flood, of a world
in chaos and flux, bears a strong resemblance to passages in Nietzsche's
Thus Spake Zarathustra, a book that Harry will paraphrase during
his final scene in the novel. A few pages before, in "Old Man," the
convicts had regarded the water as bland and innocent, almost without motion; then, when they arrived at a bridge, they had realized
that beneath the surface there was "terrific and secret speed" and all
the masked fury of the flood. In the Third Part of *Thus Spake Zarathustra* (the part Faulkner seems to draw on chiefly), there is the
following passage:

> When the water hath planks, when gangways and railings o'erspan
> the stream, verily, he is not believed who then saith: "All is in flux."
> But even the simpletons contradict him. "What?" say the simple-
> tons, "all in flux? Planks and railings are still *over* the stream!"
> "*Over* the stream all is stable, all the values of things, the bridges
> and bearings, all 'good' and 'evil': these are all *stable!*"
> Cometh, however, the hard winter, the stream-tamer, then learn
> even the wittiest distrust, and verily, not only the simpletons then
> say: "Should not everything—*stand still?*"
> "Fundamentally standeth everything still"—that is an appropriate
> winter doctrine, good cheer for an unproductive period, a great
> comfort for winter-sleepers and fireside-loungers.
> "Fundamentally standeth everything still"—: but *contrary* there-
> to, preacheth the thawing wind!
> The thawing wind, a bullock, which is no ploughing bullock—a
> furious bullock, a destroyer, which with angry horns breaketh the ice!
> The ice however—*breaketh gangways!*
> O my brethren, is not everything *at present in flux?* Have not all
> railings and gangways fallen into the water? Who would still hold to
> 'good' and 'evil'? [4]

In "Old Man" the bridges are down, the flux, the movement of life is

[4] Friedrich Nietzsche, *Thus Spake Zarathustra*, trans. Thomas Common, in
The Philosophy of Nietzsche, ed. Willard Huntington Wright (New York:
Modern Library, 1934), 207. The passage comes from Part III, Chapter LVI,
"The Old and New Tables," section 8.

revealed. And some—like Harry and Charlotte—will try to live beyond good and evil.

The second allusion is to Dante's *Inferno*. The opening scene of "Wild Palms" draws on Dante's vision of the third ring of the Seventh Circle of hell, as we have seen. Dante and Virgil leave the seventh circle on the back of the monster Geryon; Geryon flies backwards (Canto XII), and Dante's imagery is, somewhat oddly, aquatic: "As the bark goes from its station backwards, backwards, so the monster took himself from thence." Here in "Old Man" the convicts also travel backwards—on a train, though they are soon to see their journey transformed to aquatic terms, too. Later on, the tall convict's adventures in the runaway skiff and Harry and Charlotte's trip on the mining train will be backwards, and both stories will contain further allusions to Dante's poem as Faulkner explores or discovers affinities between Dante's experience of romantic love and the affairs of the two sets of characters in *The Wild Palms*. At the end of the love story, when Harry debates suicide, there is a crucial juxtaposition of Dante and Nietzsche which will help greatly to resolve the meaning of Harry's experience.

Now, on the train, the convicts jostle each other to be nearest the stove, although it has no fire in it. For all their animal and even inanimate qualities on the levee, the convicts behave instinctively at last. There have been many pointed references in the book thus far to fire and to hearth, symbols of security, of the life force, and of the continuity of home and family. There will be more. The symbolic hearth with its ritual fire is an ingredient that seems to be lacking in the modern world. Harry's difficulties as a student are increased because the only way a boy can work through college now, the author says, is to carry a football or stop those who do; dormitories are steam-heated and do not require the furnace-stoking services by which Harry's father had supported himself in his day (31). In Rittenmeyer's house the cold hearth is the backdrop of Harry's visit, a pointed indication of the coldness of Charlotte's marriage. Later there will be a strong contrast between the tall convict's careful nursing of flames to heat food and fashion tools and Harry's superfluous woodgathering.

Men who have lost most of their instincts still run to the symbol of fire and warmth while the too sophisticated do not know what to do.

The convicts are cast completely upon the alien now; the engine of the train whistles "wild and forlorn," "unechoed," "four short harsh blasts filled with the wild triumph and defiance yet also with repudiation and even farewell, as if the articulated steel itself knew it did not dare stop and would not be able to return" (69–70). The forlorn whistle of the backward train speaks for the lovers, too, both as they leave New Orleans and, later, as they depart Chicago the last time: repudiation and farewell and fear of stopping (Charlotte has said that if Rat stays on the train she might go back) and the knowledge that there is no retreat. Appropriately, the last sign the convicts have of ordinary human life is another tableau of domestic disruption and tragedy, a burning plantation house: "Juxtaposed to nowhere and neighbored by nothing it stood, a clear steady pyre-like flame rigidly fleeing its own reflection, burning in the dusk above the watery desolation with a quality paradoxical, outrageous and bizarre" (70). Here is more chaos brought home to them, cast again in terms of paradox and disrupted family life. The clear steady flame might stand for the kind of love Charlotte wants, like Tamar Cauldwell's desire in the Jeffers' poem for a "love sterile and sacred as the stars." But it is pyre-like, and this funerary burning of the isolate house foreshadows Charlotte's immolation in searing pain on the burning sands of the dead, Dantesque beach. The lovers resemble the illusion of the burning house, since they, too, are fleeing their own reflection, paradoxically running away from conventions which they cannot escape. They have already consummated a marriage of minds and bodies; it will become increasingly like any other marriage—habit, inhibition, society's pressure, boredom, and the nature of things will see to that.

Once more the convicts transfer to another mode of travel. They are loaded into a shackled string of boats this time, although they have been travelling on water, even in the train, practically since they began their odyssey. The train they have debarked from vanishes "completely in steam" when its firebox is emptied, another touch by Faulkner which adds the color of illusion and myth to the convict's tale. There is a kind of hellishness about it, as well, and when Harry and Charlotte leave Chicago there will be a similar disappearance in a cloud of steam. Still docile, the convicts "would no more have thought of asking where they were than they would have asked why and what for" (70). At the levee, the knots of refugees are animal-like, displaying the fatigued calm of all creatures displaced by the flood. Watchful like forest creatures, "eyeballs glinting in the firelight" (71), they follow the movements of the chained convicts. But at least the refugees huddle around their camp fires; they are free. The shackled convicts are herded along in the wet while, by contrast, even the cows and mules on the levee are left untethered.

The River awakens cognition in the tall convict and sets him apart momentarily from his dumb and acquiescent fellows, although the image used here does not contribute to an elevated view of mankind. The "profound deep whisper" of the river intrudes upon his consciousness, a sound he has been hearing all day in miniature, "as oblivious of it as an ant or a flea might be of the sound of the avalanche on which it rides" (71–72). When he stops short, the sub-humans behind him crash into his back "like a line of freight cars stopping, with an iron clashing like cars" (72). They proceed past the untethered mules, which have more curiosity about the convicts than the convicts have about their surroundings. Then, "like dogs into cramped kennels" (72), they are forced into overcrowded tents. William Faulkner is not glorifying prison life or implying that it provides "order" in a world of chaos, as Frederick Hoffman suggested in his discussion of *The Wild Palms.*[5] Prison life has made these convicts less than human. They have forgotten what freedom is like; they have forgotten what it is like to be men. When it comes to deciding why the tall convict and Harry accept prison at the end, one should recall this picture of the dehumanization of prison life, but one must also see that the final understanding which each man reaches probably has less to do with the nature of prison than with the particular experiences each has lived through. Though prison is dehumanizing, the awesome force of the Mississippi in flood reduces all mankind to inconsequence. The

[5] Frederick J. Hoffman, *William Faulkner* (New York: Twayne, 1961), 84.

effect of the "Old Man" upon those who dwell precariously and at his pleasure upon the banks is portrayed in a reiterated set of images. The first hint of the furious motion of the flood comes to the convicts when they cross the backward-running stream in the prison truck. Beneath the phenomenon of flood is the usual stream, "murmuring along in the opposite direction, following undisturbed and unaware its appointed course ... like a thread of ants between the rails on which an express train passes ... as unaware of the power and fury as if it were a cyclone crossing Saturn" (62–63). The convict himself has been as oblivious as an ant of the source of the flood noise he has been hearing (71–72). He watches "while a crowd of negroes swarmed" over an intact wooden barn, stripping the wood for fires, the barn dissolving "exactly as a dead fly vanished beneath the moiling industry of a swarm of ants" (73–74).[6] On two occasions the tall convict is so bemused by what he sees that the guards must shout him forward (72, 73). At first he doesn't even know what he sees, asking "What's that?" To which the answer comes, "Dat's de Ole Man." Someone tells him later what he is going to learn anyway about "Old Man": "He dont have to brag" (72).

When daylight comes, the tall convict's education continues. The river, which he can now see for the first time, has a "rigid steel-colored surface" and the levee he is standing on must appear from the other side as fragile as a hair (73). The first stage of his paradoxical and imposed freedom begins; he and his partner are unshackled and set "free" upon the water. At this point Faulkner cuts away from the tall convict and shifts abruptly to a later scene, for which he has carefully laid his plans. On the levee the tall convict observes an incoming load of

[6] These images have been taken as one of the allusions to Hemingway (cf. *A Farewell to Arms* [New York: Scribner's, 1929], 338–39). The differences, however, are revealing. Frederick Henry makes a subjective judgment about the meaninglessness of life when he remembers what happens to the ants on the log. In *The Wild Palms*, the flood reduces proportionately the stature of mankind. See the discussion in Chapters One and Eleven. George Sidney, in "Faulkner in Hollywood: A Study of His Career as a Scenarist" (Ph.D. dissertation, University of New Mexico, 1959), 75, points out a more analogous ant–image in the movie scenario of *Today We Live* (1933) and *Absalom, Absalom!* (1936). Cf. also the sketch "The Beggar" (Jan.-Feb. 1925 *Double Dealer*) in *New Orleans Sketches*, ed. Carvel Collins (New York: Grove, 1961).

refugees among whom a young Negro, provisionless as the grasshopper in the fable, plinks his guitar. Near midnight on the day the tall convict and his mate are shipped out, another scene is played. A penitentiary deputy warden, the plump convict, and a "small man with a gaunt unshaven wan face still wearing an expression of incredulous outrage" (76) make their way to martial law headquarters to report to the Warden that the tall convict is presumed drowned. The gaunt white man is "the fellow on the cotton house" whom the convicts were supposed to rescue along with the woman in the tree. When the man tells his story, it is like finding the second half of a torn bill. He had not been saved earlier because there was room in the boat "for a bastard nigger guitar but not for me—" (79). This scene is as full of mordant humor as Jason Compson's section of *The Sound and the Fury* and to paraphrase it is ruinous. Faulkner sets it up carefully, however, and he will play back to it again in one of the funniest lines in the book, the tall convict's statement to the deputy when he surrenders the woman, the boat, and himself, but not the "bastard on the cottonhouse" (278).

Amid the humor is a real irony and a picture of society's tendency toward hypocrisy and corruption. The deputy suggests an honor to the memory of the tall convict, "Drowned while trying to save lives in the great flood of nineteen twenty-seven" (79–80): something for his folks to hang on the wall "because after all they sent him to the Farm to raise cotton, not to fool around in a boat in a flood" (80). Like the recurrence of the "bastard on the cottonhouse," this works later too. When the tall convict has come back, similar consideration will be taken for this deputy in the name of economy and political expediency. As they leave on their way back to the prison farm, the deputy teases the plump convict with the observation that his partner is "free." The plump convict's answer is swift: "Free. He can have it" (80). Between captivity and nothing, he will take captivity.

CHAPTER VI

The Tragic Deception
of the Hero

...life swings like a pendulum backwards and forwards
between pain and ennui. This has also had to express itself very oddly in this way; after man had transferred all
pain and torments to hell, there then remained nothing
over for heaven but ennui.

SCHOPENHAUER
The World as Will and Idea

CHAPTER FIVE of *The Wild Palms* is the structural and thematic
center of the novel. In it everything turns upon a quiescent interlude
in solitude and a Christmas scene, then plunges inexorably downward
to tragedy. The impetus shifts from Charlotte to Harry, though in the
beginning Charlotte is still very much in control. She has brought them
to the Windy City, Chicago, another example of urban wickedness,
like the Crescent City on the river. The identification of both places
with Babylon and Rome is made clear in many ways, and it was
underscored by the deleted typescript title, "If I Forget Thee,
Jerusalem."

Brooks has discussed the place of "community" in Faulkner's work,
noting that Faulkner's fictional region (like the real one on which it is
founded) still had "a basically agricultural economy...an old-
fashioned set of values, and a still vital religion with its cult, creed, and
basic norms of conduct."[1] Such values are an important backdrop to
the romantic love which Charlotte and Harry are seeking to create.
They provide our typical romantic lovers with obstacles which help

EPIGRAPH: Arthur Schopenhauer, *The World as Will and Idea*, trans. R. B.
Haldane and J. Kemp (London: Routledge and Kegan Paul, 1883), I, 402.
[1] Cleanth Brooks, *William Faulkner: The Yoknapatawpha Country* (New
Haven, Conn.: Yale University Press, 1963), 1.

to establish the powerful, unresolved experience that fits the arche-type. As Brooks writes in his section on *The Town*, "In Faulkner's world ... the myth [of romantic love] still carries lethal power. Passion still costs something. .... Marriage is still a stable institution and the community mores cannot be flaunted with impunity."[2]

The lovers in *The Wild Palms* flee from city to city, or go into boring isolation; they are not in a community but in an indifferent impersonal world. And as Denis de Rougemont has pointed out, nothing is more devastating to passionate romantic love than a society which does not put obstacles in its way. With no social norms to flaunt and nothing to hide from, no tangible enemy, the lovers slip into mechanical roles among the faceless and anonymous myriads mentioned by the doctor (4) and Harry (54). Possession, as Schopenhauer has said, takes away the charm. The greatest illusion of the life of the will is love. It is true that the myth of romantic love will have lethal power in *The Wild Palms,* but Nature, rather than society, exacts the final price from Charlotte. Both Harry and the tall convict must pay society, but with an absurd irrelevance, and for their "crimes" rather than because of love.

In the city, from the very beginning, Harry and Charlotte have no trouble setting up a rather conventional household. On the second morning in Chicago, Harry sees plenty of evidence that Charlotte is in control. Like a bridegroom conducting a new bride, Charlotte introduces him to the apartment she has selected. Even the cab that takes them there is a strong touch: Harry's inability to afford a cab was a recurring symbol of his penuriousness and love's frustration in New Orleans. The apartment is unilaterally Charlotte's, "*a place not to hold us but to hold love*" (84).

So far so good. The primacy of love over the mere lovers is part of the romantic archetype. Harry makes an observation at this point betraying his own romantic inclinations (which do not hold up in practice) and denying to Charlotte the complete abandonment she probably believes she expresses. For women, he thinks, "even the

2 *Ibid.*, 208.

71

love-nest under the rose" must "follow a rule and a pattern": "*It's not the romance of illicit love which draws them, not the passionate idea of two damned and doomed and isolated forever against the world and God and the irrevocable which draws men; it's because the idea of illicit love is a challenge ... because they have an irresistible desire to ... take the illicit love and make it respectable ... trim the very incorrigible bachelor's ringlets which snared them into the seemly decorum of Monday's hash and suburban trains*" (82). Whether he is correct or not, at this moment, in this case of all for love, love is still uppermost. "*There's a part of her that doesn't love anybody, anything*" (82), he thinks, and he gets a straight answer when he charges her with the evident truth: "So it's not me you believe in, put trust in; it's love. . . . Not just me; any man." "Yes. It's love" (83). Charlotte wants "heaven, or hell: no comfortable safe peaceful purgatory between for you and me to wait in" (83). She gets her wish in a sense, but heaven turns out to be a purgatory or limbo, featureless and ridden with boredom. Hell will be real enough, thanks to Faulkner's use of Dante. Harry makes a bad and perhaps unwitting pun: "*she did not just run from one man to another; she did not merely mean to swap one piece of clay she made a bust with for another—*" (84). There is nevertheless a relevance to what he says. Art is one of the touchstones of the novel. Charlotte's artistry is either a complete lie or the dilettantish dabbling of a pseudosophisticate. Harry's own initiation into the world of art carries him only to the writing of cheap moronic fiction. His watercolor and painting are doomed from the beginning because he is color-blind and does not know it. Charlotte's chief claim is that she is a sculptress: symbolically she tries to fashion love, with Harry and herself as the raw materials. Her actual art gradually reveals what to expect from her symbolic efforts.

Like the tall convict, Harry has slipped out of one channel only to be swept away, volitionlessly, in another. He continues to drift, because he cannot escape himself: what he is, his long-time habits; not yet anyway. "*I'm not embracing her but clinging to her because there is something in me that wont admit it cant swim or cant believe it*

The Tragic Deception of the Hero

can" (84).[3] This follows logically what Charlotte has said about preferring to "drown in the ocean" instead of being "urped up onto a strip of dead beach" (83), and it points to their fate, their own *noyade* of marriage. Harry is still beset by two other bugaboos: time and money. He has trouble getting a job because he served an internship of twenty months, instead of the required twenty-four: "*I have been confounded by numbers*" (85), he thinks. It is not the last time. Charlotte projects their days in cold figures, calculating that they will be without money on a certain date in September. But she forgets to write her husband on the appointed monthly time to let him know she is all right, and his detective makes inquiries that cause Harry to lose the only job he has been able to get.[4] He does not tell Charlotte about the job; he pretends to go to work each day and then sits on park benches to calculate their rapidly approaching bankruptcy with the same passivity that marked his drifting through medical school.

Harry has difficulty using his medical knowledge because his twenty months' internship arouses suspicion. He thinks bitterly, in words that pick up one of the controlling images of the book, "it is apparently more seemly to die in the dulcet smell than to be saved by an apostate from convention" (85). He finally secures a position making Wasserman tests for syphilis in a tenement district hospital, but he is fired from this job, "which existed because of moral turpitude, on the grounds of moral turpitude" (96). Paradox is everywhere and society is corrupt, hypocritical, and strong.

Harry is resigned to failure anyway. At any given moment he is prepared to yield to the most innocuous pressures. On the train he expects Charlotte to back out. He is fatalistic about getting a job, and stoic when he loses what he gets. Charlotte fights to hold the dream, in the very act defeating both herself and it. She forces Harry to admit that the kind of hunger they must fear is not emptiness of

[3] The "or" in this passage is not italicized in the published book, but ought to be, as the typescript shows.
[4] Charlotte's monthly carelessness foreshadows the carelessness which causes the unwanted pregnancy. When she conceives and tells Harry that her period is 16 days late (205), he will be confounded by numbers in another way.

belly but emptiness of heart, the failure of love; yet they are always looking at the larder, or buying and fixing chops, to the point that eventually groceries instead of money become the means of exchange in Harry's computations of time.[5] As if that were not sufficient evidence of the ordinary and quotidian to tarnish the dream, Charlotte sets out to earn the money that Harry cannot. She destroys their life together completely. Her art is not merely "sophisticated and bizarre" and "fantastic and perverse" (87), but commercial. Her figurines sell, and she brings home the money she has gotten for them, "her yellow eyes like a cat's in the dark, not triumph or exultation but rather fierce affirmation" (87). Whether her art, or her conviction about love, seems to her to have been vindicated is not clear; perhaps both. In any case she is self-deceived. She believes that by her art she is going to keep the romantic vision intact. She likes "bitching"—her euphemism for intercourse—and making things with her "deft untiring hands." So she earns money to do one by doing the other, working upon her perverted art at night when Harry is in bed, often asleep, and bringing a club of sophisticates into their apartment (88), friends and hangers-on like the bohemian crowd she ran with in New Orleans.

Charlotte and Rat had separate money: she had the one hundred and twenty-five dollars from her brother and would not take anything from her husband. The middle-aged doctor and his wife have separate money too (290). And now so do Harry and Charlotte: Harry refuses what Charlotte has earned. Already they have reached two of the meaningful points in their transformation to the "ordinary couple": separate money and separate lives. Only Charlotte's powerful personality is still capable of holding Harry, her "unwinking yellow stare in which he seemed to blunder . . . like a moth, a rabbit . . . an envelopment almost like a liquid" (87). She is still capable of striking a pose. When the sales of her figurines stop, she is as quick with a rationalization as Harry was about his hospital job, but hers

[5] In Sherwood Anderson's *Dark Laughter* (New York: Boni & Liveright, 1925), Bruce Dudley notices that his wife's friends never leave their secure jobs to perform the artistic tasks they talk about: " 'We have to eat,' they said. What a lot of talk there had been about the necessity of eating" (35).

The Tragic Deception of the Hero

is not resignation. She says it not to Harry alone, but to the assembled company of the evening club: "But I expected it. Because these are just fun . . . Like something created to live only in the pitch airless dark, like in a bank vault or maybe a poison swamp, not in the rich normal nourishing air breathed off of guts full of vegetables from Oak Park and Evanston. And so that's it and that's all. And now I'm not an artist any more" (89–90). Words for public consumption; surely they have no meaning for her. They are not sincere and she does not realize their implications. Among things which are just fun, "bitching" must rank high, as she herself would be the first to say. There is however always the chance that what is produced by "bitching" will be killed by letting the air in before it ever sees light. Her pronouncement is meant to be ironic, a condemnation of those high bourgeois in Oak Park and Evanston and other middle-class suburbs, just as the phrase "And now I'm not an artist any more" is not seriously intended, though in fact it is true. Being an artist is not to be turned off and on at will. Her dedication to art may be compared to her younger brother's dedication to the newspaper business at which he had "cubbed" in a "dilettante and undergraduate heeler manner" (88). She resumes her art, and the effect is the same as before: the same kind of figures, the same disruption of her life with Harry.

The figures that Charlotte fashions have a significance of their own. In her first set was a Mrs. O'Leary with Nero's face and a cow with a ukelele. This directs attention back to the first chapter of "Old Man," in which the convicts were compared to the "slaves . . . who watched the mounting flames of Rome from Ahenobarbus' gardens" (29). Ahenobarbus is Nero,[6] and the point of linking him with Mrs. O'Leary and her cow, and Rome with Chicago, is to reinforce the title that is no longer there, with its reference to the Babylonian captivity, and to emphasize the lurid picture of city life that is drawn. The other figure is a Kit Carson with Nijinsky's legs, and it is hard to say whether the choice carries extra meaning: the frontiersman

6 The chief reference to Nero as Ahenobarbus—that is, in terms of his family name—is in Suetonius, *The Twelve Caesars*, a copy of which was in Faulkner's library (the 1931 Modern Library edition).

75

and the by-then crazed dancer. Perhaps the perversity is apparent. Charlotte's early pieces portrayed Chicago's past and were quite small. Now she switches to literature and creates objects "almost as large as small children" (91). The Don Quixote "with a gaunt mad dreamy unco-ordinated face" bears some relation to the screaming convict on the truck in the preceding chapter and helps to put the tall convict's chivalry in place. Charlotte is quixotic in the same way as he, having taken her ideas about romantic love from what she has read and trying to act as if the world were like what she had learned in books. The appearance of a Falstaff in a novel about a young man named Henry (31) or Harry is worth noting too. Charlotte's version of the old knight is overcome by his own carnality: "with the worn face of a syphilitic barber and gross with meat" (91). The figure holds meaning for the Harry here (no Hotspur he, though heir to his father's profession), who pays this statue more attention than he does any of the others. When "he looked at it he seemed to see two: the man and the gross flesh like a huge bear and its fragile consumptive keeper ... the man struggling with the mountain of entrails ... not to overcome it but to pass it, escape it, as you do with the atavistic beasts in nightmare" (91). The phrases in Harry's mind are echoed later in the tall convict's struggles with the flood and his solitary combats with the saurian monsters of the poison-swamps of Louisiana. Flesh has its day in this novel. Harry and Charlotte's affair is no pure unrequited Petrarchan passion, but a carnal engagement where "bitching" is frequent and fun. Harry might have been able to avoid his entanglement, as a matter of fact, if he had only had a little experience of the flesh before he grew too old: "the passionate tragic ephemeral loves of adolescence, the girl- and boy-white, the wild importunate fumbling flesh, which had not been for him" (34). He will have recourse to the memory-bearing flesh—"memory could live in the old wheezing entrails" (324)—at the end.

Charlotte's Cyrano de Bergerac is the "low-comedy Jew in vaudeville," while her Roxanne is cast as the gum-chewing ten-cent store song plugger. Rostand's play is called a "heroic comedy" and thus may be likened to the story of the tall convict. Like the tall convict,

The Tragic Deception of the Hero

Cyrano loses his beloved to another man: Roxanne pines for Christian and the tall convict's passenger is already pregnant, while the girl for whom he projected his heroic deeds has become Mrs. Vernon Waldrip. Each hero suffers because of his nose (in Cyrano's terms: "a great nose indicates a great man" and "When it bleeds—The Red Sea'; [7] in the tall convict's: "I done seem to got to where if that boy was to shoot me in the tail with a bean blower my nose would bleed" [260]. Both put up good fights against great odds, though the tall convict does not come out as well as Cyrano. The perversity of all these figures is the twist of modernity that Charlotte has given them, whether because she cannot do them any other way or for a satirical purpose. They fit perfectly into a world where a new avatar of Venus would be "a soiled man in a subway lavatory with a *palm* full of French post-cards" [italics added] and where a returned Christ would be crucified again "quick in our own defense, to justify and preserve the civilization we have worked and suffered and died shrieking and cursing in rage and impotence and terror . . . to create and perfect in man's own image" (136).[8]

---

[7] Edmond Rostand, *Cyrano de Bergerac*, trans. Brian Hooker (New York: Modern Library, 1923), 43, 51.

[8] The similarity of this image to the "Grand Inquisitor" section of *The Brothers Karamazov* is noted by a questioner at the University of Virginia (*Faulkner in the University*, ed. Joseph Blotner and Frederick Gwynn [New York: Vintage, 1965], 72–73). Professor Keen Butterworth of the University of South Carolina has pointed out to me that in *The Brothers Karamazov* Dostoevsky uses the verse from Psalms which gave Faulkner his original title. Aloysha observes as an unsympathetic doctor advises the impoverished captain to take his dying son to Sicily, an absurdity under the circumstances. The boy tries to console his father: "when I die get a good boy, another one." The father rushes from the room. "I don't want a good boy! I don't want another boy!" he muttered in a wild whisper, clenching his teeth. "If I forget thee, Jerusalem, may my tongue—" Aloysha asks his companion, Krassotkin, "What was that he said about Jerusalem? . . . What did he mean by that?" Krassotkin explains, "It's from the Bible. 'If I forget thee, Jerusalem,' that is, if I forget all that is most precious to me, if I let anything take its place, then may—" The sense of Faulkner's title seems to come directly from Dostoevsky, as do the three clinical doctors in *The Wild Palms*, all of whom are as matter-of-fact as the physician in this moving scene. As she dies, Charlotte tells Harry to go away; and Catherine Barkley, whom Faulkner apparently had in mind when he was working on *The Wild Palms*, tells Frederick to get another girl when she is gone. Harry's decision to live rests on his understanding of the preciousness of his memories.

77

Charlotte's disturbing child-sized figures come between her and Harry. She is gone all day and most of the night, so that Harry must eat and sleep alone, though often she returns to wake him, savagely and peremptorily, with a wrestling movement (92) which recalls the fight with her brother during which she was burned. Harry spends his time, after he loses the job making tests for syphilis, on park benches. Yet Charlotte can speak as if their life "were a complete whole without past or future in which themselves as individuals, the need for money, the figures she had made, were component parts . . . none more important than another" (92). If the parts are perverse and grotesque, can the whole be sound? The scripture Charlotte misused on the train out of New Orleans could be repeated here: "And if thy right eye offend thee, pluck it out, and cast it from thee: for it is profitable for thee that one of thy members should perish, and not that thy whole body should be cast into hell" (Matthew 5:29). She will follow this dictum from the Sermon on the Mount, but not in the way that is intended.

From his passive point of view, Harry sees "their joint life as a fragile globe, a bubble, which she [keeps] balanced and intact above disaster" (92). This is her chief work of art. Charlotte as artist is, however, a caricaturist at best. Then "the puppet business" ends, and she plunges as completely into a parody of domesticity as she had into her false art, like someone reaching after straws. Her work bench becomes a table covered in chintz, her dirty overalls are supplanted by a "curiously frivolous apron" (93), she has chops to cook—symbol *par excellence* of tame bourgeois respectability—and flowers on the table. She continues to dominate Harry sexually; at the end of the first day of domesticity she comes naked into the room where Harry reads and orders him to get his clothes off. In her desperation, with no call to make things with her hands, she falls back on the other activity she enjoys: "The hell with it. I can still bitch" (93). "Bitching" remains the only thing she and Harry can do together, and they cannot do that all the time. Besides certain hard realities like the need

Fyodor Dostoevsky, *The Brothers Karamazov*, trans. Constance Garnett (New York: Modern Library, 1950), 679–82.

for money, boredom is a force to be reckoned with when one is trying to sustain a magical and idealized love affair. The pendulum has swung in that direction now, and Charlotte and Harry are no better off than they were upon that frustrating occasion in the cheap New Orleans hotel.

Unable to tell Charlotte that he has lost his job, Harry deceives her by spending the working hours of the day in the park subtracting his daily expenditures and watching the time approach when their money will be gone and, presumably, their affair ended. He confesses a kind of profound faith in Charlotte (93), yet he expresses his faith in a peculiarly inverted way: *"God wont let her starve ... She's too valuable. He did too well with her. Even the one who made everything must fancy some of it enough to want to keep it"* (93–94). Harry sounds here like Tennyson in sections 55 and 56 of *In Memoriam* asking the question which Nature answers simply: "I bring to life, I bring to death." Schopenhauer provides an even more pertinent answer in this particular case: "Nature ... the inner being of which is the will to live itself, impels with all her power both man and the brute towards propagation. Then it has attained its end with the individual, and is quite indifferent to its death, for, as the will to live, it cares only for the preservation of the species, the individual is nothing to it." [9]

Harry's faith resides not so much in Charlotte as in God as a principle of conservation. Process and nature however are impersonal, as the voice of Nature speaking out of the flood in "Old Man" makes plain, and the only meaning that can exist in the world these people inhabit is what they give to it. They have purposely cut themselves loose from everything, and their own acts show just how far out of turn Harry speaks. When the market for her figurines dropped, Charlotte gave them away. She gives away their household god, the Bad Smell. And when they make a child, she does not want to keep it and Harry finally concurs. Why should the God in whom he pretends to trust be any more careful of His creations than they are of theirs? They are a mirror of nature themselves, the over-fecund, the

[9] Schopenhauer, *The World as Will and Idea*, I, 425.

continuing, the "female principle" and its necessary consort. When they try to hold time, stop process, deny nature, they bring what is also natural, death.

The money which Harry has found and that which Charlotte makes trickles away, but Harry still carries the 300 dollar cashier's check that Rat gave him to buy Charlotte's return passage. The check is a presence, a symbol, and Harry treats it ritually, though he knows that his toying with ways to spend the money is only "a form of masturbation" (94), a substitute for using the money and not really a prelude to doing so. He has too much respect for the idea of money to get rid of it, thinking that if he were to destroy the check even Rat would not get the money back (101), and so he carries it like his sense of resignation. Harry and Charlotte deal frequently in symbols. Charlotte is fashioning the Bad Smell on the day she learns that Harry is jobless and that they are too broke to pay the next quarter's rent. The Bad Smell stands in Charlotte's mind for that unworthiness which makes love cast one up like the ocean. By modeling a fetish she perhaps hopes to keep that evil outside their affair. It is like the metal rabbit which Doctor Martino gives Louise King: " 'That's my being afraid,' she said. 'A rabbit: don't you see? But it's brass now; the shape of being afraid, in brass that nothing can hurt. As long as I keep it I am not even afraid of being afraid.' " [10] Charlotte has talked about making things in clay and brass and stone that cannot be hurt (40–41), but her chef d'oeuvre is a flesh and blood love affair. The little papier-mâché symbol only three inches tall is appropriately inadequate to its task, if indeed it was ever a proper conception.

Harry's confrontation with Charlotte is auspicious. Here they meet at a difficult pass in their affair, each with a characteristic symbol in hand: Harry the check, Charlotte the Bad Smell; Harry with money and resignation, Charlotte with perverse art and hope for love. Charlotte immediately proposes a "black" celebration: they must go out to dine and to "find a dog" (96). The dog is the key to the scene,

10 William Faulkner, "Doctor Martino," *Collected Stories* (New York: Random House, 1950), 574. The story was first published in 1931.

and is another fetish like the Bad Smell. In this function it is related to a long passage in *The Unvanquished*, the book which immediately preceded *The Wild Palms*. Drusilla explains to Bayard that she has quit sleeping because she is "keeping a dog quiet." When Bayard fails to understand the metaphor, saying that he has not seen a dog, she replies: "No. It's quiet now . . . It doesn't bother anybody any more now. I just have to show it the stick now and then" (*Unv.*, 114). Then she speaks a moving but cynical evaluation of times in which everything has turned upside down—normal life disrupted, houses burned, slaves wandered off to drown themselves in a "home-made Jordan" and all the young men (including hers) dead. One doesn't even have to worry about "getting children," since the young men are gone. And, she says, "you don't even have to sleep alone, you don't even have to sleep at all; and so, all you have to do is show the stick to the dog now and then and say, 'Thank God for nothing' " (*Unv.*, 115). Her dog is an aggregation of griefs and fears which she must keep back in order to go on with life.

Charlotte's dog has a number of other possible referents. The scene in which Charlotte, Harry, McCord, and their Chicago friends hunt the invisible dog has served as the key to parallels between *The Wild Palms* and Hemingway's work because of the pun that occurs there: "Set, ye armourous sons, in a sea of hemingwaves" (97). Incidentally, Drusilla's speech ending "Thank God for nothing" has the ring of Hemingway dialogue, and both scenes call to mind Bill Gorton's talk about a stuffed dog in *The Sun Also Rises* ("Road to hell paved with unbought stuffed dogs," he says).[11] Harry and Charlotte are, appropriately, on a road to hell themselves, and the chops to be given to the dog they seek are in that regard like the traditional sop thrown to distract Cerberus, who guarded hell's gate. The scene is properly set: "the hot August, the neon flashed and glared, alternately corpse- and hell-glowing the faces in the street and their own too as they

11 Ernest Hemingway, *The Sun Also Rises* (New York: Scribner's, 1926), 72–75. Melvin Backman, "Faulkner's *The Wild Palms*: Civilization Against Nature," *University of Kansas City Review*, 29 (Spring 1962), 199–204, notes that Faulkner's pun "armourous" refers to Hemingway's pun on Swift and Armour in "The Snows of Kilimanjaro."

walked" (96); and, "neon flashed and glared, the traffic lights blinked
... above the squawking cabs and hearse-like limousines" (97). They
have a Virgil in McCord, to whom Charlotte says, "Have you no
soul?" (97). They have lost "two members of the party." The parallel
is to Dante and perhaps to Book XI of the *Odyssey*, where Faulkner
had found the title for *As I Lay Dying*. Charlotte had wanted heaven
or hell, no peaceful purgatory between (83). They soon depart to
such a haven, however. After this scene, McCord drives them into
the Wisconsin woods for the peaceful idyll that precedes a return
through the inferno of the city and on into the lowest frozen depths
of hell at the Utah mine. Besides the Dantean parallels and the mythic
allusions, there is a relevant biblical reference in the dog passage. The
dog "was named Moreover now, from the Bible, the poor man's
table" (97). The scripture is Luke 16, the parable of Dives and
Lazarus. The beggar desired "to be fed with the crumbs which fell
from the rich man's table; moreover the dogs came and licked his
sores." [12] Once again, the scripture has been turned upside down.
The ritual propitiation is undertaken for yet another reason. "Chops"
were a controlling image and symbol for bourgeois respectability
in *Dark Laughter*. In *The Wild Palms*, Harry puts them into the
same context when he is illustrating to McCord how respectable he
and Charlotte had become. Charlotte lays them at the feet of a cast-
iron Saint Bernard in a wealthy suburb to propitiate the force which
she believes is their chief threat.

Charlotte flaunts respectability another way. She says they have
forty-eight dollars too much; she rids them of the excess by running
out the money in taxi fare—the old symbol of Harry's poverty. He
does not fail to react. When she asks how much is left, he can look
at the meter and tell her practically to the cent. McCord keeps trying to interrupt Charlotte's fantasy to tell her about the cabin in the
woods, but she babbles on. After he found the money, Harry thought
he could keep his taxi fare, not because he wanted to ride but because

[12] Herman O. Wilson, "A Study of Humor in the Fiction of William Faulkner," (Ph.D. dissertation, University of Southern California, 1956), is first to
point out the source of this quote. Luke 16, like the verse of Matthew which
Charlotte paraphrased earlier, is an admonition against adultery.

he wanted to *"make everything last so there* [wouldn't] *be any gaps"* until he could hide behind his white jacket and *"draw the old routine"* (51) over his head; Charlotte is creating illusions too. What she planned for them, before McCord came up with the cabin, is unknown.

Like Bernice Dudley's friends in Anderson's *Dark Laughter*, the lovers have to eat. They convert their cash into groceries, but Harry will account the diminishing bags and cans as assiduously as he did the turned pages of his textbooks or their fleeting dollars. He says to McCord, "You dont realize how flexible money is until you exchange it for something . . . Maybe this is what the economists mean by a normal diminishing return" (99). Charlotte has already made a number of financial remarks about love: "the value of love is the sum of what you have to pay for it and any time you get it cheap you have cheated yourself"; you "live *in* sin; you cant live on it"; and "You stole the money we've got now; wouldn't you do it again? Isn't it worth it, even if it all busts tomorrow and we have to spend the rest of our lives paying interest" (48, 83, 88). Here and in Harry's remarks (34, 84–85) there is a nexus between love and money which hardly fits the romantic ideal. Harry's statement to McCord, then, is not put there idly. Diminishing returns, defined simply, are a return upon investment that at a certain point fails to increase in proportion to additional investments. Harry and Charlotte have reached this point in their affair. Nothing they do from now on, no matter how hard they try, will increase their "yield"—whether that is taken as happiness, love, or joy in each other. Given more time together during this "golden interval" in an idyllic setting, they become bored and go off separately to spend their days doing nothing.

Melvin Backman discusses briefly their lack of rapport with nature in the Wisconsin woods.[13] When they arrive, their first sight is a buck standing "pink in the Sunday dawn" (99); it disappears immediately and the only other wildlife is a loon whose cry they hear much later. Charlotte believes she has discovered Nature, however,

[13] Melvin Backman, *Faulkner: The Major Years* (Bloomington, Ind.: University of Indiana Press, 1966), 133–34.

and plunges after the deer with the same enthusiasm she has previously devoted to art and housekeeping. In fact, the context of her
excitement is art: she squeals, "That's what I was trying to make!
... the motion, the speed" (99–100).[14] The cynical McCord's answer
brings back to mind the passage about would-be artists from *Dark
Laughter*: " 'Sure,' McCord said. 'Let's eat' " (100). Charlotte again
is only talking. Her art has been perverse and commercial. Insofar
as is known, neither her subject matter nor her approach has given
any promise of what she is saying. She does not capture the deer.

Wilbourne remains under her spell. He is even happy because he
believes he knows where he is going (101), meaning that he can see
the termination of the affair clearly at the end of the "two rows of
cans and sacks, fifty dollars' worth to a side" which they have brought
to the woods. He sounds like Charlotte on the train out of New
Orleans. He seems to be regarding a watery and romantic death—
solitude and peace described in autumnal, faintly subaquean, terms:
"This is a solitude. Then the water, the solitude wavering slow while
you lie and look up at it ... And then fall will come ... leaves drifting
down, the double leaves, the reflection rising to meet the falling one
until they touch and rock a little, not quite closing. And then you
could open your eyes for a minute ... and watch the shadow of the
rocking leaves on the breast beside you" (100). As he did for Charlotte's squeals of delight over the deer, McCord has a squelching
answer for Harry's poetic response to the lure of death. Part of his
rejoinder is in terms of food: "You haven't near done your share of
starving yet" (100), he informs Harry. But his most telling remarks
are these: " 'For sweet Jesus Schopenhauer,' McCord said. 'What
the bloody hell kind of ninth-rate Teasdale is this?' " (100) He has
read Harry accurately on two accounts. The autumnal resignation
is straight out of Sara Teasdale, who "had learned from many an

14 The importance of "motion" was one of Faulkner's preoccupations as an
artist. Cf. *Lion in the Garden: Interviews with William Faulkner, 1926–1962*,
ed. James B. Meriwether and Michael Millgate (New York: Random House,
1968), 253, and the laconic foreword to *The Mansion*. What Charlotte really
wants to do, however, is to arrest life, which is motion, and the result of that
is death.

84

autumn/The way a leaf can drift and go,/Lightly, lightly, almost gay/Taking the unreturning way." [15] The profane apostrophe refers to the kind of death-wish pessimism often interpolated out of Schopenhauer's philosophy: "If you're not careful, you'll talk that stuff to some guy who will believe it and'll hand you the pistol and see you use it," McCord adds (101). It announces the presence of an undercurrent of philosophy that runs throughout the novel. McCord is as correct about the Schopenhauer as he was about the Teasdale, except Harry is not actually expressing pessimism, if only because for the moment he is unacquainted with the will.

Schopenhauer says that "the will proclaims itself primarily in the voluntary movements of our own body." [16] But Harry has proceeded from one volitionless drifting (34) to be drowned "volition and will" in Charlotte's sober yellow stare (39). He has been borne along on their journey by the force of her will, and even sexually he has merely responded passively to her forays upon him. By an accidental short-cut, Harry seems to have arrived at a Schopenhauerian will-less

[15] Sara Teasdale, "Foreknown," in *Collected Poems* (New York: Macmillan, 1939). 262. Any of her books of poetry will provide one or two poems to which Harry's words fit: cf., e.g., "Autumn" out of *Dark of the Moon* (1926). Faulkner's own poetry often evokes a similar mood and uses similar imagery.

Harry's repeated references to the solitude in the woods (100,103,138) call up Thoreau and Emerson, and also a phrase from the German Romantic poets: *waldeinsamkeit* (woods solitude). Heinrich Heine took the term from Ludwig Tieck to use as the title of a poem about disillusionment in *Romancero* (1851). Faulkner's passages seem to have no affinity with Heine's poem, but the chance that he knew poem and poet is strongly suggested by two other lyrics in *Romancero*: a paean to the mule which is a hint for Faulkner's own in *Sartoris* (278–79) and "Jehuda Ben Halevy," which begins with the same verse from the 137th Psalm that Faulkner used for the original title of *The Wild Palms*. There were numerous editions of Heine in translation for Faulkner to have seen, but in 1937 his old publisher, Harcourt, Brace, issued Louis Untermeyer's two-volume Heine, a biography and translations which included "Jehuda Ben Halevy": "And if ever I forget thee,/O Jerusalem, may my right hand/Wither and forget its cunning," (*The Poems*, 369). Added to this is what may or may not be coincidence. Heine was "originally called Harry after an English business friend of the family, a name the boy changed to the more familiar German" (*The Life*, 9–10). Heine's "[d]arling and much-loved sister" was named Charlotte (*The Life*, 255).

Emerson's poem "Waldeinsamkeit" is a possible analogue, too; his "Maia" has been noted as an alternate source for the "veil of Maya."

[16] Schopenhauer, *The World as Will and Idea*, I, 137.

state. He has never asserted his will. What McCord interprets as a wish for death is merely absorption in an ideal, indicated by his vague references to "this"—"I started this too late" and "I'll still take this" (101)—by which he evidently means the love affair that Charlotte has made. His posture is symbolic and somewhat effete: he squats by the water with his hand submerged wrist-deep (100, 101). He believes that they have at last found a place, a solitude, in which the ideal can exist, and this is what he is contemplating will-lessly. Here is how the state is described by Schopenhauer: "If . . . a man relinquishes the common way of looking at things . . . gives the whole power of his mind to perception, sinks himself entirely in this, and lets his whole consciousness be filled with the quiet contemplation of the natural object . . . inasmuch as he *loses* himself . . . forgets even his individuality, his will, and only continues to exist as . . . the clear mirror of the object. . . . he who is sunk in this perception is no longer individual . . . but he is *pure*, will-less, painless, timeless." [17]

Harry indicates that he has accepted totally Charlotte's conception of pure and perfect love. From the first, her intention has been to transcend the useless and despair-producing cycle of pain and ennui by trying, as if by art, to fashion the Platonic Idea, so to speak, of love affairs. Art is the second way, in Schopenhauer's explanation, to escape the round of everyday life, because it "repeats or reproduces the eternal Ideas . . . plucks the object of its contemplation out of the stream of the world's course." [18] But the fact is that neither Harry nor Charlotte has achieved real transcendence. The conception that Harry contemplates and the art object that Charlotte has fashioned are not ideal but flawed. Already apparent is that her art is a sham, only satire and caricature. There is no reason to assume that the "fragile globe" (92) she conceives and tries to hold intact is any more successful. The flaw in her scheme is her sexuality. From the very first—the moment on the train when she said "it" had to be cut— Charlotte has desired consummation. She likes "bitching." But consummation profanes the ideal. It takes away the charm, relieves the

[17] *Ibid.*, 231.
[18] *Ibid.*, 239.

pressure that sustains passion, begets satiety. Consummation runs counter to the romantic ideal, where unrequited love was the rule. Consummation also puts the individual back into time; the sexual act is the most basic expression of the will to live in Nature, which, as Schopenhauer writes, is "always true and consistent, here even naive ... the intensity of the [sexual] impulse, teaches us that in this act the most decided *assertion of the will to live* expresses itself ... as the consequence of this act, a new life appears in time and the causal series, *i.e.*, in nature." [19]

Charlotte has no true ideal, merely a desire, and the satisfaction of that desire will bring ennui. The proof of this formula comes in the Wisconsin woods where the lovers play Romeo and Juliet on an extended honeymoon, Tristan and Isolde in the forest without the naked sword to divide them—they become bored to death. Harry is not deeply absorbed in the false ideal; as the scene with McCord suggests, he is in only up to the wrist, that part of him which Charlotte has grasped like a shackle. He has realized in the past that *"It's all exactly backward. It should be ... the people in the books inventing and reading about us ... males and females but without the pricks or cunts"* (52). The strong language lends emphasis. He means that real people with the potential for desire and disappointment should not read about the unreal people in books. Fictional characters are sexless; men and women are not. When real people copy characters in books they suffer real pangs, like Dante's Paolo and Francesca. Charlotte, presumably, has taken her ideals from books, basing a flesh and blood affair on them, and the sexual nature of the death she suffers reflects the truth of Harry's words. The tall convict's experience with pulp fiction, "shades who had written about shades" (25), provides a comic gloss.

McCord may be right when he accuses Harry of not having the courage of his "fornications" (101). In a profane affair, he and Charlotte like to believe that they have a sacred ideal. Even on her own terms, Charlotte is short of the mark. Love, she says, "just leaves you, goes away, if you are not good enough, worthy enough. ... It's

[19] *Ibid.*, 423.

like the ocean: if you're no good, if you begin to make a bad smell in it, it just spews you up somewhere to die." (83). Several allusions to different kinds of unworthiness are made at the beginning of the lake idyll. Charlotte's illusions about her art recur as she takes watercolors and goes to capture the motion of the deer. McCord refers to "that junk she made" (102), and Charlotte returns from sketching with a blank pad, though the paints show use (103). The Bad Smell reappears. She has brought it along in a coffin-like carton in order to set it up as their household god, pouring a libation of whiskey into the hearth. This improperly dedicated hearth now has a fire on it, but McCord was the one who laid it, and it is he who cooks the first meal at the lake, doing both things despite Harry's concern about extravagance. Harry's fears for the wood are absurd, since there is forest all the way to the Canadian line. His only chore during this idyll will be to stockpile wood for the fireplace. The symbolic gesture will become ironic in his hands as he finally cuts more than they can possibly use. McCord is a realist who keeps offering the couple practical alternatives to their own bad ideas. He reacts brutally to their attempts to justify themselves romantically, crying "Shit!" (101) to Harry's soliloquy by the water. It is the same expletive that was supposed to end the book, taken from the mouth of the tall convict by Faulkner's editor. McCord goes on to suggest that Harry carry his resignation further: "move into the woods and eat ants and play Saint Anthony in a tree and on Christmas you can take a mussel shell and make yourself a present of your own oysters" (102–103).[20] The avowed quietude to which McCord is responding is like Harry's

[20] McCord hits the mark once more, bringing together two traditions of resisting the flesh. Saint Anthony was the first of the desert fathers, whose struggles are well known from Flaubert's novel, one Faulkner liked and owned (See Blotner's *Catalogue* and *Lion in the Garden*, 225, 243). St. Anthony engaged temptation spiritually; Origen emasculated himself. Faulkner seems to be evoking the second stanza of "Mr. Eliot's Sunday Morning Service" by linking ascetic emasculation and Harry's contriving the monkish calendar on the basis of Charlotte's menstrual periods: e.g., "at the mensual turn of time/ Produced enervate Origen." He alludes to the passage at the beginning of Act Two of *Requiem for a Nun*; see James B. Meriwether, *The Literary Career of William Faulkner* (Princeton: Princeton University Library, 1961), 36, for Faulkner's note on the subject.

previous looking back upon "the empty years in which his youth had vanished . . . with that peace with which a middleaged eunuch might look back upon the dead time before his alteration," (34) but this time "it was not the twenty-seven barren years he looked at" (103), it was the "path straight and empty and quiet" between their stacks of food and Charlotte waiting for him and the recurring vague premonition of watery death *"in the wavering solitude"* (103). The goal seems to be either death or the ideal, but it is never spelled out clearly, and Harry is as wrong as he can be. Though Harry rejects McCord's categorizing—*"Mac and his ninth-rate Teasdale who seems to remember a hell of a lot of what people read"* (103)—it does seem that the newspaperman has an objective view of the lovers. He discerns the contradiction in Harry's retaining the check from Rittenmeyer while engaged in an affair of "all or nothing." By remembering what people read, he may be able to see that the affair is a pale copy of storybook romance. He foresees their doom, predicting that Charlotte will pay the greater price, while Harry, like "an old lady being led across the street by a policeman," will survive when the "damned bloody wild drunken car" comes along and "busts hell" out of the "cop" (104). He has Harry pegged.

Left alone, the lovers prove they are not special. Even though it is late, Charlotte is not undressed. She is arranging their artifacts from the Chicago apartment—books, a copper bowl, the chintz cover, and "the old man, the Bad Smell" (105). Fleeing civilization, they have brought many of its symbols with them. Harry again marvels "on the ability of women to adapt the illicit, even the criminal, to a bourgeois standard of respectability" (104). They have fled their own reflection again. Like Tristan and Isolde, they sleep separately (in two cots on the porch), but no sword lies between them; and at dawn Charlotte comes to Harry roughly. On the first dawn in the Wisconsin woods they have their second and last experience with wildlife. Harry hears the wild and lonely cry of a loon, "the raucous idiot voice, thinking how man alone of all creatures deliberately atrophies his natural senses . . . how the four-legged animal gains all its information through smelling and seeing and hearing and distrusts all else while the two-legged one believes only what it reads" (105). Although it is unlikely that Harry means this to be self-condemnation, a contrast set up later in "Old Man" will once again be proof for what is only suggested in "Wild Palms." Charlotte and Harry see a deer, but it escapes them totally. Harry supposes that he and Charlotte emanate "an aura of unsanctity and disaster like a smell" (60), but he does not take it as a warning. Now he hears a bird, a loon, and reflects on man's loss of instinctive powers without observing himself in his own words. The tall convict follows a swimming deer to safety. When he sees a bird it is a hawk, and he kicks it into the air in order to take its prey for himself and his woman passenger to eat. He has been a victim of what he has read, but he has not lost his instincts.

Harry and Charlotte are symbolically moving away from life and toward death, from the lush tropical garden in New Orleans to the cool Wisconsin woods. The season turns toward the dead of winter. It will come upon them suddenly, though at the present moment Harry is "not fooled" as he cuts wood in the September sunshine on Labor Day, because "in these latitudes Labor Day and not equinox marked the suspiration of summer, the long sigh toward autumn and the cold" (106). Lest they forget what they are fleeing, the stranger Bradley from across the lake brings them a box of food. He has predatory eyes and a wolfish manner. He is looking at the Bad Smell and at Charlotte with "eyebrows and mouth in accord, quizzical, sardonic, ruthless" (107). When she made the Bad Smell, Charlotte had explained to Harry that it was not "a wolf at the door. Wolves are Things. Keen and ruthless. Strong, even if they are cowards" (95). Thanking Bradley for the food now, Harry says "The more we have in the house, the harder it will be for the wolf to get in." And Charlotte adds pointedly, "Or to crowd us out when he does," causing Bradley to laugh "with his teeth. His eyes did not laugh" (107). He is, in Charlotte's terms, one of the "brutes" (108) of bourgeois society, and the visit is an almost derisive taunting of the lovers. His gift prolongs their idyll but reminds them that society will still be there when the food runs out. Charlotte gives him the Bad Smell and bids him farewell sarcastically: "You must need it much worse than we do" (108). Harry is furious and wants to fling the food back, reckless with provisions for the first time in his life, for the first time really acting the romantic part, but Charlotte stops him. She arouses him sexually, takes off his clothes, and leads him to bed. Ironically, particularly in view of McCord's recent comparison of Charlotte with the eagle scout leading an old lady, she calls her lover "you damned home-wrecking boy scout" (108). This may be a step up from "You damned pauper," but Charlotte has used sex to halt him in the first heroic gesture he has ever tried to make. And with more foreboding than she realizes, she jokes: "Only this is supposed to be bad luck or something in the forenoon, isn't it?" (109) For lovers who want to dwell in the bright passion of the ideal and die in the "dulcet smell" of uncorrupted love, "it" is always bad luck.

Their sylvan paradise, where Charlotte goes naked and calls Harry "Adam" (109), is actually a limbo, a purgatory. Not only do they find no rapport with nature, they do not even achieve true rapport between themselves. Their lives remain distinct, ununited, except for the "bitching." They sleep in separate cots most of the time. After breakfast, Charlotte swims while Harry sleeps or lies in "a drowsy and foetuslike state, passive and almost unsentient" (110). The womb image has obvious general application, but it will be picked up in a specific regard by Harry at the end of this chapter. They spend their days apart, Charlotte out alone with the paper and water colors which never produce anything, and Harry by himself at the house meditating as he had done on innumerable park benches. He is bored, unneeded. This is still Charlotte's affair; and though she is away and absorbed in her own activities most of the time, she is also omnipresent, entering and leaving his static presence like an apparition. He is passive, even indifferent to the excitement of her body. Shortly before, he has thought "*She dont need to touch me. . . . Nor the sound of her voice even nor the smell, a slipper will do it, one of those fragile instigations to venery discarded in the floor*" (109), but already he does not follow her with his eyes when she leaves to swim naked the first time, "or he would have had to raise his head" (110). Everything is unreal; time seems to stop. Then Charlotte's sexuality in its most

WILLIAM FAULKNER'S *The Wild Palms*

basic, purely biological terms brings Harry back to an awareness of time. Bored to extinction (112), he borrows some of her water colors, but discovers immediately that he is color-bind and cannot paint, so one day out of sheer physical idleness he starts to make a calendar, a pretty one, like a "man carving a basket from a peach stone or the Lord's Prayer on a pin head" (113). Having made it, he discovers that he can check his memory against the days of Charlotte's menstrual periods, delighted that he is making Nature serve him: "contriving for God, for Nature the unmathematical, the overfecund, the prime disorderly and illogical and patternless spendthrift, to prove his mathematical problem" (114). Nature mocks him. She is more orderly than his memory, but deceptive too, and he has been *"seduced to an imbecile's paradise by an old whore ... throttled and sapped of strength and volition by the old weary Lilith of the year"* (114–15). It is later than he thinks. The food on the shelves, which he had refused to consider during this timeless interval, suddenly takes shape in his mind in an appropriate image. The "row of cans ... the dynamic torpedolike solid shapes which up to now had merely dropped ... into that stagnant time which did not advance and which would somehow find for its two victims food as it found them breath" (114) is blotted out by time as though by a dark cloud. There is a cloud on the horizon too, betokening the first snow of winter.

There is enough ambiguity in Harry's accusations against Nature to apply them to Charlotte as well, particularly when he thinks *"The old bitch. She betrayed me and now she doesn't need to pretend"* (115) and in the next second (and the next sentence) he sees Charlotte approaching wearing trousers (his) and a sweater against the cold he had somehow ignored until it was upon them. Thus *"seduced to an imbecile's paradise by an old whore"* is roughly his own position, the statement of his captivity by Charlotte. The word *whore* follows Charlotte through the novel, anyway. Even without the analogue to Catherine Barkley's feeling like a whore, the scene in the cheap hotel suggests that something of the sort is in Charlotte's mind. In Utah, she unexpectedly says to Mrs. Buckner that "Billie" is a perfect whore's name, adding "It would be a good whore. That's what I would try to be" (179). During the time Harry declines to perform the abortion and use his medical knowledge, he suggests "a pill of some sort" (210). He had thought before, "this, a trained doctor: *whores use them*" (207–208), but Charlotte does not understand, and when she asks him where he would go to try to get an aborticidal pill his answer is anguished. "Where would I try? Who would ever need such? At a brothel. Oh, God, Charlotte! Charlotte!" (210). The implication is clear. At a later time, when she is dying and trying to persuade Harry to flee, Charlotte says she will exonerate him "and nobody ever knows just where the truth is about a whore to convict anybody" (21).

The whore of Babylon out of Revelation stood, there at the end of the New Testament, for the wicked city of that day, Rome. The statue of Mrs. O'Leary with Nero's face has already linked Rome and Chicago figuratively. Chicago is also described in terms fitting a modern avatar of wickedness, the new Babylon, and it was that city, from the very beginning (48), where Charlotte thought of taking Harry. The image is strengthened in many ways and always plays back to Faulkner's original title, "If I Forget Thee, Jerusalem." At the end of the psalm from which that passage comes, the psalmist promises that the "daughter of Babylon" shall be destroyed, her little ones dashed against the stones. In his ambiguous recriminations, Harry also refers to Lilith, the legendary first wife of Adam (Harry has been called Adam here in the woods). Lilith refused to assume the recumbent position in intercourse, believing herself Adam's equal (Charlotte is the sexual aggressor), and she became a destroyer of children. Though she has been purged from scripture, Lilith is remembered in Hebrew commentaries on the apocrypha as being one of the two harlots of Jerusalem who appeared before Solomon for judgment on the custody of the child; the one who did not protest the child's being cut in two is Lilith (I Kings 3: 16*ff*).[21]

Whatever Harry had been contemplating at the beginning of their idyll, he is happier now than he was then (115), as if he were actually pleased to end the boring hiatus. Charlotte's first reaction is her usual

21 Robert Graves and Raphael Patai, *Hebrew Myths: The Book of Genesis* (Garden City, N. Y.: Doubleday & Co., 1964), 65–69.

savage overhaul; grasping his hair and shaking him impatiently, she tells Harry again to quit acting like a husband. As when she wanted to distract him before, she uses sex. "This time she came straight and got into the cot with him, as heedless of the hard and painful elbow which jabbed him as she would have been on her own account if the positions had been reversed" (116). One thinks again of Lilith.

Harry's solution is to send her to the city to take the job McCord has found, while he remains behind in the woods until something for him opens up—undoubtedly never, if his previous luck holds. He acts as if he is ready to take McCord's advice to "move into the woods and eat ants and play Saint Anthony in a tree and on Christmas" emasculate himself (103). He is no Saint Anthony nor a self-emasculating Origen, however; the temptations of the flesh take him every time, as Charlotte well knows. Far from emasculating himself, he begins to assert his manhood. Charlotte responds appropriately as soon as she understands that he means business, getting quietly into his cot and creeping close, as she has never done before. When he has fully unfolded his plan, her grip on herself breaks entirely: "Hold me! Hold me hard, Harry!" she cries (118, 119), just as when she is losing her life at the end (46).

Charlotte's argument for remaining together is that "This is what it's for . . . what we were paying for: so we could be together, sleep together every night: not just to eat and evacuate and sleep warm so we can get up and eat and evacuate in order to sleep warm again" (118–19).[22] Yet they have slept together only in the euphemistic sense of that phrase which applies to what they still call "bitching." Otherwise, each keeps to his or her iron cot, as monkish a bed as the ones in the interns' quarters or convicts' barracks. They have pursued separate daily existences, apart from their meals together—the eating which is a necessity, the food which occupies Harry so much. They do not have the inner resources to sustain an idealized passion.[23] Harry is

[22] Cf. William Faulkner, *Pylon* (New York: Smith and Haas, 1935), 176, for a similar statement.

[23] A few years later, Faulkner spoke in general terms on the problem: "One of the saddest things is that the only thing a man can do for eight hours a day, day after day, is work. You can't eat eight hours a day nor drink for eight hours

monkish in yet another way besides his keeping to the severe iron cot. His interest in Charlotte's sex is chiefly expressed by his using her menstrual periods to create an illuminated calendar. Recommending the example of Origen and St. Anthony, McCord was at least partially correct, as we have seen, except, as noted, Harry will not defeat the flesh. That alternative will be left to the tall convict, while Harry will affirm the flesh and the trials of human existence which go with it.

Charlotte wins out against their separation, and so they resume their upside-down lives in Chicago, Charlotte supporting her unemployed partner again. Both Charlotte and McCord work inverted schedules which begin in the afternoon or night. The imagery of hell recurs: the empty store to which Harry conducts her takes on a "bizarre and infernal inverted life." Though the reader cannot know it at this point, the setting is also solemnly prophetic: the store is "like an empty midnight clinic in which a handful of pygmy-like surgeons and nurses battle in low-toned decorum for some obscure and anonymous life, into which Charlotte would vanish too" (120). Harry waits for Charlotte surrounded by mannikins which have "suave organless bodies" (120)—a mockery, like the sexless people in books about which Harry was thinking earlier (52)—and charwomen come like "another species just crawled molelike from ... the foundations of the earth" (120). The lovers live in a "new and neat" apartment in a "new and neat district near a park," so Harry does not even have to go out to hear the voices of children which have served so often as chorus to his meditations. But he is not meditating any more. While Charlotte sleeps, he tackles another art-form. As before with the painting, the tools, the symbols of craft, are suspect and tainted. Charlotte's original work had been performed in a studio with a skylight, "the handiwork of a dead or bankrupt photographer or maybe a former sculptor or painter tenant" (84); Harry's typewriter comes from among the cheap pistols and gold-filled teeth in a pawnshop (121). With this redeemed machine he writes confession stories from the female adolescent point of view. His art does reflect his experience in an ironic way, of course,

a day nor make love for eight hours—all you can do for eight hours is work" (*Lion in the Garden*, 249).

and he tells McCord later that "there seems to be no limit to what I can invent on the theme of female sex troubles"—this, too, from the pen of the author who had already created Caddy and Miss Quentin, Addie and Dewey Dell Bundren, Lena Grove, Temple Drake, and Rosa Coldfield, to name a few. Harry's writing is also a counterpart to Charlotte's sculpture, both commercial and perverse: "moron's pap" and "monotonous inventing" (122), "primer-bald moronic fable, his sexual gumdrop" (123). It also has a "smell" (126).

In the hellish city, even the season of Christian holiday is bereft of meaning. Though their customary bar is decorated in the season, the customers drink the same iced cocktails they have drunk all summer. McCord sums up Christmas as the "apotheosis of the bourgeoisie . . . when before an altar in the shape of a gold-plated cattle-trough man may . . . prostrate himself . . . to the fairy tale which conquered the Western world" [24] (130). The lovers "eat, at the wrong hour . . . the meal which none of them wanted" (124). They are like automatons living dead, meaningless lives.

The role reversal which began during the last days at the lake goes a step further. Charlotte buys presents for her children in New Orleans. Though her hands are "at nearly every other human action unhesitating and swift," the emotions which she feels apparently prevent her from satisfactorily wrapping the presents. Suddenly it is she, and not Harry, who is clumsy and inept. It is a scene which plays pointedly on the original title from Psalms, and the biting irony is that she tries to perform this Christmas ritual upon the bed, "the workbench of the child's unwitting begetting become the altar for the Child's service" (125). The ironies cut even deeper as the scene progresses, however, for it is apparently not so much her remembering the children as her fearing what is going to happen to her and Harry that has caused this emotion and ineptitude. She has covered her awkwardness with a cynical comment upon the "ruthless piracy" of children and the puerility of adults at Christmastime, but abruptly she comes out with what has

[24] Cf. William Faulkner, "Mirrors of Chartres Street": "a fairy tale that has conquered the whole Western earth," in *New Orleans Sketches*, ed. Carvel Collins (New York: Grove, 1961), 54.

been on her mind all along: the store where she works part-time will give her a permanent job. Despite all they can do, respectability and bourgeois values repeatedly overtake the runaway lovers, much as the flood keeps pursuing the tall convict. Now it is Harry who is jolted into reaction. His response is patterned after Charlotte's words at the close of the Wisconsin idyll (118–19, 126), with the addition of an observation on their present lives. The city, he says, has begun to be a prison, a "dungeon" (126); winter naturally herds "people inside walls," but the city enforces a routine even on sinning and it absolves adultery by showing indifference. The lack of community, as Cleanth Brocks has argued, is paradoxically a burden to the lovers who want to be free; a permissive society makes it inevitable that their love affair will dwindle into the ordinary.

Harry has thought about the perils of succumbing to the ordinary once before; it was as he waited on the train out of New Orleans for Charlotte to appear. He thought, "*I dont believe in sin. It's getting out of timing. You are born submerged in anonymous lockstep with the teeming anonymous myriads of your time and generation; you get out of step once, falter once, and you are trampled to death*" (54). Now he and Charlotte have been caught up in the rhythm of city life, winter and the city a "*combination too strong for us yet*" (126), as he thinks. He will deliberately try breaking step; the results are already predicted in his earlier thoughts. The tall convict, anonymous, chained in a line of broken men, and repeatedly subjected to the vagaries of the flood when he "escapes" the chain gang, undoubtedly lives as an example of these concepts. When he first becomes cognizant of the river and stops to gaze at it, the anonymous and lifeless men shackled to him crash into his back (72). The prison has a routine for sinning, too, the fifth-Sunday visiting days when women may come to be with the convicts (335).

Harry prepares to break step by leaving Chicago, convinced he is in control and doing something about the fact that they act "like we had been married five years" (126)—the length of Charlotte's marriage to Rat. "I had turned into a husband" (132), Harry accuses himself. He tells McCord he has learned "that it's idleness breeds all our vir-

97

tues ... the wisdom to concentrate on fleshly pleasures—eating and evacuating and fornication and sitting in the sun—than which there is nothing better" (133). Has Harry forgotten how bored he was in the sun-impacted solitude of the lake? Has he so misunderstood Charlotte's admonition (118–19) not to slip into the cycle of eating and evacuating and sleeping warm? Does he realize where he is taking them? There will be no sun to sit in when they get to Utah. Harry apparently has equalled his mate for talking without heeding his own words. For all his brave talk, he is still prey to the habits of respectability. He tries to talk up the salary offered him for the mining job, but Canfield backs him down—"This job is nowhere near up to your qualifications" (129)—and forces him to eat crow. Then Harry says "I will have to have transportation for *my wife*" (129) (Italics added).

They vacate the apartment where they have left no mark but the cigarette scars on the table at which Harry wrote his pulp fiction stories. Among the symbols of its respectability is the aforementioned noise of children and the promise that by spring Harry would have been hearing nursemaids and smelling "infant urine and animal crackers" from inside (134). The sounds and smells of children are not for Harry. He believes he is fleeing all forms of ordinary life that bind. He proposes a toast to "freedom," but McCord sees clearly that he will "probably be able to drink to a lot of it before [he sees] any of it again. And in water too. . . . And maybe in a tighter place than this too" (131). Harry has thought that "they were about money like some unlucky people were about alcohol: either none or too much" (126). He has similar trouble with time: either he is running out or he has too much to kill. Waiting for the train, he has more than he needs: "twenty-two minutes yet. *While it will only take two minutes to tell Mac what it took me two months to discover*" (131–32). "*Fourteen minutes to try to tell what I have already said in five words*" (135). Yet he keeps talking, maundering merely because he has the time to kill or because he is trying to keep from thinking about what he is going to do; perhaps trying to convince himself. At any rate, for all his words, he never gives McCord an answer to the pertinent question which the reporter asks. McCord picks at Harry's inconsistencies, just as at the lake he goaded him for keeping the check from Rittenmeyer. He points out that Harry, talking in disgust about his regular employment as a pulp-fiction writer, is clinging to his "damn typewriter." McCord wants to know "what it's all about" (131), but as Harry is ready to get on the train, McCord is still asking that unanswered question: "But why go to Utah in February to beat it? And if you cant beat it, why in hell go to Utah?" (141). Providentially, Harry's "Because I—" is cut off by the steam hissing out of the train and the sudden, apparitionlike appearance of the porter at his elbow.[25]

Between McCord's two questions Harry spends a lot of words trying, as he puts it, to explain to McCord what he has already said in five: "I had become a husband." What he does not realize is that having once been a husband to Charlotte, he can never again be her lover. While she, long since a mother and now twice a wife, in effect, is no longer a maid. The consummation of their love shattered the tension that must exist in an idealized affair. They are real people, not sexless figures with "suave organless bodies" like mannikins in a store (120) or characters in books (52). Significantly, after McCord scoffs at the idea of drinking to freedom, since they are going into the service of the corrupt mining operation, Harry proposes instead a drink to love, with as little thought as in the first toast. Harry speaks ill of the world, crying out that the world is against them; it has become no place for love, yet in the name of love he puts himself into the service of corrupt society (the hospital where he tested for syphilis, the crooked mine) or seeks aid from its institutions (the whore house and the shady druggist's where he seeks the aborticidal pill) or performs an act contrary to both nature and moral society (the surgical abortion). He and Charlotte lost their chance for the ideal at the very beginning; "bitching" is the fatal flaw for this tragic couple, and everything else that happens to them proceeds from that fact. Carnality

---

[25] Apparitionlike arrivals and departures in both plots and the use of imagery out of stagecraft reinforce the illusory character of ordinary reality. Schopenhauer says, "Life and dreams are leaves of the same book," and he notes that Indian and Western (i.e. Platonic) philosophy "have no better simile than a dream for the whole knowledge of the actual world"—what the Hindus call the web or veil of Maya (Schopenhauer, *The World as Will and Idea*, I, 21–22).

kills Charlotte. They keep picking the wrong time to try to make their love an ideal. Nature will take its own course. Even if it were not too late, the life Harry describes—"eating and evacuating and fornication and sitting in the sun"—is the shortest road to unhappiness he could take, for these are the pleasures of the senses, desires which are never capable of gratification, but forever lure man on to disappointment and incompleteness. Fornication, we recall, is the chief means by which the will in Nature achieves its end of continuing forever this meaningless round of life. Harry ought to be aware of this, because part of what he has to say in his nine-page circumlocution sounds like a difficult paraphrase of Schopenhauer. It has profound implications for the final meaning of the book.

Harry is trying to explain to McCord how he was "in eclipse" and "out of time" until he took charge of the love affair. He had begun in a will-less state, the volitionless drifting of medical school and the drowning in Charlotte's will, though he says it began the night he told Charlotte he had twelve hundred dollars (137). He did not come out of it until the "night she told [him] the store would keep her on" (137). The nature of his experience in between these two moments is what he wants to convey to McCord:

> "I was outside of time. I was still attached to it, supported by it in space as you have been ever since there was a not-you to become you, and will be until there is an end to the not-you by means of which alone you could once have been—that's the immortality—supported by it but that's all ... insulated ... from ... the current of time that runs through remembering, that exists only in relation to what little of reality ... we know, else there is no such thing as time. You know: *I was not.* Then *I am*, and time begins, retroactive, is was and will be. Then *I was* and so I am not and so time never existed" (137).

This was the "drowsy and foetus-like state" in the "womb of solitude and peace" (110) he exhibited at the lake. Unborn symbolically, he was outside of time: only at the beginning of life does one emerge into "time and the causal series." [26] He was static, in the equivalent of a will-less state. But time still existed, as did space, which must be true

---

[26] *Ibid.,* 423.

so long as there is an individual to perceive them (the "you" of Harry's speech) or a will, that is, primal reality ("the 'not you' by means of which alone you could once have been") to be objectified in an individual manner. The will exists both as one, the individual, and as multiplicity, all creation. The birth and death of individuals is merely a rapid vibration that constitutes one of the attributes of the will, which is enduring, permanent ("that's the immortality"). Time that "runs through remembering" is a construct of a man's endless present ("*I am* and time begins, retroactive, is was and will be. Then *I was* and so I am not and so time never existed"). As Schopenhauer says, "The world is my idea" and that fact is "obviously true of the past and the future, as well as of the present. . . . All that in any way . . . can belong to the world . . . exists only for the subject," that is, the individual, who alone perceives in his moment of existence "what little of reality we know."[27]

True will-lessness is a blessed state, according to Schopenhauer. It frees man from the cruel bonds of life. It consists in complete indifference to everything, the cessation of hope and desire, the refusal to be led by the illusory blandishments of phenomenon, and the absolute denial of "the assertion of the will to live beyond the individual life."[28] The sexual act is thus explicitly denied, for it is the means by which the will to life most strongly expresses itself. Harry is correct to characterize this "eclipse" of his in sexual terms. The long period during which he was "outside of time" was "like the instant of virginity, it was the instant of virginity: that condition, fact, that does not actually exist except during the instant you know you are losing it; it lasted as long as it did because I was too old" (137). On one level of meaning Harry is saying that he has had a symbolical virginal orgasm lasting approximately nine months (they left New Orleans in early May; it is now late January). These nine months have also been a proper gestation for him, at the end of which he has come into objectified

---

[27] *Ibid.*, 3–4. In volume III these ideas are elaborated in "On Death and its Relation to the Indestructibility of our True Nature," 249–317. Thomas Buddenbrooks reads this selection and uses it as a rationale for suicide in Chapter Five of the novel of Mann's which Faulkner seems to have admired most.

[28] Schopenhauer, *The World as Will and Idea*, I, 424.

reality, into time, by asserting the will through the agency of sex. He is figuratively born, parented, as he says, by Charlotte and McCord (141). He has also gained an insight that is almost too much to bear: "... the precipice, the dark precipice; all mankind before you went over it and lived and all after you will but that means nothing to you because they cant tell you ... what to do in order to survive. . . . You must do it in solitude and you can bear just so much solitude and still live. . . . And for this one or two seconds you will be absolutely alone: not before you were and not after you are not, because you are never alone then ... you are secure and companioned in a myriad and inextricable anonymity" (137–38). Harry seems to be going back to what he had already said about life—that it is a continuous present and the only reality the individual knows. Before and after life he has no existence except as a part of the Will which is the source of all being. He has changed his views of solitude from the interlude in the woods; having been brought into time he has had a glimpse of the true nature of things. Solitude is hard to bear because in it one discovers the secret of life, the nature of the will, the miniscule and uncontrolled part one man plays in the round of nature. The sexual act, in terms of which Harry is speaking, is what Schopenhauer calls "the decided and strongest assertion of life": "to man in a state of nature, as to the brutes, it is the final end, the highest goal of life." [29]

Nature is interested in perpetuating itself, and that is really all. The individual has no other importance and no greater function than to be a part of this scheme. Sex, says Schopenhauer, "does away with that carelessness, serenity, and innocence which would accompany a merely individual existence." The experience of sex is, in the philosopher's terms, as much an organic shock for everyone as it is for Harry: "the young, innocent, human intellect, when that great secret of the world first becomes known to it, is startled at the enormity! ... from the standpoint of pure, and therefore innocent, knowing, is horrified at it." [30]

[29] *Ibid.*, 425.
[30] *Ibid.*, III, 376, 380.

The Tragic Deception of the Hero

The remainder of the passage is cast in even more explicitly sexual terms:

"... you herd the beast you have ridden all your life, the old familiar well-broken nag, up to the precipice.... Maybe you thought all the time that when the moment came you could ... save something, maybe not, the instant comes and you know you cannot ... you are one single abnegant affirmation, one single fluxive Yes out of the terror in which you surrender volition, hope, all—the darkness, the falling, the thunder of solitude, the shock, the death, the moment when, stopped physically by the ponderable clay, you yet feel all your life rush out of you into the pervading immemorial blind receptive matrix... grave-womb or womb-grave, it's all one" (138).

The beast, the precipice, the fluxive Yes, the receptive matrix and the little death are all basic sexual symbols and understandable on their own terms. But there is another set of referents too. The "fluxive Yes" is simply that affirmation of life expressed in the process of generation. The "beast ... the well-broken nag" is that piece of "ponderable clay," the mortal body.[31] The conjunction of "grave-womb or womb-grave" reflects that the "pain of birth and the bitterness of death are the two constant conditions under which the will to live maintains itself." The individual exists only by owing "to nature the debt of death ... the periodical payment of the toll, birth and death," while "our inner nature, untouched by the course of time and the death of races, exists in an everlasting present."[32]

Harry is saying, in Schopenhauerian terms, that for him this prolonged hiatus was metaphorically both gestation and procreation. When it was completed he broke into time. He was born as an individual and simultaneously, sexually, asserted the will to live. There is a resemblance between this state of Harry's and one he believed Char-

[31] Cf. "The Beggar," in Collins, *New Orleans Sketches*: "When I was a boy I believed ... life was more than just eating and sleeping, than restricting a man's life to one tiny speck of the earth's surface and marking his golden hours away to the stroke of a bell.... Ah, to have mounted heart and sight and sense on such a sorry nag!" (46–47). Harry's remarks also seem to owe a lot to the thoughts of the poet-tramp in "Carcassonne."

[32] Schopenhauer, *The World as Will and Idea*, III, 270, 377.

lotte to have been in. In Chicago earlier he had observed of her: "*She had a father and then four brothers exactly like him and then she married a man exactly like the four brothers and so she probably never even had a room of her own . . . and so she has lived all her life in complete solitude and she doesn't even know it as a child who has never tasted cake doesn't know what cake is*" (82). This may help to explain Charlotte's illusions about perfect love. She has been raised in a family of brothers, she has married, she has borne children and taken a lover, yet she still is capable of attempting a passionate romantic affair like something from the middle ages. She had "solitude" without being aware of it. She was perhaps in that "instant of virginity" all those years, "alone" and outside of time in a purely individual existence. When she came into time, when she entered life, she did so sexually just as Harry did. But no insight came to her; she was in fact deceived, veiling the act behind the romantic ideas she had taken from books, assuming that affair to be a lofty and special passion which was only the urge to procreation and the continuance of the will.[33] There is double irony here: Charlotte has had experience with sex, yet gains no insight, and therefore goes off self-deceived; Harry has had no experience with sex, yet he gains the insight, and then he overlooks what he has learned and also goes off self-deceived. This cycle of innocence, experience, knowledge, and return to innocence is a recurring motif in *The Wild Palms*. It is expressed in terms of solitude, the shock of recognition, and figurative birth and rebirth. It is finally resolved for the central characters by the ultimate dropping into place of the last piece of a pattern of which they become increasingly conscious. But that must wait for the end of the novel. Charlotte's chance is over, the cycle of desire, attainment, desire which she instigated is complete. She carried Harry from one wicked and indifferent city to another which was even worse, an Inferno. Harry's attempt begins, and he will carry Charlotte to a barren frozen wasteland like the ninth circle of hell and then back to where they began.[34]

[33] See Schopenhauer's chapter, "The Metaphysics of the Love of the Sexes," *The World as Will and Idea*, III, 336ff.
[34] Harry plays with time constantly and sets up various ways to measure it—food, money, Charlotte's menstrual cycle—a clear indication that time is a

The Tragic Deception of the Hero

He is such a complete, but confused, convert to Charlotte's half-formed and romantic ideas about love being everything that he has even stopped worrying about money. "I can make all the money we will need," he says (136), which is as accurate as Charlotte's claims for her artistry. He says he has beat both money and respectability. The forces against them "will have to find something else to force us to conform to the pattern of human life which has now evolved to do without love" (140). But "They" will not have to go out of the way to beat these lovers; "love" will beat them, the act of love, by causing that most natural and patterned event, the conception of a child. When Harry is condemning the forms of human life which have evolved in the modern world, he ignores himself and Charlotte, who choose the frozen wasteland as their trysting place, who choose abortion as the

---

human construct, not a universal reality. Time's only *a priori* existence, according to Schopenhauer, is as the "principle of sufficient reason" of becoming, that is, causality. Harry may divide his days and his life any way he likes, but he cannot change the basic nature of causality or its effects. He makes this belated discovery in the Wisconsin woods when winter creeps up on him. Elsewhere in his fiction, Faulkner explores similar concepts, particularly the definition of time as a continuum which exists only in the present along with the individual who perceives it and whose perceptions create past and future. Compare *As I Lay Dying* for Darl's "sleep is is-not ... And so if I am not emptied yet, I am is" (New York: Cape and Smith, 1930, p. 76); Quentin's "*One day he was not. Then he was. Then he was not. It was too short, too fast, too quick*" (*Absalom, Absalom!*, 152); the Judge in "Beyond": "So what I have been, I am; what I am, I shall be until that instant comes when I am not. And then I shall have never been. How does it go? *Non fui. Sum. Fui. Non sum*" (Faulkner, *Collected Stories*, 792). Quentin's section of *The Sound and the Fury* is loaded with similar time-consciousness. His "Again. Sadder than was" (118) seems particularly Schopenhauerian—i.e., that for life to go on, repeat itself, rather than cease, is sadder. Quentin's assertion, "*my fathers Progenitive I invented him created I him*" (152), may be due to Schopenhauer's doctrine, "The world is my idea." Quentin's own assertion of "*Non fui. Sum. Fui. Non sum*"—"Peacefulles: words"—is on page 216. Harry refuses the peace and oblivion which such death-wish pessimism offers.

Faulkner's conception of time, he himself said, was Bergsonian, and he once told Joan Williams, whom he was trying to train as a writer, to read Bergson's *Creative Evolution*, where the philosopher's conception of duration is spelled out, because "it helped me." Joseph Blotner, *Faulkner: A Biography*, Vol. II (New York: Random House, 1974), 1302. But there would not seem to be a great deal of incompatibility between Schopenhauer's conception of the Will in nature and Bergson's *elan vital*. Faulkner was, of course, capable of understanding—or at least using for his own purposes—the ideas of more than one philosopher.

means to prolong their affair, who flee home for one final stab at the abandoned husband, sham though he is, and the children, instead of going off into the wilderness to disappear decently like injured animals. No wonder McCord reacts so contemptuously when Harry says, "there is something in me you and she parented . . . that you are father of" (141). Harry has managed to pervert even McCord's honest cynicism into something weak and ignoble. Here is one more perverse and sterile birth image in this love story of inverted values, a man-child who is the distorted product of Charlotte's erring romanticism and McCord's cynical realism. This is a harsh judgment, one which the ending of the novel will not allow. And, in fairness, McCord's words to Harry are probably well-intentioned. If Harry, so self-deceived, wants a blessing, perhaps a "curse" will put him right. It is the same logic that lies behind the buying of the expensive nightgown when Harry and Charlotte want the hemorrhaging to begin. Illusion, self-deception, inversion rule in the world of *The Wild Palms*—a fact made even more explicit by the adventures of the convict.

It is apparent to everyone that the lovers are doomed as they leave Chicago. Even Harry knows it, although he still does not quite understand why. McCord does not have to repeat his dire prediction; Harry does not have to voice it. It comes silently to Harry's mind: *"You wont see us again"* (141). Their fate is sealed. The first chapter of the novel showed where it brought them: the dead beach on the Mississippi coast. The last two sections of "Wild Palms" will depict its final working out and the crucial aftermath.

CHAPTER VII

Counterpoint:
The Comic Deception
of the Hero

The life of every individual, if we survey it as a whole and
in general . . . is really always a tragedy, but gone through
in detail, it has the character of a comedy.

SCHOPENHAUER
The World as Will and Idea

THE TALL CONVICT has been sent to prison and virtually destroyed
as a man. He is launched forcibly into a devastating and death-dealing
flood to perform rescue work for which he has no experience. He
suffers pain and hardship to fulfill his obligations as he understands
them and despite great odds he succeeds. He is rewarded for his faith-
fulness to a corrupt society by an increased term behind bars. Yet we
see it all in comic detail.

Having followed the lovers this far, one should perceive at least
one of Faulkner's purposes in making "Old Man" richly comic and
why Faulkner conceived his novel in the form of two alternated tales.
The emotional tone of "Wild Palms" is so intense and unrelenting that
it would go flat if it were sustained unbroken throughout. In *Absalom,
Absalom!* (1936), where Faulkner set the complete story at the highest
pitch, he dealt with the problem of undeviating tone by employing a
relative and multiple point of view, narrators within narrators, that
filtered parts of the story through different, but equally intense,
characters. There is no relief in the story of the two lovers in *The
Wild Palms*, not even during their "golden interval" (111) in the

EPIGRAPH: Arthur Schopenhauer, *The World as Will and Idea*, trans. R. B.
Haldane and J. Kemp (London: Routledge and Kegan Paul, 1883), I, 415.

Wisconsin woods. They are always "on" emotionally and psycho-
logically, always reacting to one another or projecting complicated
rationalizations for their actions or caught up in something outside
themselves that hastens them to their doom. The tall convict's adventure is foil to the love affair. It is developed chiefly in terms of natural
force and human physical endurance. A simpler tale, it provides a
running commentary upon the story of the lovers, sometimes parallel,
sometimes in contrast, though there is no mere dichotomy here, no
clear-cut debate between primitivism and modernity, unsophistication
and oversophistication, instinct versus reason. "Old Man" provides
counterpoint for "Wild Palms" not by dropping pitch but by shifting
into a complementary and contrasting mode. More than one critic has
called the alternation fugue-like. It actually sustains pitch. There is
perhaps more catastrophe in "Old Man" than in "Wild Palms," but the
mode is essentially comic, not tragic. It is primordial and nightmarish,
while "Wild Palms" is modern, human, even, in a sense, filled with
everydayness. What happens in "Old Man" helps explain what has
happened in "Wild Palms." The physical events of the one correspond
to the emotional events of the other. The psychological tale is counter-
pointed by its "visionary" equivalent in a manner to be discussed later
on. The mingling of the two tales creates a balance in the novel; each
is full of movement which leads forward to the next episode, and each
is cyclic, following similar patterns of development.

The emphasis which the presence of a "tall convict" puts on the
theme of captivity has been noted. Prison life has done for the tall
convict what convention and circumstance have done for Harry Wilbourne. The tall convict has come to prison at the dictates of others,
just as Harry has attended medical school under the terms of the outdated bequest left by his father. Whatever the justice of circumstances
which have brought the convict there, like Harry he does not rebel
but instead accepts willingly the rules of his servitude. His life is without meaning, sub-human and sterile, so that it does not matter if he
plants "pebbles" or weeds "papièr-mâché" cotton and corn (30). His
companion is womanish and impotent; his most cherished possession is
his mule, John Henry. The tall convict's life prior to prison, as a farm

boy in the Mississippi hills, has prepared him for coping with the flood of the century no better than Harry's celibate provincial youth has fitted him for headlong flight in an adulterous romantic love affair. The tall convict had never even seen the River, as the virgin Harry had never been in love. It is not surprising that both become disoriented when they are swept out of their torpor into new and different lives by powerful forces. The difference between their experiences is that the tall convict's jeopardy is more immediate and crucial in a quite personal way: if he does not struggle, he is going to drown literally, and he knows what that means. Harry goes along with Charlotte and still proceeds under his old compulsions; roughly nine months pass before, in his own estimation, he takes control. But it is harder to understand the process of drowning in a sober yellow stare than it is to feel the suffocating grasp of the flood. The River, the "Old Man," unlike Charlotte, "dont have to brag" (72).

Even so—and this is only a seven weeks' tale, not a twelve months' one, and the scale is smaller—the tall convict does not immediately adapt himself to the new conditions. The medium upon which he has been cast is not merely unfamiliar, it is also gone wild. He can think with rage of the "firm earth fixed and founded" somewhere beneath him (144), because he can see the tops of trees which he knows to be anchored in it, but everything else he knows from ordinary experience is useless: he is wrong about his speed, wrong about the distance he has come, even wrong about the direction of upstream and downstream. As before in "Old Man"—and in the preceding sections of "Wild Palms" to a smaller degree—there is an aura of marked unreality. The plump convict has vanished out of the boat "like in a translation out of Isaiah,"[1] while the tall convict and his skiff disappear theatrically, "like a tableau snatched offstage intact with violent and incredible speed" (143). The boat moves down a bayou empty of

---

[1] There are no actual translations in Isaiah; perhaps Faulkner was thinking of Enoch in Hebrews 11:5. But see Isaiah 51:6: "Lift up your eyes to the heavens, and look upon the earth beneath: for the heavens shall vanish like smoke...." There are several smoky vanishings in *The Wild Palms*, and the last third of Isaiah takes up the Babylonian captivity and the fall of the wicked city of harlots and idolators.

current ever since the "old subterranean outrage" (144) that first created it, though the water has plenty of force now. The boat moves *through* the water, propelled like the Ancient Mariner's craft, rather than merely riding upon the flood, so that the convict hangs in a "trough" behind the boat between "gouts of cold yellow" water thrown up on each side (144). Until this moment, the flood has been brown or chocolate (62–64,66,69,73), but henceforth it will be the color of Charlotte's eyes, yellow (39).

Against this fantastic and often antic force the convict opposes instinct and will. At first he does not even have time to think. Instinct operates automatically to prevent his drowning, so that eventually he hauls himself and the paddle he has clutched unconsciously into the boat. He muses furiously upon the self-victimization occasioned by his own morality, and he curses the "arbitrariness of human affairs" (146) which had afforded the other man safe refuge in a tree and consigned him to the spinning boat merely because he would be the only one to attempt the rescue. Nature, though providential after all, is risible too, for as he paddles furiously, getting nowhere, about to strike a pile of debris for the second time, he feels beneath the boat a "current of eager gleeful vicious incorrigible wilfulness" (146). Will, according to Schopenhauer, is the underlying reality, it exists in all things: "every force in nature should be thought as will," [2] he says, a truth that may be observed, for instance, in "the strong and unceasing impulse with which the waters hurry to the ocean . . . which, just like human desire, is increased by obstacles."[3] Man occupies his higher position among the degrees of objectification of the will due to his greater knowledge; but since the higher "objectification of will can only appear through the conquest of the lower"—no "victory without conflict"—"it endures the opposition of these lower Ideas, which . . . constantly strive to obtain an independent and complete expression of their being. . . . Thus the will to live everywhere preys upon itself . . . till finally the human race, because it subdues all the others, regards nature as a manufactory for its use. Yet even the human race . . . re-

2 Schopenhauer, *The World as Will and Idea*, I, 144.
3 *Ibid.*, 153.

veals in itself . . . this conflict, this variance with itself of the will, and we find *homo homini lupus* [man is a wolf to man]."[4] Bradley, the wolfish interloper of the preceding chapter, is a perfect example.

That the "will to live everywhere preys upon itself" accurately describes the state of Nature in "Old Man." The Mississippi (a "lower idea") comes to the full expression of its being—"the river was now doing what it liked to do" (160)—shoving back the man-made boundaries set upon it. Among other feats, the tall convict struggles for his life against this force of nature. In order to get food he robs birds of prey; to earn money he kills alligators. Nature is not malevolent, but it is willful. Man is merely a part of it, winning his way like the rest as best he can. To the tall convict, the world may appear to have gone mad, for he has lived in a kind of foetal state himself, insulated from the normal strife, provided for by the State. It is taking him a while to get used to dealing with raw Nature suddenly out of its bounds. So when he is thrown to the bottom of the boat by the second collision, he thinks: "He would have to get up sometime, he knew that, just as all life consists of having to get up sooner or later and then having to lie down again sooner or later after a while" (147). The "alternation of victory" in nature, the constant opposition of the different manifestations of the will to live, produces the "burden of physical life, the necessity of sleep, and, finally, of death."[5] But life is also renewing itself constantly, awakening and being reborn, so long as there is will. And thus the tall convict is right. He, like Harry, will go through a number of figurative deaths and rebirths as he learns and decides finally what he must do. Momentarily he is in a timeless state like Harry's. Everything is out of joint and he is "being toyed with by a current of water going nowhere, beneath a day which would wane toward no evening; when it was done with him it would spew him back into the comparatively safe world he had been snatched violently out of and in the meantime it did not much matter just what he did or did not do" (147). Harry's sense of idyll was ended when he realized that he had been "*seduced to an imbecile's paradise by an old*

---

[4] *Ibid.*, 190–92.
[5] *Ibid.*, 191.

whore" (114–15). The tall convict's feeling lasts only so long as he is alone; in the next moment after thinking it, he hears the voice of the woman in the tree and his situation alters radically.

"Old Man" is a kind of modern fertility ritual set against the aborticidal tragedy of Harry and Charlotte. It begins in the Spring, in May. Following the hiatus caused by the rampaging but fertilizing waters of the flood, it ends in time for a belated planting season compensated by a soil so rich that the mere sight of a seed suffices to bring forth a bountiful crop. The tall convict and his consort, the pregnant female who descends from a tree, act as King and Queen of May, whose comic ritual marriage and childbearing symbolically cause the fecundation of the earth. In primitive times ritual marriages between symbolic gods and mortals, or between mortals impersonating gods and goddesses, were widespread. The purpose was to ensure fertility of the earth and of certain crops, according to Frazer; "the sacred marriage of the powers both of vegetation and of water has been celebrated by many peoples for the sake of promoting the fertility of the earth . . . and . . . in such rites the part of the divine bridegroom or bride is often sustained by a man or woman." [6] Frazer discusses at length the particular nuptial of this type celebrated annually by the kings of Rome: the king masqueraded as Jupiter and wed a surrogate of Diana or of her counterpart, Egeria, nymph of wood and water, who was, like Diana, sacred to pregnant women because she "could grant them an easy delivery." [7] So far in the mating of the tall convict and the pregnant, treed flood refugee there is merely an interesting analogue of the fertility ritual which Frazer describes. The dating of the tale in May—when April was the time of the actual events, which Faulkner follows otherwise quite closely—points to the Kings and Queens of May distinctly. And one other piece of evidence supports the identification sufficiently to suggest that Faulkner drew in fact from his mem-

---

[6] Sir James George Frazer, *The Golden Bough* (abridged; New York: Macmillan, 1922), 146. According to Carvel Collins, "Faulkner and Anderson: Some Revisions," Paper read at MLA Convention, Chicago, 28 December 1967, this is the edition which Faulkner read in Sherwood Anderson's New Orleans apartment.

[7] Frazer, *Golden Bough*, 146–48.

ory of Frazer. Among the attributes of Jupiter, whom the kings of Rome impersonated at the annual fete, was a reddened face. During the festival days not only the face of the king-impersonator, but also the faces of all the statues of Jupiter in the city's plazas, were reddened with vermillion.[8] The convict likewise has his face dyed red. Every time he is struck by the boat, whacked by a tree limb, switched by an alligator tail, the blood flows over his face. The indignity and unmanliness of the crimsoning is another comic turn to the comparison, but the most humorous and devastating element is strongly sexual. The ritual marriage being parodied was usually consummated by actual sexual intercourse, a homeopathic device to insure the fertility of the symbolically impregnated earth. In the tall convict's case, and to use terms he would understand, his crop has been plowed, planted and laid by. His ritual bride is already expecting and all he is doing is transporting her.

The comic irony of his situation does not escape his notice, for he is as capable of fostering romantic illusions as Charlotte, despite his lack of sophistication. In prison ("even in durance") he had continued to read the implausible pulp fiction that had precipitated his original downfall; thus "who to say what Helen, what living Garbo, he had not dreamed of rescuing from what craggy pinnacle or dragoned keep when he and his companion embarked in the skiff" (149). He has achieved a small symbolic victory, nevertheless; he started out with the plump womanish convict, whom he was seeking when he found the pregnant woman. On his return up the river he will even find a woman he can actually use, but she turns out to be "a fellow's wife" (334); and thus his experience with women is complete, that which was merely theoretical (148) is now proved, and he comes back to prison and to the plump convict.

The Frazer connection seems sure and conforms to the generally mythic patterns in which the tall convict's tale is told. It works in the

[8] *Ibid.*, 148. Another possible analogue is Tammuz-Adonis, whose ritual death was associated with spring flooding: "Every year...Adonis was wounded to death in the mountains, and every year the face of nature itself was dyed with his sacred blood...the red anemone, his flower, bloomed among the cedars of Lebanon, and the river ran red to the sea" (*Ibid.*, 382).

113

context of "Wild Palms" too, just as fertility myth works in Eliot's *The Waste Land*. The modern age has corrupted traditionally rich and fruitful symbols, Harry has said, so that the goddess of love would be a man selling filthy postcards in a public lavatory (136). But the imputation that Nature is a wasteland is anthropocentric. The year, to use Jeffers' words out of "Tamar," may be going up to its "annual mountain of death," but it will come down again; the devastation of the flood is prelude to a richer spring. Death is part of a cycle that begins with birth and continues with birth. Nature is not man's tool nor his manufactory. He is merely a part of it, in necessary conflict with all the other parts and even with himself. The cycle will be worked out as *The Wild Palms* proceeds to its climax. The images of fertility and sterility, of birth and death, will resolve themselves at the end in terms of the state of nature which has already been described, and Frazer will come into it again.

The vocabulary out of chivalry ("durance" and "craggy pinnacle or dragoned keep") in which the tall convict's hopes were expressed leads back, if only vaguely, to Charlotte's statuettes of Don Quixote and Cyrano. The similarities between the tall convict and Charlotte's perverse caricatures are only suggestive, but strongly so in light of Faulkner's other deliberate links between the two tales. Another subtle point is the substitution of the word *palm* where *hand* or *fingers* had served better or as well. This occurs in both plots, a reminder that *wild palms* may refer not only to the clashing trees that figure symbolically in "Wild Palms," but also to Harry, whose bungling hands cannot *hold* Charlotte but cause her death; to Charlotte, who uses her hands to make things and to do with Harry what she pleases; and to the tall convict, who seems so skillful with the crude tools nature allows him. Faulkner did not choose carelessly when he wrote that Charlotte drew Harry's fingers along the "base of her other palm" (40) to demonstrate that she was a sculptress, any more than when the tall convict, just before he hears the woman's voice, was made to touch his *palm* to his bleeding nose (147). Even the tree in which the woman has found refuge is probably no more a piece of inanimate and normal scenery than the wildly clashing palms that give Harry and Charlotte's story a title and an ending mood. Egeria, Diana's counterpart and a frequent bride of the kings of Rome in their annual impersonations of Jupiter, was a tree nymph as well as a nymph of water. And in general, according to Frazer, among the beneficent aspects of trees, fertility ranks high, a connection in which the palm is frequently mentioned. In the one-volume abridgement of Frazer which Faulkner is said to have read, in the section on trees and tree-worship, the anthropologist reports a widespread belief that the souls of the dead animate trees. Frazer gives the particular information that in one culture the souls of women who die in childbirth are believed to "invariably take up their abode in trees." [9] The possibility that Faulkner applied this lore purposely will appear even greater in Harry's final scene.

The advent of the pregnant woman does nothing to better the tall convict's position. She only increases his predicament and adds to the boat another burden for him to return to its proper place. He and the woman are in greater evident jeopardy than are Harry and Charlotte. The wild element upon which he has been cast threatens at any moment to overwhelm him and bring the kind of watery death that Charlotte and Harry court glibly. Consequently, he has an immediate incentive to work a great deal harder than Harry does. His goals are more tangible and even more personal, since in this case at least both the boy scout and the old lady, however they are identified, will perish together. He is still either ignorant of his surroundings or deceived by them. At one point, "they were in an eddy but did not know it" (151). Later, in the Yazoo River, he is unaware that the water is running backwards. As he tells the woman, "I dont even know where I used to be. Even if I knowed which way was north, I wouldn't know if that was where I wanted to go" (152). He speeds his paddling, believing erroneously that he must soon come to a town, when actually he paddles away from civilization. He is unaware that a forty hours' accumulation of flood water "was somewhere ahead of him, on its way back to the River" (155). And

[9] *Ibid.*, 115.

finally, when the flood wave has reached the skiff, he "did not know what it was" (156).[10]

Faced with the giant wave, once again the tall convict is denied time to think, or even scream, and the action is abruptly telescoped so that now it is midnight and, at the end of one of the richest paragraphs in the novel, his "native state, in a final paroxysm, regurgitated him onto the wild bosom of the Father of Waters" (158). He is abrupted onto the river with a "rolling cannonade of thunder and lightning . . . as though some forty hours' constipation of the elements . . . were discharging in clapping and glaring salute" (157). This thunderous salute stands out as the only clap of thunder in a storm-drenched novel, and it calls sufficient attention to the trauma that is taking place. Like everything in the convict's story except its final implication, this is comic: a regurgitation, a cosmic dissolution of constipation (the skiff "was in a seething gut"), with great laboring of the elements and a single vast cannonade, a crude parody of birth and evacuation, and a possible allusion to the thunderclap which opens Canto IV of *The Inferno*. But the transformation is no less real for being comic. Compared to where the tall convict finds himself now, the streams and rivers he has traversed heretofore are mild forms of chaos indeed. A "wind filled with the smell and taste and sense of . . . boundless desolation" (158) strikes him as he moves onto the river, images of odor and wind which coincide with those used to set the barren beach scene. But there is a difference: this is cold and wet instead of hot and dry; in place of the dying year this is the year struggling to be reborn, the working out of the spring thaw latent with hope of regeneration.

Faulkner shatters conventional suspense in "Old Man." He carries the tale immediately to its end, writing "This is how he told about it seven weeks later" (158). The narrative henceforth appears in a framework. The story will be interrupted repeatedly with references

---

[10] The wave which almost falls on him has a crest that "swirled like the mane of a galloping horse and, phosphorescent too, fretted and flickerd like fire" (156). Compare the well-known image in "Carcassonne," the buckskin pony with "eyes like blue electricity and a mane like tangled fire." William Faulkner, *Collected Stories* (New York: Random House, 1950), 895.

to time (161,163–65,168,169,171), interrogation by the plump convict (161,171,172,239–40,242,246–47), and dialogue guides which indicate that the tale is *told* by the tall convict (168,169,170,171,172,173,174, 230,244). He is telling it in prison. He has returned to base, come full circle just as Charlotte and Harry have done, as we know from the first chapter of the novel. As in their case, what we know from the "ending" of the novel colors what we learn as the first part of the story unfolds. Harry's statement that he is a painter (18), for example, is revealed false and the falsity occurs in the context of Charlotte's own aspirations in art, giving a general source for evaluating the lovers. Knowing that the tall convict is in prison as he tells the tale of his adventures, we gain a similar insight. We know that he has tasted freedom and given it up, retreating from knowledge like the doctor in the first chapter. It remains for us to learn why.

Out on the river at last, the tall convict begins to make discoveries. One is about nature—that the present state of the river is "no phenomenon of a decade," but what "it liked to do" (160). Another is that fear, like pleasure, cannot be sustained forever. There comes a point when it ceases to agonize and only itches, "as after you have been burned bad" (160).[11] At the full mercy of the flood now, the tall convict wants "so little," desires only "to come to something, anything" so he can rid himself of the woman. "That didn't seem like a great deal to ask" (161). Charlotte and Harry think their desires are equally simple: as she says, "I like bitching, and making things with my hands. I dont think that's too much to be permitted to like, to want to have and keep" (88). Part of the trouble is that these people are talking about permission when what they actually want is something between endorsement and aid. The problem they all have, in different ways, is that they want to follow their heart's desire, as the tall convict thinks, and do it "the right way" (161). He has a standard to meet in getting rid of the woman which is just as restrictive for him as the standard Charlotte and Harry have for

---

[11] The burn which Faulkner sustained in New York in 1937 (see Chapter One) and his experience with doctors and hospitals at that time may find its way into the novel here and elsewhere. The phrase also reminds one of Charlotte's scar.

their remaining together. If there is an answer at all to such wishes, it probably is that one does not ask of life, one takes from it.

Both the tall convict and the lovers want to evade the realities of life. Charlotte and Harry want release from the bonds of time, they want to live and love without fulfilling the prerequisities or accepting the consequences, they want to be free from worrying about eating and sleeping and free from the intrusion of pregnancy. The tall convict wants to "turn his back ... on all pregnant and female life forever and return to that monastic existence of shotguns and shackles where he would be secure from it" (153). His view of his companion's unborn child is equivalent to Charlotte and Harry's view of theirs. He thinks of "it" as a "senseless millstone" and even makes a crueller analogy. Musing on the "aberration of eye or hand which would suffice to precipitate her into the water ... he felt sorry for her as he would for the living timber in a barn which had to be burned to rid itself of vermin" (154).[12] Vermin may not be desirable, but like a child in the womb it is a living part of nature. The mistake he makes is suggested by his term "living timber," which is wrong, a perversion. In a sense different from Harry's, he feels the oppression of the fleshly. It seemed to him that the "swelling and unmanageable body ... was not the woman at all but rather a separate demanding threatening inert yet living mass of which both he and she were equally victims" (154), a perception that coincides with Harry's interpretation of the Falstaff figure as "two: the man and the gross flesh ... the man struggling with the mountain of entrails ... to pass it, escape it, as you do with the atavistic beasts in nightmare" (91). The convict makes another error, but this is merely folly. Like Harry trying to keep Charlotte from dying, he pleads with the woman, when her time comes, to "hold on" (171). He might as well tell the river to cease flowing.

In other respects he is learning to accept the conditions that nature offers him. The next time the skiff runs up a tributary, he is aware that it flows backwards (162), and he paddles with intent in the direction he really wants to go. When another wave is gathering

12 Cf. Faulkner, "Golden Land," *Collected Stories*, 708, 710.

ahead of him, he knows what to expect. But he is still not enough the realist to seek any means to get out of the flood's way. He runs up on a shanty boat as he flees and tries to explain to the three people aboard his desire to get back to the familiar comfortable companioned life of the prison farm—the bug screens, the ball games, the movies, the "good stoves in winter and someone to supply the fuel and the food too" (166). As wretched as these shanty boat folk are, however, they do not desire any part of a man who cannot wait to give up his freedom. They will take the pregnant woman or give the castaways food, but they do not want him. "He never did even get on the other boat" (164). As he tells this part of his tale, his hand shakes so badly that he spills the tobacco of the cigarette he is rolling and snaps the paper in two, an act pointing to the novel's original title. He has forgotten Jersualem, freedom, and his hand has lost its cunning. Appropriately, when he tries to explain his reasons for wanting to get back, the strong impulse to give up his freedom, he does so "not for justification because he . . . knew that his hearers, the other convicts, required none from him" (165). They are as comfortable as he is, and as oblivious of their freedom. The paragraph in which this phrase is set is replete with hints of impotence. Among the comfortable things in prison he thinks about are the mules "with characters he knew and respected as he knew and respected the characters of certain men" (165–66). He also recalls that two years before he had declined the job of trusty by deciding "I done already tried to use a gun one time too many" (166). Faced with the implacability of the shantyboaters, like Harry in the preceding chapter the tall convict realizes that he is doomed, fated "never to get rid of" the woman, "just as the ones who sent him out with the skiff knew that he never would actually give up" (168). He is imputing an intention that never existed. The powers-that-be were as indifferent to his qualifications as nature herself is. The "ones who sent him out" are merely the tall convict's equivalent of Harry's imaginary "They" (140). The tall convict makes another equation that sounds like Harry's. When the intern looked at the food he and Charlotte received for $100, he saw the goods in terms of time, mentally measuring it into the days it would last them. The tall convict looks at the single can of condensed milk which the shantyboat woman has thrown into the skiff, among other scraps of food, and finds it a presage that he will not reach a "flat stationary surface" for the woman's child to be born on. As with Harry, "Time: that was his itch now" (169).

Time is not all. He had "wanted so little...yet there had been demanded of him in return the one price out of all breath which" he could not pay (169). The figure recalls Charlotte's talk in the beginning about the value of love being the price you had to pay for it and sets up Harry's anguished cries in the following chapter that the price he must now pay—performing the abortion—is too much. Cast loose again, the tall convict must resume his flight from the second wave; and thus nature comes down behind the boat as inexorably as it proceeds on its course within the boat before his tortured eyes. He transcends the quotidian again, fleeing or borne away from reality, crossing into a timeless hiatus, like Harry's solitude: "he and the wave...hanging suspended simultaneous and unprogressing in pure time, upon a dreamy desolation" (170), the alternation of day to night and back to day "anachronic and unreal as the waxing and waning of lights in a theatre scene" (171).[13]

The tall convict's experiences differ greatly in one respect from Charlotte and Harry's. He never sees a city (157,276,336), though he passes quickly in and out of New Orleans as an unwilling refugee. Here, instead of dealing with the corrupt and hypocritical members of the bourgeoisie, he has sought help from the shanty folk who are outside society, outside the law, and they do not want him at all.

[13] This is the third image out of stagecraft in "Old Man," the second in this chapter (see 143, 171), all suggesting the fabulous and illusory nature of life. The suffusion of yellow in both plots—the river, the sky, Charlotte's eyes— evokes Wagner's *Tristan and Isolde*, which was apparently often lighted with "sorrowful" yellow in the third act: "the yellowish obsession of the fevered," as Denis de Rougemont calls it (*Love in the Western World*, trans. Montgomery Belgion, Revised Edition (New York: Pantheon, 1956), 230). There is no chance that Faulkner had read Rougemont before *The Wild Palms*, but he might have seen, or read about, traditional productions of the opera. He knew about Wagner and Bayreuth, as dialogue in "Ad Astra," for instance, testifies (Faulkner, *Collected Stories*, 412–13.

Counterpoint: The Comic Deception of the Hero

For them, the penitentiary suit is just as good as an odor of unsanctity and disaster. From them he rebounds onto more respectable elements. He comes into the Atchafalaya Basin in Louisiana, where a "neat white portrait town" appears "abrupt and airy and miragelike" (172). Here is familiarity—skiffs, railroad cars, khaki-clad figures—everything from which he departed only a few mornings ago and toward which all his energies had tried to return him. But they do not want him either. They do not understand. Under the conditions, he is not behaving like a convict. When he tries to surrender, the soldiers assume he is trying to escape, and they fire away at him and drive him back under the water, the Freudian birth image coming to use again. His flight must continue, so once more he departs. Harry was rejected by a corrupt society for being corrupt; the tall convict is rejected by respectable society for being respectable. Illusion beguiles everyone.

The river becomes the only reality he is allowed to know, the towns all "unattainable and miragelike" (175). The tall convict is a quick learner in some respects. From now on he dreads the thought of passing a town or of being taken into one by the steamboat. As he says, "*I tried that once. They shot at me*" (247). So he is really doomed now, the towns "less than the figments of smoke or of delirium" (175). The woman is straining in labor, a thin trickle of blood on her chin like the thread of blood at the corner of Charlotte's mouth when she is suffering from a related but different cause (286). The wave catches them, but the convict sees the swimming deer in time and instinctively he follows it to safety. Another of the apparitionlike phenomena, the deer seems to run on the surface of the water, "soaring clear of the water . . . vanishing upward . . . the entire animal vanishing upward as smoke vanishes" (176), like one of the "translations out of Isaiah" with which the chapter began.

The tall convict has never really shown a death wish, although his frustration with his predicament reached a point at which he sought "anybody he could surrender her to, something solid he could set her down on and then jump back into the river, if that would please anyone" (161). He gets his goal. The woman's child is born

121

on the Indian mound they reach, and the tall convict slips back into the fluid world "from which he himself had never completely emerged" (177). This is the classical Freudian dream image of birth. John Feaster's psychoanalytic approach to "Old Man" provides a number of illuminating observations upon the imagery of this part of the novel. He quotes Trigant Burrow on the birth trauma: "With the infant's forcible expulsion from the paradise of peace and plenty, he enters a totally different world of experience." [14] This is rather self-evident, and it is one of the things that happens to the tall convict, who is taken from the secure life of the prison farm and sent out upon the chaotic and unfamiliar River. But the River becomes a kind of womb for him too, and over and over again he must suffer the traumas of both birth and death, departure and return, entering and climbing out of the water. The numerous departures which he begins in company with the other convicts, all roughly in terms of water voyages, have been discussed. His experiences in and out of the skiff, his eruption out of the Yazoo River onto the "Father of Waters," his being chased under water by the soldiers' guns, his emergence on the banks of the Indian mound only to slip back into the amniotic medium in which he has existed for so long–all combine elements of birth and death from the psychoanalytic point of view. If the chains linking the convicts are "umbilicals" (67), so is the grapevine painter that links the convict to the skiff and hence to the water. It is also a manacle like Charlotte's grasp upon Harry (who falsely calls himself a "painter" in Chapter One), something which binds him to that which supports him on the flood. Similar ambiguity and paradox occur throughout his experiences upon the land, where he adapts with the same nearly foetal complacency as

---

[14] John Feaster, "Faulkner's *Old Man* [*sic*]: A Psychoanalytic Approach," *Modern Fiction Studies*, 13 (Spring 1967), 90. By an interesting coincidence, Burrow was a friend of Tennessee Mitchell's and Anderson's. There is a probable portrait of him in "Seeds," in *Triumph of the Egg* (1921), along with one of Tennessee, who sculpted the clay figures photographed and used as illustrations for the book. See Dale Kramer, *Chicago Renaissance*, where the Burrow-Anderson friendship is traced, though Burrow's name is spelled wrong (i.e., "Trigent Burrows") and the index entry on him contains a typographical error. See also Anderson's correspondence.

Counterpoint: The Comic Deception of the Hero

Harry to wherever he happens to be, whether in the blood-heat of the cajan's cabin or jackknifed into his bunk back on the penal farm. Feaster makes his points in relation to "Old Man" alone, even beginning with the statement that "Old Man" has been studied little as an independent work (which is unfortunately not quite true), though often as thematic contrast to "Wild Palms," as if that were undesirable. Thus, he has failed to appreciate that most of what he says about the tall convict applies strongly to Harry, for whom the tall convict is merely a foil. Bunks, park-benches, daydreams of floating in water, periods of timelessness, drowsings in woods-solitude—all are womblike experiences for Harry, and very much more self-imposed than the circumstances to which the tall convict merely adapts. The importance of doors and rooms in "Wild Palms," the constant departure and return, the lakes over which the lovers travel leaving New Orleans, the frozen "iron lake" on which Chicago sits (119), the Wisconsin lake in which Harry soaks his hand up to the wrist, the womblike aspects of the Utah mining camp—a multitude of images reinforce the impression that much is being made of symbolic birth and death. The experience of the middle-aged doctor is likewise expressed in these terms: from his womblike but barren house he passes through the gap in the oleander hedge that veils him from reality into the harsh wind of the sea (like the icy and wet wind which struck the tall convict after he had come through the "gut" into the river and also like the black wind that casually seeks entry to the broken cottage the lovers rent).

The tall convict's experience is also expressed in terms of will. He is too busy struggling for existence to talk, as Harry does, in Schopenhauerian terms. But he is a pawn of the will to live. He fights just to stay alive, and seeks a safe place for the woman to have her baby. Eventually, he yields to the primal urge of sex, though with another man's wife instead of with his passenger. In the telling of the last part of the tale, the part about the second wave, there comes a moment when he is calm. He makes the cigarette he could not make earlier, and it is as if he has passed "into a *bourne* beyond any more amazement" (174, italics added). Part of

123

his memory is how he "half pushed and half flung" the woman up the mound "as if his own failed and spent flesh were attempting to carry out his furious unflagging *will* for severance at any price, even that of drowning, from the burden with which...he had been doomed" (177, italics added). The elements of Harry's surname, and the passage from *Hamlet*, are evoked. This is not the last time in the novel for a significant conjunction of memory and flesh and will. That "bourne" is the convict's will-less state after he has returned to prison, but he is not irrevocably committed to it. He has exhibited the will to live several times. He tells these experiences now. The possibility exists that his memories will push him on either side of the fence, so that he either affirms or denies life. He must unfold the whole story, and remember what he could not tell them at his first trial, before his choice is resolved. It will have everything to do with the preciousness of his memories.

CHAPTER VIII

The Price
of Sleeping Together

... the empty hands still now ... those curious appendages
clumsily conceived to begin with yet with which man has
taught himself to do so much, so much more than they
were intended to do or could be forgiven for doing. ...

WILLIAM FAULKNER
The Unvanquished

THE TALL CONVICT has come to temporary shelter on an Indian
mound where he and throngs of other creatures take common refuge
from the flood. In general, there is harmony here, as much because
of as despite the disruption of normal order. Life renews itself even
here as the woman's child is born, the nameless offspring of a nameless mother, apparently fatherless and homeless, but thriving. For
all the chaos and death and destruction, the river that cannot be held
within its banks cannot in turn prevent life from continuing. The
flood is not all death and destruction anyway. As was noted earlier,
it is also a force for renewal. The damage is compensated by a rich
residue of soil when the waters recede. The crops that have been
delayed will sprout and grow faster than ever. The harvest will be
good and life will take up where it left off. Spring will be late, but
truly it will be beautiful in the spring.

Harry and Charlotte have had their turn with natural harmony
and beneficence in the Wisconsin woods. That was in the fall, not
the spring, and the year was hastening toward the death of winter.
After a Christmas season perverted into a buying spree, they
abandoned the neon corpse-glare of Chicago for a different kind of

EPIGRAPH: William Faulkner, *The Unvanquished* (New York: Random
House, 1938), 272.

hell: cold, static, dead. The scene is ugly: a "snow-choked railhead" (180). Monstrous creatures like the "grimed giant" meet them (revealed later as no giant at all). The canyon itself is a scarred and blemished "gutter." Even the sky is "dirty." The "lovers" with whom they share their retreat are a hardfaced couple without delicacy, compunction, or love. The Buckners—Buck and Bill—are another perversion of the relationship between the sexes. There is no romance in their lives, merely the open and frequent practice of fierce stallionlike sexual romps. Bill lets Charlotte know quickly how to hang on to a man: marry and put the license away. It "dont do a girl any harm to be safe," she says, particularly if she is "jammed"—her word for pregnant (179–80). Like everyone else they have met, Bill Buckner can sense that Harry and Charlotte are not married. Charlotte and Harry have come to this barren, womblike place to flee the world, but, as Cleanth Brooks has noted, they find that they have taken the world to bed with them.[1] Their experience with the Buckners has two results. Harry told McCord that the pleasures to be sought were the "fleshly" ones: "eating and evacuating and fornication and sitting in the sun" (133). Clearly there is no sunbathing at the Utah mine, where one can never hope to get warm. The food supply from the commissary is not a gourmet's choice. And though no reference to evacuating is made, undoubtedly even that is a hardship in a place where people sleep in woolen underwear and still are cold. Fornication is all that is left to them, but the Buckners inhibit them so much they are unable to make love. The Buckners do give them something. They introduce Charlotte and Harry to the possibility of abortion, they provide the means to try out the operation, and they give a false sense of hope for the operation's success. In fact the Buckners may be indirectly credited with Charlotte's pregnancy, since the events which allow conception to occur are a result of what happens the evening the Buckners leave, when Charlotte and Harry make up for lost time.

There is less difference between the Buckners and the young

[1] Cleanth Brooks, "The Tradition of Romantic Love and *The Wild Palms*," *Mississippi Quarterly*, 25, No. 3 (Summer 1972), 265–87.

lovers than is immediately apparent. Both women are masculinized. Charlotte was called "Charley" in New Orleans (38) and either wears her own clothes as if they were overalls or puts on Harry's trousers. Mrs. Buckner is known as Bill and is dressed identically with her husband (182). Bill is given the name of whore by Charlotte, who claims the possibility of the title for herself, too. Both Buckner and Harry support a dishonest enterprise, with full knowledge of its crookedness. Both do less than their best for the poor unpaid Polish workers; Buckner runs out and Harry and Charlotte take their own food supply before they allow the miners to divide the stores in the commissary. Buckner has used his knowledge of the corruption behind the mining operation to advantage: undeceived about the possibility of ever getting his pay, he has chosen to remain at the barren site. Because Bill is pregnant with a child they do not want, Buckner has kept the fruitless mine open—and kept the Poles working it—to await a doctor. Buckner undoubtedly knows that Callaghan will have to send another doctor or close up and stop selling stock, and that any doctor taking the job will be amenable to performing abortion.

The house the couples share is made of sheet-iron,[2] and in place of a hearth or a stove it is supplied with a modern gasoline-burning contraption that explodes violently whenever it is relighted but has little effect against the infernal cold. The storeroom with its depleted shelves seems to Harry "a thermometer not to measure cold but moribundity" (184). Since neither Harry nor anyone else who works for the mine will be paid, the shelves of food, instead of money, become a measure of time, which in Charlotte's case will soon tick off moribundity too. The cold of the place is a "dead cold," the mine entrance is a "lifeless scar" (184). The mine galleries are like an "Eisenstein Dante,"[3] (187) where even the dirty light

2 More prison imagery; cf. "iron" Lake Michigan; the "ironlike" convolutions of water that shackle the convict (145); the railroad cars "knee-deep, bedded and fixed forever in concrete" (140). Like captivity and freedom, stasis and motion are contrasted throughout.
3 In his TS Faulkner had "Demille," then altered it to "Eisenstein" by hand, perhaps a reflection of his Hollywood experience. The revision emphasized

bulbs express sham and moribundity. Already Wilbourne has thought, *"We should have brought the Bad Smell"* (184), but they gave that away in a gesture of defiance to Bradley. As a fetish to ward off the unworthiness Charlotte feared, it was ineffective anyway, and it actually may have become a sign of the "smell of unsanctity" which Harry believed they emanated on the train leaving New Orleans. A "smell" has in fact preceded them to the mine. Buckner tells them that the Chinese workers had pulled out in October: "They smelled it" (187).[4]

Charlotte and Harry's experience with the cold leaves "an ineffaceable and unforgettable mark somewhere on the spirit and memory like first sex experience or the experience of taking human life" (182).[5] Charlotte has been marked previously by the fight with her brother during which she fell into the fireplace; both the experience and the scar have figurative value in the novel. Harry thinks that *he* has "marked" her, telling McCord at the lake that if he "hadn't marked her by now" he would refuse "to believe" in the power of love. He is self-deceived, as McCord's succinct and vulgar comment at the time suggests (101). However he will *mark* Charlotte in the novel's near future, impregnating her and cutting into her womb with a scalpel, ineptly; but he has not yet marked her, simply because she cannot be touched in the same manner as he has been. Charlotte has been in love before (43). The scar she bears is a sign of an experience with her brother, which, if not the real and desired one forbidden by the incest taboo (40), is at least symbolically sexual. She could not sleep with her brother, so she married Rat, and she has borne him children. She knows enough about "bitching" to know that she likes it. Thus, unlike Harry, who was a twenty-seven year old virgin, she cannot succumb to Harry's feelings about "first sex experience." She already

---

the starkness of the scene; Sergei Eisenstein, more than Cecil B. Demille, was known for austere black and white settings.

[4] Like Harry and Charlotte, who are always trying to close doors between themselves and reality, the miners labor furiously, and futilely, inside the mine portal. More illusion.

[5] Houston's murder leaves this mark on Mink Snopes: "the dead who would carry the living into the ground with him; the living who must bear about the repudiating earth...the deathless slain" (William Faulkner, *The Hamlet* [New York: Random House, 1940], 249).

bears that mark from other times. In fact, it is she who will leave Harry marked with both the "ineffaceable and unforgettable" experiences mentioned: sex and the taking of human life.[6]

The young intern is already aware that she has introduced him to sensuality, and he has accepted it so fully—"she has marked me too forever" (133)—that he preaches McCord a doctrine of *carpe diem* while they await the departure of the Utah train. Charlotte has tried to transcend the disappointing alternation of desire and ennui in the life of the individual will by her art. She hoped to fashion an ideal love affair, but she failed, profaning the ideal and asserting the will to live in its most basic manifestation by celebrating sex. Now Harry takes his turn. But he has misread his Schopenhauer, or his Epicurus, and also attempts the right thing in the wrong way. Schopenhauer identified the peaceful state of will-less contemplation of ideas apart from motive as akin to "the painless state which Epicurus prized as the highest good and as the state of the gods." [7] It was, according to Schopenhauer, the other way, besides the singling out of the Ideal by means of art, to escape the Ixion's wheel of willing. But Epicurus did not celebrate the *fleshly* pleasures: it was in selected intellectual pleasures that he found the equableness and peace which Schopenhauer—and Harry—is talking about. So Harry labors under a double irony: he is doing the wrong thing, and he is going to the wrong place to do it. By putting "fornication" on his list he proves that he is caught in the prison-house of the will to live.

Harry demonstrates his acceptance of the continuance of life in another, more orthodox and understandable way. He begins immediately refusing to perform the abortion that the Buckners want, though he admits that the operation is simple: "A touch with the blade to let the air in" (192). A month passes: it is "almost March now and the

---

[6] The same connection is made in Thomas Mann's *Magic Mountain* (first pub. in English in 1927 by Knopf): "It is absurd for the murderer to outlive the murdered. They too, alone together, as two beings are together in only one other human relationship, have, like them, the one acting, the other suffering him, shared a secret that binds them forever together. They belong to each other" (trans. H. T. Lowe-Porter [New York: Knopf, 1944], 462).

[7] Arthur Schopenhauer, *The World as Will and Idea*, trans. R. B. Haldane and J. Kemp (London: Routledge and Kegan Paul, 1883), I, 254.

spring for which Charlotte waited that much nearer" (193). In the face of the renewal of the earth, Charlotte persuades Harry to perform the operation on Bill Buckner. For pay he accepts not money but a claim upon a hundred dollars worth of supplies in the mine commissary. In a sense, he is back where he began at the lake, with a hundred dollars worth of food on the shelves. Despite Buckner's comment that the commissary is now all Harry's, the intern believes the agreement "will keep the books balanced" (195).

Their first night alone they are able to make love again. Seven weeks later Harry learns that Charlotte is pregnant because the perverse heating contraption had gone out that night, causing Charlotte's douche bag to freeze and break. The explosive, warmthless surrogate for a hearth, Nature, and Charlotte's carelessness have betrayed them in this frozen hell. Charlotte seeks justification again in something she had heard about love, "that when people loved, hard, really loved each other, they didn't have children, the seed got burned up in the love, the passion. Maybe I believed it." (205)[8] This is another of her mistakes.

The lovers are completely alone again, having sent the unfortunate Poles on their way. Charlotte's art served her well for once. These people could understand the drawings she made to tell them why they had to go away because the pictures were caricatures. The miners and their families point up two things. Among them are five women and two infants, one of which is less than a month old, obviously born since Harry's advent and without his knowledge or assistance. He seems amazed that the people did not know he was a doctor, without realizing that he has done nothing to inform them. So for all its barren aspect, this dirty, scarred, icy womb is capable of harboring new life, just like the snake-infested Indian mound in the middle of the flood. Harry and Charlotte learn this to their dismay. The couple give the departing miners what is left in the commissary, having removed their own $100 worth of food first. "Maybe it wasn't ours," Charlotte says,

[8] Cf. Mink Snopes' wife: " 'I've had a hundred men, but I never had a wasp before. That stuff comes out of you is rank poison. It's too hot. It burns itself and my seed both up. It'll never make a kid.' But three years afterward it did" (*The Hamlet*, 274).

thinking of the people who had not been paid in over five months, and when Harry suggests that it was Buckner's, who in turn gave it to them, she adds "But he ran away. They didn't" (203). A strange time for her to be talking about running away in such terms. As before, she and Harry are participating in the corruption that is everywhere.[9]

Now the message from Buckner comes and Charlotte wants an abortion for herself.[10] Harry thus finds another menstrual scale upon which to mark time. Charlotte believes she is 16 days past the first period that ought to have come. Harry wants to argue that one "can never be sure until two" periods are gone, hiding behind his medical training from the more likely facts, but Charlotte logically counters, "That's just when you want a child" (205). Because he does not want to perform the abortion, the time during which the operation is possible passes slowly for him. At the mining camp he has no park benches to sit upon while he broods and counts, so he takes walks, "slogging and plunging in the waist-deep drifts" (206–207) like the tall convict struggling in the water and marshland he encounters. He had believed he was taking them to safety, getting away from the infernal city and out of the rut they had fallen into. Instead, he has plunged them into an icy hell from which there is no easy escape. He has reduced their alternatives to the worst possible. Their life together is as miserable as it was in the Wisconsin woods. Harry stays outside until the "cold—something—would drive him back" (207). Perhaps the "something" is solitude, only so much of which one can stand and still live, as he told McCord after he had gotten his fill of *waldein-*

[9] Harry says about staying at the mine: "We've still got three-quarters of the hundred dollars in grub ourselves, and if everybody left here, somebody would hear about it and he might even send a man in here to pick up the other three cans of beans" (198). This is balanced by the Warden's remark to the deputy about getting the tall convict's name off the books "before some politician tries to collect his food allowance" (80; cf., also, 329).

[10] Buckner's note comes as magically as the lovers' meeting, the $1200 in the trash bin, and other events of the novel. It is brought by a mountaineer searching for "one of them big airplanes" which had fallen just "before Christmas" (204). An airliner carrying nineteen—big for that day—crashed in the Utah mountains in mid-October 1937, about the time Faulkner was in New York. *New York Times*, 19 October 1937.

samkeit in Wisconsin (138). They still sleep together "to keep from freezing," and still make love: "in a kind of frenzy of immolation" (207), which presages once more the fate that waits for Charlotte, the death by fire and not by water.

Harry has nothing to do, not even wood to gather. He throws out the empty cans from which their food came, a form of "evacuation," but hardly one of the fleshly pleasures he came seeking, and also a form of accounting the days of their existence against their dwindling supplies. Like the tall convict on the flood, he is disoriented, walking in the unfamiliar landscape, wallowing and plunging in the "drifts which he had not yet learned to distinguish" (207). The pregnancy of his companion becomes an obsession, though he argues against the fact. He cries mentally in protest that he does not flee outside in order to avoid looking at her (207). But he protests too much. Ignoring his medical education, he debates getting some kind of pill: *"whores use them"* (208). He runs up the account on his life to this moment: *"this is the price of the twenty-six years, the two thousand dollars I stretched over four of them . . . the dollar and two dollars a week"* (208). At that, his price is less than what Charlotte will have to pay, though perhaps more than what the tall convict was talking about (169). The price one pays for love has been resolved for Harry by Charlotte: the abortion is what she demands of him. Money has taken them about as far as it can. At the moment, Wilbourne is defeated. His fancy runs to the sardonic, like the convict thinking of the moment's aberration of eye that would suffice for him to drop the woman and her "millstone" overboard. Harry suggests he can take them to a warmer climate, where they can have the child and he will support them by setting up as a professional abortionist (208). Charlotte does not even bother to argue with him. Once again she is in command, knowing "that one of them must keep some sort of head and she knew beforehand it would not be he" (208).

Two months after the Buckners' departure, Harry and Charlotte leave the abandoned mining camp themselves. By this time they could, if they knew its signs, "see the beginning of the mountain spring which neither of them had seen" (203). They flee through snow into a more familiar climate, to San Antonio,[11] Texas, where the oleander blooms as in New Orleans and cabbage palms explode "shabbily in the mild air" (209) like the palm in the courtyard where they met nearly a year before. The money has dwindled to "a hundred and fifty-two dollars and a few cents" (209), not counting the check from Rat which Harry still carries. They rent a wretched room with a "decrepit gas plate" for the next-to-final avatar of house and hearth they will use. They are there in time for what would have been Charlotte's second period, and Harry still will not perform the abortion. His refusal leads him to a decorous but savage brothel,[12] to a drugstore clerk who dispenses fake abortion pills,[13] and to a dance hall that forbodes death: a revolving globe on the ceiling gives the dancers "the faces of corpses" and creates the illusion of a "marine nightmare" (215), suggestive of the tall convict's difficulties and of the unattainable death by water.

Return to the wicked life of the cities has given Harry access to park benches again, and he uses them for refuge as before, sitting there to curse himself and to read the newspapers he grubs out of garbage cans. He is not so fortunate this time; no lost wallets appear. But money would not help them now anyway. The price has been set at abortion for the moment and it will be raised. Money, although it has seemed to each at different times and in slightly different ways the crux of their misfortune, has never been the answer. Like the groceries from Bradley, it merely prolongs the torture.

They cannot have the child because it would come between them. What Charlotte is thinking when she says "They hurt too much" comes to Harry gradually: "He was about to say, 'But this will be ours,' when he realised that this was it, this was exactly it" (217). Children have hurt her already because she has given them up: "she

---

[11] In a novel as complexly wrought as this one, the choice of San Antonio is no accident, bringing up St. Anthony again, the resister of fleshly temptations to whom McCord had referred (103).
[12] *Sanctuary, Light in August, The Town, The Mansion,* and *The Reivers* have such brothels.
[13] In *Soldiers' Pay* and *As I Lay Dying* similar clerks peddle similar pills, though to the ladies in need, not to the male involved, and for a different price.

had already and scarcely knowing him given up more than he would ever possess to relinquish, remembering the old tried true incontrovertible words: *Bone of my bone, blood and flesh and even memory of my blood and flesh and memory*" (217). Harry seems to have in mind the maternal-child relationship, but the insertion of "memory" into what he thinks links it to the ending of the novel and his discovery there. The words he uses are paraphrased from Genesis, and they do not apply to children: "And the rib, which the Lord God had taken from man, made he a woman, and brought her unto the man. And Adam said, This is now bone of my bone, and flesh of my flesh: she shall be called Woman. . . ." (Genesis 2:22–23). Harry and Charlotte have long since left the Eden where she went naked unashamed and called him Adam, but they were not particularly happy there. By Harry's performing the abortion on Bill Buckner, at Charlotte's urging, they have gained the fatal knowledge of good and evil that will doom them to death and travail. When he has performed the operation on Charlotte, they will have passed the limits to "*that of love and passion and tragedy which is allowed to anyone lest he become as God*" (280). Transcending good and evil, he will know the secret of life itself.

Harry tries to delay the operation (217). Already, says Charlotte, he knows by his "own hand" that the operation is simple (206), and during his park bench meditations he can even agree mentally to the abortion and "hold his hand out and it would not shake" (217). But in her presence he cannot agree. Thirteen days before the time of her third period, when she will be going into the fourth month of pregnancy and it will be too late to perform the operation, she extracts a promise from him. If he cannot find a job by the crucial time, he will operate. The job he comes home with is a travesty, an ironic and cruel parody: a ten-dollar-a-week position as a W.P.A. school-crossing guard, protecting children. Charlotte once called him a "home-wrecking boy scout" (108); McCord characterized him as the old lady under the scout's protection (104); now Charlotte puts him in the class of simple pervert: "So you can rape little girls in parks on Saturday afternoons!" (220) She sets up the operation, readies the surgical tools, encourages him: "Just a touch. Then the air gets in ... and I will be all right and it will be us again forever and ever" (220). But his hand will not cease its shaking for a long while, and even when it seems to, evidently it does not. The act is put flatly in sexual terms: "We've done this lots of ways but not with knives, have we?" "Ride me down, Harry" (221). Here is another of the paradoxes of the novel: the coupling of generation and aborticide, the simultaneous affirmation and denial of the will to live.

The scene shifts abruptly to New Orleans where Harry sits once more in a park inventing in his mind the farewell scene between Charlotte and Rat. The lovers have come full circle, just as the tall convict will. The convict returns the boat and the woman where he was supposed to; Harry brings Charlotte and the $300 check to Rat. Charlotte must know already that she is going to die. She has come back to see the children, to return Rat his check, and to try to set Harry free from the consequences of the botched abortion. Her actual feelings are hinted but never fully revealed, for the scene between her and Rat is presented as Harry imagines it, and his version is not altogether accurate. In his mind's eye he sees clearly the "neat and unremarkable though absolutely unimpugnable door" (221) which had once closed between him and Charlotte and was never thereafter opened to him again. Harry made the discovery on the train out of New Orleans that Rat was capable of suffering. He will grant him little more, however. He cannot overcome the stereotyped view of the husband, and so he misreads both Rat and Charlotte. The bedroom scene in the first chapter of the novel revealed that Charlotte did extract a promise from Rat (20–21). She is successful at that sort of thing, as the act of abortion proved, and she puts no limitations upon what she may ask. Harry, however, believes that Rittenmeyer will make no promise and that Charlotte will ask none, save that in the name of "justice" she will hope that Rat does nothing against her lover (225). Harry imagines her saying that a promise is "*too much to ask*" (226). He is wrong, as he will learn later. Nothing is too much for Charlotte to ask. She has already asked for the world.

He imagines Rat responding sardonically to the suggestion of "justice," when the fact is that Harry himself is guilty of the fault he ascribes to Rat. He sees the husband as if the man wore a mask, *"this face impeccable and invincible"* (227), "the impeccable face ... beneath the impeccable hair which resembled a wig" (56). "Justice," in one sense, consists in not inflicting suffering on other individuals, and it proceeds from the awareness that "other persons are not ... mere masks, whose nature is quite different" from one's own; to act justly is to see through the veil of Maya.[14] Though Harry once sees Rittenmeyer's suffering (55–56), the experience does not really teach him anything. He fails to see what is common between himself and Rittenmeyer. So it is indeed ironic that he imagines Charlotte asking and being refused "justice" as she casts herself and her lover before the betrayed husband as among *"all the men and women who ever lived and blundered but meant the best"* (225). He cannot recognize the possibility that Rittenmeyer may fit into that category himself. Misunderstandings like this play a significant part in *The Wild Palms*, from the middle-aged doctor's rejection of his own piercing of the veil, to the various achievements and losses of rapport that occur between the central characters throughout, in "Old Man" as in "Wild Palms," as they go toward finding meaning in life.

It must not be forgotten that Harry is imagining this scene and that he is demonstrably wrong on a point which can be checked by what occurs later. When Rittenmeyer asks Charlotte what he is to do, Harry imagines she says "Nothing" (225), meaning "nothing against Harry." The intern is evidently wrong about this, as later events will show. Rittenmeyer promises to do "something." When he discovers the facts of this visit between the husband and wife, Harry will come to a new view regarding himself and his relation to the past and the future. He will find absolution better than exculpation, grief better than "nothing." He will do so in terms relevant to everything that has transpired in the novel. But for now he imagines this scene while sitting on the park bench, surrounded by "cries of children and the sound of pram wheels like the Chicago apartment had been" (221), a recurring motif. Upon a "dead noon," there is a "general exodus"

14 Schopenhauer, *The World as Will and Idea*, I, 478.

The Price of Sleeping Together

of nursemaids and children from the park (224), reminding him of Time. Shortly, he thinks of their departure from Chicago "last year," and suddenly comes upon the realization that actually it was only "five months ago" (225). The winged chariot is at his back. Money comes into it too. He imagines Charlotte refusing the three hundred dollars for the last time, replying to Rat's sarcastic observation that they "*have money for coast vacations*" with an affirmative "*We have money*," while in his lap Harry holds all their funds: "the six bills in his hand, the two twenties, the five, the three ones" (225).

Now that the time for glib talk about death has ended, Charlotte demonstrates plainly that she does not believe the "world well lost for love." She does not want to die (206). Harry may have realized what Charlotte meant when she said children hurt too much, but he cannot yet appreciate the full implication of her words, how magnified and cruel the hurt is now that she, dying from the effects of aborting the child in her womb, has just seen her little girls again to bid them farewell. The ending of the chapter is intense and understated. Harry asks her "They were both well?"—a conventional innocent query that shows his ignorance. She ignores it and tells him that he must flee when she is about to die. In a moment he asks her again. The last sentence in the chapter is her answer, simple and dramatic: " 'Yes,' she said; the scaling palm trunks fled constantly past. 'They were all right' " (228). She is probably already listening to one of her "own flagging organs," as the middle-aged doctor correctly observed (5), but it is not the heart. Her suffering is in the womb, and it has a lot to do with children.

CHAPTER IX

Counterpoint:
The Birth in the Flood

> Throughout and everywhere the true symbol of nature
> is the circle ... the most universal form in nature ... from
> the course of the stars down to the death and the genesis
> of organised beings.

SCHOPENHAUER
The World as Will and Idea

THE BABY BORN on the Indian mound was not due for a month (167),
but Nature cannot be accurately clocked or put off. It may even
hurry those who would like to make It wait. Both Harry and the tall
convict have discovered this to their dismay. Nature is the over-
fecund, as Harry once said (114). Even in the frozen wastes of Utah,
children are conceived and born. The Indian mound, despite its nightmarish qualities, is also a refuge and a place of birth. Nature can afford to be careless of the individual and to be intolerant of those
who deny It. Like the "Old Man," It "dont have to brag" (72). This
chapter is an immediate reflection of the preceding segment of "Wild
Palms," and the first sentence reintroduces the principal element of
Harry and Charlotte's tragedy: the woman asks the tall convict for
a knife and his reaction is an inarticulate, raging impotence at the
utter absurdity of such a request. She gives him directions and he
performs an operation, though in this case, and without Harry's
training, the result is successful. He ties off and severs the umbilical
cord, a very symbolic act for him to have performed, as John Feaster
notes in his psychoanalytic study of this part of the novel, and an-

EPIGRAPH: Arthur Schopenhauer, *The World as Will and Idea*, trans. R. B.
Haldane and J. Kemp (London: Routledge and Kegan Paul, 1883), III, 267.

138

other instance of the convict's involvement in the birth trauma, either figuratively or as a witness. His role is more strange to him than abortion is to Harry, who had been shown the procedure during medical school ("maybe to show us what never to do" [191]) and who practiced on Bill Buckner. In his ignorance, the convict has not even realized immediately why the woman wants the knife or the can; but, given a natural act to perform, he succeeds. Unlike Harry, though, he has no stake in what he does.

The woman passenger and Charlotte are both resourceful, but there is a great distance between the serenity of the one and the agitation of the other. Charlotte wants the dream at any price; the anonymous woman is quietly content with reality, however hard. Charlotte's first regard is for love, and then for her lover; a child has no place in the scheme. The woman may have neither husband or lover. She is interested almost exclusively in her child. Charlotte and she both set up and direct operations, but the woman does not even boil the crude instrument that severs her from her baby, though she does produce matches, miraculously, to kindle a fire for food and warmth and to heat the water with which she cleans the child. She says very little, while Charlotte says too much. These women have to be resourceful, at least in the sense that they initiate action, for both their partners have given up to the conditions of the moment. Before Charlotte persuades Harry that the abortion will enable them to live and love again as they had intended, he is ready to make the best of the circumstances, taking a pitifully inadequate job and planning vaguely for the child. The tall convict has acquiesced to the chaos of the flood and cannot think beyond it, so that the simple request for a knife or a match sends him into suffocation and speechlessness. Anything merely ordinary seems out of the question, given what he has already been through, and so the woman provides.

The convict's reflections on the birth of the "terra-cotta colored creature" take a double meaning: "*And this is all. This is what severed me violently from all I ever knew and did not wish to leave and cast me upon a medium I was born to fear, to fetch up at last in a place I never saw before and where I do not even know where I am*" (231).

He is talking about his recent eruption onto the Father of Waters, his removal from the prison farm and the subsequent command to go out and fetch the woman who was pregnant with this child. He is also talking about the process of birth into this life. The second of those two purposefully ambiguous sentences is as pure and excellent a metaphor for the mystery of life as the image of the swallow in Bede's *Ecclesiastical History*. In the "psychoanalytical approach" to "Old Man" already mentioned, Feaster points out this and similar birth imagery in descriptions of the convict's experiences.[1] The convict is wrenched from the womb-like security of his prison bunkhouse, and he eventually returns to it gladly, hunched in a lower bunk while he tells his story. Feaster's approach is stimulating, but short of the mark, as noted, because it ignores the total novel. Harry repeats the birth trauma; so does the middle-aged doctor. And the tall convict goes through more than Feaster recounts: for instance, that dramatic and Freudian passage in which, accompanied by a cannonade of thunder, he shoots through the pillars of the railroad trestle over the Yazoo River and onto the Mississippi. Though there is a crude joke in the word *gut* and the phrase *constipation of the elements*, nine days after this experience the convict comes to life and action on his own terms at the cajan's camp.[2] Feaster writes of the convict's attachment to the water as being due to his failure in the "cathartic repetition of the birth process" to succeed "in abreacting his primal fixation on the womb-substitute."[3] But the convict longs for the land, not only for the familiar earth he plows at the prison farm, but for any dry earth. Consider the joy with which he lies upon the solid mud of the Indian mound, after putting the woman and the child into the boat and pushing them back out upon the water in order that they may lie evenly and safely and in an altogether dif-

[1] John Feaster, "Faulkner's *Old Man*: A Psychoanalytic Approach," *Modern Fiction Studies*, 13 (Spring 1967), 89–93.

[2] He arrived there on the "tenth day of terror and hopelessness" (241), but he was not ejaculated onto the river until the end of the first terrible day: i.e., it was after midnight (157). He also spends nine days in the camp's "blood-heat" (252) before he is forced to leave because the levee is being dynamited.

[3] Feaster, "Faulkner's *Old Man*," 92.

ferent medium. The solid earth represents something real and familiar and substantial: "if you fell upon it you broke your bones against its incontrovertible passivity sometimes but it did not accept you substanceless and enveloping and suffocating, down and down and down" (232–33), a passage that necessarily recalls Charlotte's stated preference for hard sculptured objects made of earth elements (41). The convict does not long for water. It is the unfamiliar, though there was one time in the boat when he would have accepted drowning merely to escape "the belly" (161). At least in terms of his struggles against being swallowed by the flood, he is very much opposed to extinction and in favor of life. But then water is not pictured here as the peaceful fluid that cradles the foetus in the womb. He is led to realize early in the adventure that this wild chaos is the river's normal state—and Nature's—while "the intervening years during which it consented to bear upon its placid and sleepy bosom the frail mechanicals of man's clumsy contriving was the phenomenon" (160).

He has met the Father of Waters, the Old Man. But the flood, like many characters in the novel, is depicted in androgynous terms. Using the provocative criticism of Gaston Bachelard, especially *L'eau et les rêves*, Maurice E. Coindreau observed in his preface to the French translation of *The Wild Palms* that the "little piddling creeks that run backward one day and forward the next" (244) are fickle, while the ability of the water to accept Harry "enveloping . . . down and down and down" (232–33) and to sweep him "thrall and impotent for days against any returning" (233) is much like Charlotte's captivity. But the great river is masculine, and a worthy adversary,[4] while earth, Mother Earth, the passive, the fruitful, the dependable, in which the static trees and posts are firmly set, upon which man by difficult effort of plowing and other labor may get some bounty, is in eclipse. The tall convict has inadvertently gotten himself in the center of a wild and tempestuous love affair of the elements. The Father of Waters overwhelms, covers and fertilizes the unresisting

---

[4] Maurice E. Coindreau, *Préface* to *Les palmiers sauvages* (Paris: Gallimard, 1952), i–xiv.

patient Mother Earth to which the convict would like to cling. Nature is doing what it "liked to do" (160)—a fact that reflects strong light on Charlotte's preference for bitching and making things. Later, in the cajan's camp, the convict finds himself in the same position under slightly different terms, between the "furious embrace of flowing mare earth and stallion sun" (255–56).

In addition to the description of real and symbolic birth and procreation, which mirrors the real and symbolic elements of sterility, perverse creation, and aborticide in "Wild Palms," "Old Man" presents the struggle of the tall convict in primal terms suggesting the development of the life of mankind from the "old subterranean outrage which had created the country" (144), from the biblical Genesis already evoked in "Wild Palms" (109,217). Although the title "Old Man" refers explicitly to the great river, it may also extend to include the convict himself: "old man" in the sense of feral or primitive man. Considering Faulkner's double application of *palms* in the title of the main story, such an extension is to be expected. Charlotte has "blank feral eyes" (11); she and Harry play Adam and Eve, though it hardly needs pointing out that as progenitors of the human race, romantic and tragic lovers would fail. Whether the tall convict would be any better is not to be answered yet. Though it is much against his wishes, he and the woman and child already represent a family. And right now, on the Indian mound, he is very much a primordial creature. Darkness is spread upon the waters, suggesting first creation, and then the quarter-acre Indian mound becomes both an "earthen Ark out of Genesis"[5] and a primordial "cypress-choked life-teeming constricted desolation" (232). When his oar is lost, the tall convict sets about fashioning another in the most primitive manner. As a toolmaker he is not even in an age of chipped stone. He has no weapon to find food either, but, in primitive fashion, he must act as scavenger, taking the prey of hawks. A descendant of some hill-bred Abraham, he is merely the current avatar in the "long generations of himself" (276), a kind of Everyman.

[5] The purpose of the Deluge in Genesis was to "destroy all flesh" because of the corruption and violence in the world (Gen. 6: 1–17).

Counterpoint: Birth in the Flood

Like the lovers at the time of the "Child's service," the tall convict has reached a turning point in his venture, the top of his cycle. *"I dont know where I am and I dont reckon I know the way back to where I want to go . . . But at least the boat has stopped long enough to give me a chance to turn it around"* (233). But before he can even set out, he must endure some of those "deeds and vexations . . . the mishaps of every hour" which make the details of a man's life the "scenes of a comedy." [6] Shoving off to depart, he asks for the oar. The woman tells him it is gone, and he feels like a man "who, having just escaped a falling safe, is struck by the following two-ounce paper weight which was sitting on it" (234). Back on the mound, he must make a paddle, and "for an instant in which he knew he was insane" (234–35) he considered trying to saw down a proper tree "with the flange of the bailing can" (235). While he burns down the tree and then chars its flanks to form a paddle, it rains, and he must build a shelter for his passengers, shaking off the snakes; but when he finishes, "the rain stopped at once and did not recommence and the woman went back to the skiff" (235). The water comes up on him as he sleeps, intruding into his consciousness as a funny dream (in which the wet bed and other elements suggest, as Feaster points out, a form of infantile regression). He is forced to pole away from the Indian mound, flinging the snakes aside and telling the shrieking woman "I wish I was a snake so I could get out too" (237).

Back on the flood, he experiences another of those terrific translations that have marked his voyage. He hears again "that sound which he had heard twice before and would never forget" (something which has left an ineradicable mark on him)—"deliberate and irresistible and monstrously disturbed water" (237). A monster is hinted —"something bellowed tremendously above his head"—and the "mist vanished as when you draw your hand across a frosted pane" (237). The air cleared into a "sunny glitter" [7] and he saw upon the water

[6] Schopenhauer, *The World as Will and Idea*, I, 415.
[7] He seems to be emerging from the twilight world of dream into hard reality. Moments before the sun had been a "pale and heatless wafer disc" (237), recalling Crane's well-known wafer image in *The Red Badge of Courage*. Cf. Faulk-

143

a crowded steamboat. Though the imaginary monster is thus dispelled, the unreality does not immediately cease. The cursing of the riverboat captain comes down on him in "roaring waves of blasphemy and biological supposition" as if the "water, the air, the mist had spoken it" (238). Then, incongruously, paradoxically, the calm voice of the man who is revealed to be a doctor cuts in: "more foreign and out of place than even the megaphone's bellowing and bodiless profanity" (238). The tall convict's sense of alienation is compounded further by the fact that the refugees on the boat are not "Americans," that they sound to his innocent ears like this: "Gobble-gobble, whang, caw-caw-to-to" (240). He has no experience to tell him that these people are cajans and that he is near the bayou country of Louisiana. Like the lovers on the returning leg of their circular flight, the tall convict must also pass through a kind of hell. His descent begins here among jabbering incomprehensible demons as he is ferried across the river by the angry Charon. The doctor with the incongruously mild voice is a kind of Minos (the judge in Canto V, *Inferno*, who punishes carnal sinners) who judges him and lets him pass on. The captain, among other unrecorded profanity, cries out "Do you expect me to hang here on stern engines till hell freezes" (238). The boat is "burning coal" just to talk to him (239). The remembered effect of whiskey is a "fierce turmoil in the hell-colored firelight" and the present effect includes a "bright hot red wave" (240–41). Even as he tells it, the tall convict has "his cigarette going now, his body jackknifed backward into the coffinlike space between the upper and lower bunks ... the blue smoke wreathing across his ... face" (242). "Hell fire" is what the plump convict exclaims during the discussion. And the doctor produces a "pack of cheap cigarettes" and says "Smoke?" before he condemns the convict to the increasingly coppery landscape, where he must descend the levee through "a swirling cloud of mosquitoes like hot cinders" into the bottom-land terrain "broken ... by thick humps of arsenical green ... and by writhen veins of the color of ink" (251). The "poison swamp" of

---

ner's *Mosquitoes*: "Pontalba and cathedral were cut from black paper and pasted flat on a green sky" ([New York: Boni & Liveright, 1927], 14–15).

Counterpoint: Birth in the Flood

which Charlotte spoke (89) has appeared. Within it he finds the bayou rat's cabin, "like a shabby and death-stricken (and probably poisonous) wading creature" (251).

The confrontation between the doctor on the boat and the tall convict is detailed. The doctor, like the middle-aged physician at the beach and even like Harry on the evening when he likened putting on his white intern's jacket to pulling the covers over his head, has lost himself behind the special medical identity. He is more doctor than man. He begins, like the middle-aged doctor, from an unsympathetic point of view, coldly regarding what has happened to the tall convict in a perfectly clinical manner. He prescribes whiskey over the convict's knowing protests that he cannot tolerate it, and then he congratulates the convict on the skull-breaking and self-injurious fight he puts up under the influence. He has the "coldest eyes the convict had ever seen" (242). The convict quickly stops thinking of him as "the mild man" and considers him merely as "the doctor" (242). And when the doctor examines the convict after the fight, he has "eyes which the convict said were not looking at him but at the gushing blood with nothing in the world in them but complete impersonal interest" (242). The two men regard each other without understanding, separated by the masks of individuality, the veil of Maya. The doctor is being his glib confident self as the tall convict tells him about the attempted train robbery. The doctor says that he can do better the next time, now that he knows what went wrong: "they wont catch you next time" (248). But the convict says there will not be a next time and he explains himself in terms which the doctor evidently can understand:

> The convict looked at the doctor steadily. They looked at each other steadily; the two sets of eyes were not so different after all. "I reckon I see what you mean," the convict said presently. "I was eighteen then. I'm twenty-five now."
> "Oh," the doctor said. Now ... the doctor did not move, he just simply quit looking at the convict. He produced a pack of cheap cigarettes from his coat. "Smoke?" he said.
> "I wouldn't care for none," the convict said.
> "Quite," the doctor said ... He put the cigarettes away (248–49).

145

Apparently they reach an understanding; "the two sets of eyes were not so different." Presumably each has found something common behind the mask of individuality in the other; the veil of Maya has been pulled aside. The details which Faulkner offers invite an interesting speculation. Among the first things revealed about the middle-aged doctor was that he did not smoke cigarettes because he had been "sixteen and eighteen and twenty at the time when his father could tell him (and he believe it) that cigarettes . . . were for dudes and women" (3). Like him, and at the same age (eighteen), the tall convict has been irrevocably influenced by the experience of train robbery. When the convict tells this to the doctor on the boat their eyes meet in recognition. The doctor on the boat seems not to smoke: he has "cheap" cigarettes, which apparently are, along with the whiskey, his *materia medica*, something for offering around but not for his own use. There is hardly enough evidence to say assuredly that the doctor on the boat is the doctor at the beach ten years younger, but the weight given to the scene at least arouses suspicion that Faulkner may have broken here what seems otherwise an inflexible adherence to the separation of the two stories, perhaps by accidental adherence to an earlier conception of the material of the book.

The suggestion that the convict's nose bleeds are due to his being hemophilic causes a humorous and malapropian discussion of hermaphroditism by the convicts—"You know what that means?" "You let him call you that?" (242). It brings to mind something Harry said to their landlord when he and Charlotte were leaving Chicago for good. The landlord "expressed regret at the dissolution of mutually pleasant domestic bonds. 'Just two of us,' Wilbourne said. 'None of us are androgynous' " (129).[8] But is that true? The opposite, rather, seems to be in effect in *The Wild Palms*, where almost

---

[8] In *A Reader's Guide to William Faulkner* (1964), Edmond Volpe misses the humor of the convict's speculation and then fails to pick up the other images which make the scene important. Faulkner, among other things, seems to be alluding to the legend of Hermaphroditus. The youth was loved by the water nymph Salmacis; when he resisted her, she united their bodies into one and pulled him into her lake.

everyone is depicted in androgynous terms. Charlotte is definitely feminine, with that "profoundly delicate and feminine articulation of Arabian mares" (38), but she looks at the world with a sober masculine stare and is a better man than Harry, as he knows. He, on the other side, responds in a feminine passive fashion to her sexual forays, but he eventually asserts his manhood strongly. Quite a list can be made of characters similarly divided: the middle-aged doctor and his wife, the tall convict and his plump companion, the woman on the shantyboat (who is dressed in men's clothes and stares soberly like Charlotte did [167]). Even the convict's pregnant passenger is touched, for she is dressed in men's shoes and an old army tunic. "Bill" Buckner is dressed exactly like her husband. The water too has stereotypical characteristics of both sexes, as Coindreau has noted: fickle and capricious in the little streams, virile and threatening as "Old Man." This repeated ambiguous sex differentiation functions in a number of ways. In the strongest sense, it is part of the paradox inherent in nature, which is emphasized by other means as well, a denotation of the one-ness of life beneath the apparent diversity of individuality. Male and female, like birth and death, are merely aspects of a continuing and integral thing-in-itself, the will to live. Sexual ambiguity is both comic and tragic, depending on context, and therefore another means of providing complement and contrast between character and circumstances in the two sections of the novel.[9]

After the doctor has "simply quit looking at the convict" following the momentary recognition, he decides to act in his capacity "to bind and to loose" and allow the young man, whom he recognizes as a convict, to "escape." This power has been granted "if not by Jehovah ... certainly by the American Medical Association—on which incidentally, in this day of Our Lord, I would put my money, at any odds, at any amount, at any time" (249). The contrast with the

[9] Schopenhauer, *The World as Will and Idea*, III, 355–56, provides another gloss: "one loves what he lacks....For...a truly passionate inclination to arise ...two persons must neutralise each other...manhood and womanhood admit of innumerable degrees....From both sides complete hermaphrodism can be reached, at which point stand those individuals who, holding the exact mean between the two sexes, can be attributed to neither, and consequently are unfit to propagate the species."

retribution demanded by the middle-aged doctor in the following chapter of "Wild Palms" is extreme. In this case, the medical man does not choose to make someone else suffer, he shows sympathy and justice. But then, just as when the tall convict's operation was compared with the one Harry performed, he does not have the stake in it that the middle-aged doctor does.

The tall convict's idylls away from the flood, brief as they are, suggest the stages of pause and flight in "Wild Palms." The swimming deer, the gathering of firewood, the operations, the different hell-like atmospheres, the contrast between the ever-colder and ever-warmer climates which the two sets of people seek—all relate one to the other directly. Institutionalized society (in the form of a crooked mining operator and a sardonic member of the A.M.A.) sends both couples into their respective hells, where they communicate successfully with the alien and incomprehensible native beings. Both men put skills with the knife to use: Harry remembers what he had been shown in medical school about abortion, and the tall convict uses his experience in slaughtering pigs as a guide to hunting alligators. In the final accounting, neither is paid for his particular work. Harry gets no salary from Callaghan Mines, though he lives rent- and board-free at the mining camp. The tall convict cannot negotiate his share of the alligator hides, but he lives also rent- and board-free at the cajan's cabin. At certain times in their lives Harry and the tall convict each come to what Feaster calls self-discovery, which has been seen to occur under the guise of a process of psychological birth or rebirth, like Harry's coming out of the nine-months' timelessness and the tall convict's escaping to land after nine-day sojourns upon the river. Both suffer the shattering of illusion. Harry is bored to extinction during his *waldeinsamkeit* and finds their existence in Chicago the "stinking catafalque" of love (139). The tall convict sees the pregnant woman whom he rescues as the "catafalque of invincible dream" (149), but even before that disillusionment his sweetheart, for whom he had committed a crime, had jilted him. Later, a woman who turns out to be a "fellow's wife" will cause him to move on up the river. But while Harry eschews the everyday reality of bourgeois

148

life and embraces Charlotte's vision of romantic love, the tall convict lets the dream die and deals with reality. Like the other prisoners at the penal farm, he had been indifferent to the meaning of the work he performed, denying nature, not caring if he planted pebbles or weeded papièr-mâché crops. Now, successful in his gambit against the alligators, he thinks *"I reckon I had done forgot how good making money was. Being let to make it"* (262). In similar fashion, Harry had come to enjoy his less heroic occupation: "I liked the money I made. I even liked the way I made it" (135). It is appropriate to Harry that he puts money first, while the tall convict (who never gets any money from the work he is talking about) seems to like most the *idea* of remunerative work, the act in terms of the reward, rather than simply the reward. Another difference is that the tall convict discovers himself in this experience. He realizes what the phrase *"Will have to get on back"* to prison (261) means and temporarily reclaims the memory of his freedom.

The convict's understanding of freedom is only temporary. He always has his goal before him, to return the boat and his passenger and to get himself back to the penal farm. Harry and Charlotte, conversely, are always fleeing. One of the ironic facts of life, however, is that there is no place to hide, and the lovers come as surely full circle as the convict does. Harry's calculation of money against time is a way of measuring the days he and Charlotte will have together. The tall convict also comes to think of his earnings as "a question of the money in terms of time, days" (261), but these are the days he will require to get where he is going. His reasoning is usually simpler than Harry's, as one would expect: both men flee the cities, Harry because that is where "They" would best be able to use respectability and other forces to destroy what he thinks he has, while the tall convict avoids them for the practical reason that the city is where they have used a gun against him. What they do have in perfect common is a view of the nature of the universe. The "cosmic joker" which the convict conceives as causing his troubles (264) is the same as the "All-Derisive biding to blast him" (132) of Harry's thoughts. Each has this conception confirmed for him in an experience that pro-

149

ceeds out of solitude. After the cajans have left, the convict goes out alone for the first time, "as though not only not content with refusing to quit the place he had been warned against, he must ... affirm ... his refusal by penetrating even further and deeper into it" (269). As Harry said, thinking of the period of womblike solitude which ended with his abrupt coming back into time, one can stand only so much solitude and still live. The experience is like Pip's in *Moby-Dick*: the "intense concentration of self in the middle of such a heartless immensity, my God, who can tell it?" [10] What happens to the convict is exactly what happened to Harry in the Wisconsin woods (114–15), and probably what happens at some point to Charlotte (who had always been "alone," though surrounded by men) to make her regard the masculine with hatred as she lies in the chair at the beach. For him it is described in terms of his recent encounters with the flood: "without warning the high fierce drowsing of his solitude gathered itself and struck at him" (269). The "silence and solitude and emptiness roared down upon him in a jeering bellow" (269). As if facing a wave of water, "the skiff spun violently on its heel" and he propelled it back toward the cabin in a dreamlike (270), unprogressing striving. What the tall convict and Harry both have left out of account is causality, what Schopenhauer calls the "principle of sufficient reason" of becoming. To be unaware of this chain of succession is to be blinded by the veil of Maya, to see only illusion, to live as in a dream, which is discontinuous.[11] Coming out of the same experience, Harry abandoned his "drowsy and foetuslike state, passive and almost unsentient in the womb of solitude and peace" (110) and saw that "stagnant time which did not advance" was only an illusion, that time had been operative all along and that it was later than he thought. As the convict hurries back to the cabin he knows "it was already too late" (270). When they tell him he must be evacuated in the face of more flooding, he cries "Flood? What flood? Hell a mile, it's done passed me twice months ago!" (271) He is as wrong as Harry was when the intern thought about "last year" in

[10] Herman Melville, *Moby-Dick* (New York: Harper, 1851), 462.
[11] Schopenhauer, *The World as Will and Idea*, I, 8–9, 19, 20–21.

Counterpoint: Birth in the Flood

Chicago (226), meaning a date only five months previous, or imagined the abortion a "month ago" (224). This is the tenth day the convict has spent in the cajan's cabin. Another nine-day gestation has ended and he is being removed. It is only the second such period he has spent on the water.

The convict is outraged, as Harry was when he cursed the "*old weary Lilith of the year*" which betrayed him (115). He complains not so much of the fact of the opposition as of the means employed. He is to leave this refuge where he has rediscovered the joy of work, driven out by another volume of water, a repetition of what has happened to him twice before, though "this third time was to be instigated not by the blind potency of volume and motion but by human direction and hands" (264). His outrage is that of one artist for the work of another: the force against him had no more "pride of artistry and craftsmanship" than to repeat itself (264). There is hardly any consolation in it, but Harry is given more consideration: "They" used money, and "They" used respectability, and finally "They" used sex in order to get him and Charlotte. As it happens, when the "power" comes to get the convict, it turns out to be nothing more than a group of men, trying to save him. The circumstance of his removal from the poisonous-looking wasteland where he rediscovers his freedom is ironic. The men save his life but take his freedom. His own view has been paradoxical anyway. He looks back upon his "seven wasted years" in prison (263) just as Harry looked back on the twenty-seven wasted years of his life up to the day he met Charlotte. He sees that he "had been permitted to toil but not to work" (264), as if he were a slave. Yet he has guarded the symbol of his slavery jealously. He has made the woman carefully clean the prison suit, and each night before going to bed he has looked at it where it rests, like an icon, behind the rafter. Essentially it is captivity, not freedom, he is unwilling to forget, though he can offer a reasonable rationalization for leaving this alien place where he has done so well. In spite of the affinity between river-rat and hillbilly that allows him to comprehend the hard-bitten life of the hunter and to communicate with him, he still believes this is not his way, not his real

151

gambit. He can "be no more than the water bug upon the surface of the pond, the plumbless and lurking depths of which he would never know" (266).[12] The natural question arises, however, whether or not he is self-deceived, blinded by the veil of Maya. He seems to be turning his back upon the "pure rapport of kind for kind" (256) which he has achieved. And what he does may be one touchstone for Harry's statement about his writing: he gives it up when he has become successful. Granted that the convict's gambit seems far more glorious and heroic and certainly more dangerous than Harry's, the two experiences reflect on each other. Harry had come to like writing the cheap stories, not merely for the money they brought him but because through them he was learning that he "had no idea of the depths of depravity of which the human invention is capable" (132–33). Paradoxically, this exploration of depravity is to him a symbol of respectability, since it is his equivalent of the nine-to-five job. When he rejects this—something that is cheap and quickly done and moronic—he rejects not the badness in it, but all forms of daily work, of which the writing is merely an example. At the same time, he is himself engaged in a great many forms of depravity. The parallels and contrasts between the two decisions are merely one more way of emphasizing that all along the tall convict has been able to have for free an essentially better, though slightly comic, version of everything that Harry and Charlotte must fight and suffer and fail to get. And he turns his back every time.

The story of the tall convict's adventures is comic; the contrast between what happens to him and what happens to the lovers is ironically so. The mingling of tragedy and comedy produced by the alternation of "Wild Palms" and "Old Man" has a justification in Schopenhauer, who wrote: "The life of every individual, if we survey it as a whole and in general, and only lay stress upon its most sig-

---

12 Similar imagery in "Ad Astra" spells out the kind of timelessness that both Harry and the tall convict experience: "I think of us as bugs in the surface of the water, isolant and aimless and unflagging. Not on the surface; in it ... we were outside of time; within, not on, that surface" (first published March 1931; William Faulkner, *Collected Stories* (New York: Random House, 1950), 408, 423; cf. also 421).

nificant features, is really always a tragedy, but gone through in detail, it has the character of a comedy . . . as if fate would add derision to the misery of our existence, our life must contain all the woes of tragedy, and yet we cannot even assert the dignity of tragic characters." [13] Harry and Charlotte both touch upon this notion at different times. Harry refers to the "last prone and slightly comic attitude of ultimate surrender" (46), meaning woman's position in the act of love, yet this will also be, for Charlotte, the attitude of death, as the black shape in the wind cuckolds Harry. Charlotte says sardonically that the "best joke of all" is that she has saved her money for five years and does not even have "enough to get two people to Chicago" (48). Harry muses on the aftermath of the visit to the cheap hotel, thinking how right Charlotte is: *It's comic. It's more than comic. It rolls you in the aisles* (52). In his incomplete realization of Rat's suffering, Harry also mistakenly believes that the train's pulling out *is making comedy of that tragedy which he must play to the bitter end or cease to breathe* (56).

Faulkner devotes rich prose to the tall convict's exploits, but nowhere does he match the eloquence used to describe the contests between man with mace and knife and the saurian monsters of the desolate Louisiana swamp country, those

> instants when on lonely and glaring mudspits under the pitiless sun and amphitheatred by his motionless and riveted semicircle of watching pirogues, he accepted the gambit which he had not elected, entered the lashing radius of the armed tail and beat at the thrashing and hissing head with his lightwood club, or this failing, embraced without hesitation the armored body itself with the frail web of flesh and bone in which he walked and lived and sought the raging life with an eight-inch knife-blade (266).[14]

[13] Schopenhauer, *The World as Will and Idea*, I, 415–16.
[14] One of the properties Faulkner worked on during the Hollywood trip that preceded *The Wild Palms* was a film entitled *Banjo on My Knee*, a musical set on the Mississippi or Louisiana coast and about river-rats and a pair of runaway lovers off on a trip to Chicago. The anecdote which Faulkner told more than once about cajans watching Hollywood technicians build a fake shrimping village belongs with *Louisiana Lou*, a film he worked on in 1933 while on location at the Gulf. One cannot help recalling the similarity between Faulkner's tall tale and the scene where the cajans watch the convict battle alligators. The

Life may be a wretched business—and a "gambit he had not elected" —but in these moments the tall convict ennobles it. The passage, like his thoughts upon looking at the newborn child (231), has metaphorical force, for it states the riddle of life. Throughout the convict's tale it is emphasized that he glimpses life in its truest sense. To remember this will help in understanding his final resolve. His affinity with the river-rat is based on a knowledge of hardship and austerity. He senses the reason for the existence of the spiderlegged house "enclosed and lost" in that strange land because of what he has in common with the cajan: "the same grudged dispensation and niggard fate of hard and unceasing travail not to gain future security . . . but just permission to endure and endure to buy air to feel and sun to drink for each's little while" (256). Thus from an unromantic point of view, without any illusions about life's joys, he knows things which Harry must learn laboriously and still be unable to achieve.

Faulkner's "tall men," hill-country people like the MacCallums in *Sartoris* (1929) and "The Tall Men" (first published May 1941) or the brothers in "Two Soldiers" (first published March 1942) and "Shall Not Perish" (July–August 1943), like Jewel Bundren and Jack Houston and even Mink Snopes, are a hardworking, literal minded, almost fanatically persevering set of individuals. The tall convict is one of them, with origins in some "hill-bred Abraham" (255). Like them, he could have looked forward to a life of unremitting labor on the land for no more reward than the right to keep on working until he dropped. But, sent to prison for the folly of trying to rob a train, he learned something. He learned better than to rob trains, and he found a life that meant less work, no responsibility, and no uncertainty. He found a place that provided him with his own mule and his own bunk and good food and warmth and entertainment he never could have afforded on the outside. There was a woman

anecdote appears in a 1939 interview with Michel Mok and in the 1956 *Paris Review* interview, both in *Lion in the Garden: Interviews with William Faulkner, 1926–1962*, ed. James B. Meriwether and Michael Millgate (New York: Random House, 1968), 40–41, 243. Details about the *Louisiana Lou* episode are in Joseph Blotner, *Faulkner: A Biography*, Vol. I (New York: Random House, 1974), 801–802.

Counterpoint: Birth in the Flood

in it, to be sure, but he tried to break the law. He failed, and he was put in prison. He accepted his punishment, and he accepts the additional ten years capriciously and dishonestly added to his sentence, because that is part of the rules, the price he must pay (331). The convict's nature is to fulfill his obligations by returning the skiff and the woman to their designated place and even to care for and return his other piece of government property, the prison suit. It is not surprising that he is willing to escape the difficult life that waited for him on the outside. *The Hamlet*, for example, is full of men with similar backgrounds who seek various ways to get off the land because, as Flem Snopes puts it, "Aint no benefit in farming. I figure on getting out of it soon as I can." [15] Flem has good precedents and examples in Ratliff, in the gold-seekers Bookwright and Armstid, in Houston, in the fanatical and tragicomic schoolteacher Labove, and others. Two other factors weigh in the balance, however, and the scale does not actually pitch to one side until the last sentence in the book. The tall convict rediscovers the joy of being allowed to work on his own terms and for his own profit, a pleasure he enjoys both at the cajan's camp and during his return voyage as he works his way up the river. This makes life outside of prison *better* than life inside. But at the same time he rediscovers certain facts about his own fate where the female is concerned. Perhaps it is just a weakness, like his nose bleeds or his inability to tolerate alcohol. At any rate, his crime had a woman in it, or behind it, and that she later jilted him is one of his chief memories. Now, expecting a Garbo or a Helen, he gets instead a pregnant hill woman. Here is a man who does not like to make the same mistake twice, who learns from his experiences. He is not going to rob another train or drink whiskey. But the female principle is strong, as Harry says, so once again the convict becomes involved with a woman, and then he has to leave the wood landing, where he likes it pretty well (334). These experiences cancel his new sense of freedom. He turns his back on life and retreats into prison.

The final part of his adventure is telescoped into a few pages. He

15 William Faulkner, *The Hamlet* (New York: Random House, 1940), 26.

155

will refer to it under questioning in the last chapter of the novel, where the full rationale for his behavior comes out. He does not want to leave the cajan's camp under compulsion or on anyone else's terms, but the men take him anyway, fiercely, clamping him into handcuffs which make a noise like the wild palms: "dry vicious snapping" and "clashing" (272).[16] They carry him to New Orleans and house him in a refugee center from which he escapes, using the old methods of romance, Tom Sawyer style: "there were doors in plenty ... but he had a hard time finding a window they could use," a revelation that causes the plump convict to jibe him: "You ought to tore up a sheet and slid down it" (276).[17] What is important to him is that life is back in joint. The river has "recovered from his debauch" and the earth has been fertilized and restored so that there will be bountiful crops of cotton at the summer's end. But now it is June, month of brides, and the tall convict gives up the boat, the woman, and himself, having come full circle. He has done well, except he "never did find that bastard on the cottonhouse" (278).

---

[16] There is a "dead noon" in this section to complement the one which brings Harry back into time as he sits in the park waiting for Charlotte. Symbolically, at least, the events might be said to serve the same purpose, except the convict seems unaware of any implications for him, though he has ended another nine day sojourn in a watery solitude. The launch which carries them to New Orleans stops, its engine stilled, and the helmsman explains, " 'It's noon ... I thought we might hear the dynamite.' ... but no sound, no tremble even, came anywhere under the fierce hazy sky; the long moment gathered itself and turned on and noon was past" (*WP*, 273). The function in the novel is plain; here is another of those anachronic, timeless pauses in the round of eternal return and the cycle of pain and boredom which characterizes the life of the will. But it also reflects, apparently jokingly, what actually happened on 29 April 1927 when engineers dynamited the Poydras levee to relieve pressure on the New Orleans dikes. Crowds assembled to observe the spectacle, the charge was laid and ignited, but very little actually happened. There was no great gash in the levee, no dramatic surge of water. The anticlimax was as great as it is in the fictional scene. (New Orleans *Times-Picayune*, 29, 30 April 1927, p. 1; Memphis *Commercial Appeal*, 30 April 1927. It is worth noting that 30 April 1927 is the day Faulkner's *Mosquitoes* was published.)

[17] See Nancy Dew Taylor, "The River of Faulkner and Twain," *Mississippi Quarterly*, 16 (Fall 1963), 191–99. An important image in this scene is the convict's thought that he would use lying "with respect and even care, delicate, quick and strong, like a fine and fatal blade" (276).

CHAPTER X

The Psychological
and the Visionary Modes

Even with him who approaches [denial of the will], it is
almost invariably the case that the tolerable condition of
his own body...and the satisfaction of the will...*i. e.*,
lust, is a...constant temptation to the renewed assertion
of it....Thus in most cases the will must be broken by
great personal suffering before its self-conquest appears.

SCHOPENHAUER
The World as Will and Idea

THE BLACK WIND and the invisible wild palms grow more ominous
and threatening as Charlotte's death comes closer. The doctor has ex-
amined her. He has full knowledge of how her condition came
about. Shaking his hand at Harry, he accuses him as her murderer.
His voice is "cold, precise, and convinced" (279)—dispassionate and
assured and unsympathetic like the manner of the doctor on the steamboat. His outrage is not what it seems nor even what he may believe.
Yet it is strong, because "he was too old for this:" too old to be
dragged into a "bright wild passion which had somehow passed him
up when he had been young enough, worthy enough" (279). When he
learns that Harry is not only lover but abortionist—having arrogated
to himself more of love and passion and tragedy than is allowed to
mortals (280)[1]—he saves himself from suffocation in these outrageous
facts by fleeing home to call the police and initiate punishment for the

EPIGRAPH: Arthur Schopenhauer, *The World as Will and Idea*, trans. R. B.
Haldane and J. Kemp (London: Routledge and Kegan Paul, 1883), I, 507.
[1] In "An Odor of Verbena," Drusilla sends Bayard to kill his father's assassin.
She notes that the pistols are the shape of love and promises him that he will
remember her because she has made it possible for him to taste everything, an
equation of sex and the taking of human life. William Faulkner, *The Unvanquished* (New York: Random House, 1938), 274.

157

offender. Back through the gap in the oleander and back through the veil of Maya he goes, denying his common plight with Harry and believing he can ease his own suffering by causing another to suffer.[2] Both the doctor and the "little futile moth-light beam" of his flashlight struggle "against the constant weight of the black pitiless wind" (281). But the light carries him through the screening oleander and into the sterile security of his ordinary life.

Harry remains alone in the wind. He is superconscious of his body, and he labors as if he were drowning in water, his heart pumping as if his veins held sand and not blood, his breath dying in the heavy black air (281).[3] He tries to flee the wind, believing that it alone is why he cannot breathe, "*because apparently the heart can stand anything anything anything*" (281). Charlotte's dictum is demonstrably untrue: the heart does not break after all, the heart is not where she and Harry are suffering. He has no refuge: the wind dogs him like a brute, risible and constant and teasing, declining to follow him into the house because it does not need to follow him. It need only wait. This has been apparent all along, from Bradley's visit to the present. The lovers are fated, doomed.

Charlotte lies in a grotesque sexual posture on the wretched bed of the broken cottage, "not sprawled, not abandoned, but on the contrary even a little tense" (284), as if she lay with the black wind. Yet here there is no wind, "no shape of death cuckolding him; nothing to see, yet it was there, he not permitted to watch his own cuckolding but only to look down upon the invisible pregnancy of his horning" (284).[4] What Harry had said about the "last prone and slightly comic attitude of ultimate surrender" (46) has lost any tinge of humor now. Charlotte's death is described ironically in sexual terms, a lying with

[2] Deluded by the veil of Maya, he refuses to see that "he lives in all that suffers pain in the wide world" (Schopenhauer, *The World as Will and Idea*, I, 457).

[3] Harry has been in a flood all along, swept away in Charlotte's will and held thrall in her deep yellow gaze. Now he is in peril of drowning. Cf. William Faulkner's *Sartoris* (New York: Harcourt, Brace, 1929), 48.

[4] In "Tamar," it seemed to Tamar that "a wandering power/Essayed her body, something hard and rounded and invisible pressed itself for entrance/Between the breasts, over the diaphragm." Robinson Jeffers, *Selected Poetry* (New York: Random House, 1938), 24.

the "shape of death," an "invisible pregnancy" and final throes of agony in which she thrashes as if in labor. The tall convict has been a cuckold too, symbolically, and has had to look upon the visible pregnancy of his companion; he tried to avert his eyes but could not. Confronted with his version of that same vision, Harry also tries to retreat from Charlotte, as he had done after she announced her pregnancy. Charlotte has always had two ways of holding him, however, either with her strong wild hands or by her omnivorous yellow eyes. Her eyes catch and retain him this time, the "I," the dot of ego and sentience and will rising amid the emptiness like a fish rising in water. In the pain of her laboring, not to bring life but death, Charlotte thrashes from hip to hip beneath the sound of the wind, a thread of blood at the corner of her mouth (286), like that which had marked the woman in the boat during her own labor (175). Charlotte's immolation begins; she begs Harry to "cut it out" of her so "there wont be anything left but just a shell to hold the cold air, the cold—" (286). She begs for sterility against the pain which is "just like fire" (286, 287). Her lips and hands are hot and dry and she thinks about the "snow, the cold, the cold" (287). Her memory is of the fun they had "bitching, and making things" in the cold (287), but the truth is that they had very little fun and that the things they made were either grotesque or, like the child that was a product of their "bitching," unwanted. The Utah cold was the particular natural phenomenon that caused their present inescapable condition.

In the desperation of trying to "hold on" to Charlotte, Harry once again resorts mentally to remedies that have been efficacious for whores. The reference is literary this time: "He was trying to remember something out of a book, years ago, of Owen Wister's, the whore in the pink ball dress who drank the laudanum and the cowboys taking turns walking her up and down the floor . . . keeping her alive" (287).[5] At this moment the doctor returns and his wife comes with him. She is practical and eagerly hypocritical. Like Rat Rittenmeyer, with his mask and his concern about appearances, she wants to efface from all

[5] The scene is in Owen Wister's *Lin McLean* (New York: Harpers, 1903), 253–66.

memory the deed which Charlotte's condition announces. She wants the couple out, cured or made well enough to leave and die anywhere else, "not in this house . . . in this town. Get them out of here and let them cut on one another and die as much as they please" (290). She is as strongly puritanical as her husband is, but in a different way. She does not feel the bite of conscience for which he seeks relief in punishing Harry. At the same time, she has no real sympathy for the lovers. She has performed her little charities toward them with "grim and vindictive and masochistic pleasure" (10). She is antimasculine, seeing her husband's desire to punish Harry as a form of aiding and abetting the young intern: "I never yet saw one man fail to back up another, provided what they wanted to do was just foolish enough" (290). Her lack of sympathy is expressed in her total disregard for the suffering of the lovers and in her being unaware that her husband could feel threatened by any personal involvement in this affair: "You're mad because he used a scalpel without having a diploma. Or did something with it the Medical Association said he mustn't" (290). Her final act is to turn "on (not to) Wilbourne with that cold abruptness" (290) and tell him she is going to fix him a cup of coffee that he does not want. The assumption the doctor's wife makes is that Harry wants his punishment as much as the doctor wants to inflict it on him. The way Harry's alternatives are presented makes it seem generally that this is so, because Charlotte has begged him to run from punishment, and he has not. Charlotte's main reason is solicitude. And behind that is a feeling that Harry does not fully deserve to pay for having committed a deed that she urged him to perform. Harry's apparent denial of freedom is in this case paradoxical: to accept the condemnation of a society that is demonstrably corrupt. However, as in the tall convict's choice, there is a simple mitigating circumstance to be weighed in the balance. He is showing the same solicitude for Charlotte that she is for him. She cannot flee the price Nature demands of her; he is not willing to leave her alone, even though he is as powerless to prevent her death as the tall convict is to subdue the flooding river. His refusal to run is perfectly natural. It has nothing to do with accepting his punishment. Only afterwards, when he refuses the various kinds of "freedom" which Rat offers him, does Harry choose jail and grief, and like the tall convict in a parallel decision, he devises a new rationale for doing what he does. There is no contradiction in Harry's act. The heavily worked theme of paradox that expresses itself in *The Wild Palms* (fixed and static trees amid the flux of the loosed waters, discrepancies between appearance and reality in society) is illusion. Due to the veil of Maya, the masks of individuality, man may see paradox. The ills and wickedness of life, however, like its fleeting joys and the infrequent good, are all part of the same thing, all "manifestation of the one will to live,"[6] "everywhere in nature we see strife, conflict, and alternation of victory, and in it we shall come to recognise more distinctly that variance with itself which is essential to the will."[7] Rat Rittenmeyer preserves his respectable facade while delivering his wife to her lover, but he suffers inwardly in a way that Harry and the reader can only guess. The crooked mine owner sends a doctor to the mining camp only to ward off a possible lawsuit and to fulfill the letter of the mining regulations, but he finds a doctor who will go. Buckner waits knowing that a doctor will come and that there is a strong likelihood they can persuade him to perform an abortion. And he is correct. The warden of the prison saves his own skin twice, once by discharging the convict with commendation when he thinks the man has drowned, and once by promoting his deputy to the outside and adding to the convict's sentence for "escaping." People are constantly at variance with one another, and nature seems against them all. The lovers, with their insatiable demands, are no more pure than anyone else. Charlotte imposes her will on Harry and carries him off. He pleads his conscience and delays doing the inevitable so long that it kills her. There is indeed a "heartless immensity" and a continual strife to the phenomenal universe.

Michel Mohrt in his review of Maurice Coindreau's translation of *The Wild Palms*[8] was the first to point out the similarity between Hemingway's use of rain in *A Farewell to Arms* and Faulkner's or-

---

[6] Schopenhauer, *The World as Will and Idea*, I, 455.

[7] *Ibid.*, 191.

[8] Michel Mohrt, "Les prisonniers du temps," *La Table Ronde*, No. 59 (November 1952), 160–65.

chestration of the sounds of the wind and the wild palms. In a sense, Faulkner does more with his "sound effects" than Hemingway. They change in implication and force as the final action of the novel progresses. When the doctor's wife cannot persuade her husband to let the couple go, she urges that he use "some of my money" (290). But when her suggestion is refused, she goes to fix Harry's coffee, and now Harry can hear her in the kitchen, he can hear the black risible wind and he can imagine that he hears the "wild dry clashing of the palms" (291). Amid the commonplace household noises comes the old sound of passion and the newly evoked sound of death and, rising out of it all, the "mounting wail" of the ambulance (291) which marks the real beginning of the end of the lovers' life together.

The hospital they carry her to is "almost hidden by a massy lushness of oleander" (295). Remembering the oleander screen that kept the doctor away from the reality he did not want to see, remembering all the impersonal doctors and others with self-imposed ignorance, one sees intention in this display of deliberate facade. There is still more wind and the smell of the sea is blown from the Sound across the black beach and into the hospital corridor. There is wind also in the operating room where Charlotte's body lies, only "this was not a cool wind blowing into the room but a hot one being forced out" by a hidden ventilator (305). Charlotte's immolation is ended. The final force of the realization comes across Harry like a flood wave. The ventilator is shut off and the wind ceases. The breath of passion had changed to the black wind of death and then was transformed into the whine of a siren and the whirr of a hospital exhaust fan. And now all is quiet. A "tremendous silence ... roared down upon him like a wave, a sea, and there was nothing for him to hold to, picking him up, tossing and spinning him and roaring on" (307). Solitude. It had caught Harry before, but not so strongly. It had also caught the tall convict, both in the reality of the flood wave and symbolically in the bayous: "the silence and solitude and emptiness roared down upon him in a jeering bellow" (269). Man occasionally reaches these points and this realization. But then life may go on, the will may not be denied, because something, "the tolerable condition of his own body," "the delusion of hope," or "lust" is a constant temptation to the renewed assertion of the will to live.[9] Man has it all to learn over again, if he accepts the gambit. This is the second time for Harry (the first was in the Wisconsin woods). He still does not know what he is going to do.

The deputy who takes Harry to the hospital emanates brutality and sadism. He is civil to the intern, but so impersonal that he never even says Harry's name correctly. Harry surrenders his freedom to him immediately, even saying "why dont you put the handcuffs on me?" (294). He meets more doctors, impersonal and precise and mechanical, unsympathetically recording details which carry no implication for them (296–98, 301). The nurses do not look at Harry, and when two of them laugh, he knows it is "nurses" and not "women" (303). It begins to come clear—as it has been shown all along by imagery in "Old Man"—that individual captivity makes little difference. All life is in actuality a prison. The door to the operating room "looked final and impregnable as an iron portcullis" (298). Not modernity nor corruption nor any particular thing can be blamed: life, as the phrase goes, is just life. Schopenhauer had already said it. And Harry begins to understand more fully as he sits (on a bench again) and muses upon the strange nature of such institutions: "like wombs into which human beings fled ... to surrender ... lust and desire and pride ... to become as embryos for a time yet retaining still a little of the old incorrigible ... corruption ... then to be born again, to emerge renewed, to bear the world's weight for another while as long as courage lasted" (299). Schopenhauer said essentially the same thing, talking about the renewal of the will:

> So long as no denial of the will takes place, what death leaves untouched is the germ ... of quite another existence, in which a new individual finds itself again, so fresh and original ... What sleep is for the individual, death is for the will as thing in itself. It would not endure to continue the same actions and sufferings throughout an eternity without true gain, if memory and individuality remained to it. It flings them off, and this is lethe; and through this sleep of death it reappears refreshed ... as a new being.[10]

9 Schopenhauer, *The World as Will and Idea*, I, 507.
10 *Ibid.*, III, 298–99.

Like the tall convict during the flood, Harry sees dimly that "all life consists of having to get up sooner or later and then having to lie down again sooner or later after a while" (147). The middle-aged doctor goes through the cycle himself, on a minor scale—all part of Faulkner's reiteration of the motif of the circle, the theme of rebirth, Eternal Return. When the officer arrives, the doctor asserts his medical rights, and his voice becomes peaceful: "as if it had worn itself out yet which would have, could have risen again at need quick and easy, as if it had renewed itself, renewed the outragement" (293). Whatever Harry gains by his realization, he sets it aside for the moment as he concentrates on Charlotte's death. After all it is merely an observation upon life in hospitals, not his statement of a philosophical concept. As he has time and time again previously, Harry speaks without knowledge of his words. In the luxury of his jail cell he will have the opportunity to come back to such thoughts.

When he is asked to explain why this abortion failed, after he had performed one that did not, Harry says to himself "*I loved her. He could have said it: A miser would probably bungle the blowing of his own safe too. Should have called in a professional, a cracksman who didn't care, didn't love the very iron flanks that held the money*" (297). The crude pun helps to sharpen the image. This simple realization is a step in his understanding of love, of himself, of Rittenmeyer, and it obviously fits into the context of all his money-oriented thoughts up to now. Charlotte is dead, her body "curiously flattened beneath the sheet" (305) and that due to "more than just a slackening of joints and muscles, it was a collapsing of the entire body as undammed water collapses...seeking that...primal level much lower than...the prone one of the little death called sleep...the flat earth itself and even this not low enough...gone, vanished, no trace left above the insatiable dust" (306). Her death is like the flood's dispersal, and as natural. *Her* "debauch" is also over: that which accepted him "substanceless and enveloping and suffocating, down and down and down," which had swept him like the convict "thrall and impotent for days against any returning" (232–33), has returned from whence it came.

164

Harry is left in the solitude and silence, "blinking steadily and painfully" (307).

At the jail the ubiquitous palm tree appears, a single shabby tree outside the window of his cell, representing a memory which returns to the cabbage palm in the garden where he and Charlotte kissed the first time. The symbolic force is augmented by supernatural manipulation: when Harry and the deputy pass under, "with no wind to cause it it had set up a sudden frenzied clashing as though they had startled it, and twice more during the night while he stood . . . it clashed again in that brief sudden inexplicable flurry" (307). The bars of the cell "began to sweat on [Harry's] palms" (307). The palm tree must remind Harry of his "bright passion," and of the thrashing that characterizes both sex experience and the throes of death. The dry clashing sound is the noise which some of the implements of imprisonment make in "Old Man" and, with the black wind, it has served in the two chapters devoted to the final scenes to give a Wasteland atmosphere. The connection between the palm tree and Jeffers' "Tamar" was noted in Chapter Two; another possible frame of reference is Frazer's *Golden Bough* —the observations there upon the association of various trees, including the palm, with fertility and particularly with childbirth are applicable.[11]

The old bad smells, which recall the "odor of unsanctity" that accompanied the lovers out of New Orleans and the bogus fetish, are with Harry for a while: "the sour smell of salt flats where oyster shells and the heads of shrimp rotted, and hemp and old piling" (307). But dawn brings a new day and, at last, a new color and a new smell. "Wild Palms" and "Old Man" are both sprinkled with yellow: Charlotte's eyes and the muddy river and a number of jonquil dawns.[12] At his lowest depth, the tall convict prepares to start back up the river,

---

[11] See Chapter Seven, and Sir James George Frazer, *The Golden Bough* (abridged; New York: Macmillan, 1922), 117–20.

[12] There are jonquil skies on pages 233 and 277. The image is one Faulkner liked. In *Light in August* (New York: Smith and Haas, 1932), there is a "jonquil colored sun" (314) and a "yellow day" (104); in *The Unvanquished*, a "jonquil-colored" dawn (69); and in *The Hamlet*, "jonquil thunder" (207).

lining up on the Coca-cola sign and the draw bridge which arched "spidery against the jonquil sky at dawn" (277). His adventure is essentially over, the river "now ineradicably a part of his past, his life ... a part of what he would bequeath, if that were in store for him" (277). In other words, he has been marked by his experience just as Harry has. At the climax of his flight, his lover dead, himself in prison awaiting trial for her murder, trying to come to terms with himself, Harry sees a bridge, too, "the draw bridge on which the railroad to New Orleans crossed ... against the paling sky" (307). Harry sees a roseate Homeric dawn which makes a train crossing the bridge seem "toylike and pink like something bizarre to decorate a cake with" (308). Thinking in those terms, Harry might be celebrating the memory of their departure from New Orleans. On the level of time, the herald of a new and different roseate day contrasts markedly with the yellow twilight mornings and the static middays, those jonquil dawns (233, 277) and those hard (263) or dead (225, 227, 273) or "immaculate monotonous" (111) noons given emphasis in the book. At any rate, the palm outside the window begins murmuring, not clashing, and the morning sea breeze cools him and carries away the sour smell of the salt flats and shrimp and cuts the odor of creosote and tobacco spit and vomit in his cell. The bad smell is finally gone. The air is clearer and promising, but Harry has not reached a decision yet. In several ways he is made to resemble the tall convict. He sits on the edge of his cot in the "immemorial attitude of all misery," his head dropped between his knees, the posture taken so often by the convict when his nose would bleed (151–52, 242, 259). He tries to roll a handmade cigarette and cannot, a problem met by the convict (165, 171,174) in a time of his own remembering. The emphasis in the scene is on Wilbourne's hands, which shake so badly even after he has fashioned the ill-made tube of tobacco that he must grip his right wrist with his own left hand (a hold Charlotte so often used on him) to bring the "raddled tube" to his lips. He has the same trouble with a mug of coffee. Cognizance of all that has happened to him has begun to move him. He "who had shown none before this and perhaps had not even begun to feel it yet" manifests despair (310).

166

The Psychological and the Visionary Modes

Wilbourne faces the first of his three temptations now. He is no Christ figure, but the faint ringing of bells which the christological pattern effects is an example of the way Faulkner liked to evoke motifs that he did not necessarily choose to weight heavily or employ throughout a work of fiction. Rittenmeyer offers to bail him out so he can flee, but Harry says that he cannot. Rat's "Think of her" produces a delayed insight. "I wish I could stop," Harry replies; then, thinking better, he contradicts himself: "No I dont. Maybe that's it" (312). He is on the trail of something but he does not know what. He is in no hurry to complete the thought. He is sure "it would return; he would find it, hold it, when the time was ready" (312).

Whatever Harry will hold when he finds it, his hands are occupied while he is in jail by clinging to the bars of his cell as he stares blandly and thoughtlessly at the world outside going into midsummer. His window faces west, toward the sunset: "across the river and toward the sea," where he notices now "the concrete hull of one of the emergency ships built in 1918 and never finished" (314).[13] He watches with curiosity the motions of life on the hulk, the daily chores of a fisherman and his wife. The scene, which recalls to us the convict's meeting with the shantyboaters, brings him further out of the shock he has suffered since Charlotte's death. Rittenmeyer's first visit stirred his memory; the fisher couple on the hulk stir within him the time sense. He is struck suddenly by how little time he and Charlotte had together at the last: "*It could not possibly have been just four days. It could not*" (314). But the thought drops away like the vaguely groped-for meaning aroused by Rittenmeyer's visit. Like Harry, the tall convict has slowly taken the measure of what has happened to him. He recounts some of his adventures to his bunkhouse mates. He is even sufficiently rattled by one memory to lose the skill of his hands, spoiling a handmade cigarette just as Harry has done. The

13 There was such a bridge across the Pascagoula River. In 1926, when Faulkner spent time there, three partially finished hulks stood in Yazoo Lake, near the mouth of the river (Pascagoula *Chronicle-Star*, 14 May 1926, p. 4), and in 1927, a wooden hulk left over from the first world war was destroyed by fire (Pascagoula *Chronicle-Star*, 2 September 1927, p. 1). A hurricane dipped into Pascagoula in September of 1926, the month in which Faulkner dated the typescript of *Mosquitoes* there.

167

whole story is there; as he tells it, he extracts from it the lesson he needs, though he does not reach a final decision until the end of the book. Harry comes upon the meaning of his adventure slowly, too, the way the middle-aged doctor came to slow consciousness and discovery in Chapter One. Faulkner uses scene and event in this case, as in the first one, to depict the mental process: the clearing of the air, Harry's discovery that he does *not* want to stop thinking about Charlotte, the surprise that their last days together had been so few, and the vision of a perfectly normal and insignificant family life on the old hulk that had been intended for the war. Now a hurricane "galloping off somewhere in the Gulf" sends a remnant of itself onto the shore near Harry's cell, "a flick of the mane in passing" (315). A roil of yellow tide and accompanying wind and rain cause the river to bellow and moan (the Pascagoula is known as the Singing River because near the docks in the city it makes a strange singing noise [14]). The palm outside his window continues to thrash and clash, despite the rain, with its usual dry sounds. The phenomenon reminds Harry of death, just as the black wind and the frenzied dry clashing months ago had shown him death. It is the quietude and peace in the aftermath of death that he envisions, knowing that inland the effect of the storm would be less: "It would be even quieter inland, it would become only a bright silver summer murmur among the heavy decorous trees, upon the clipped sward . . . a good deal like the park where he had waited . . . the very best . . . a headstone soon, at just exactly the right time, when restored earth and decorum stipulated, telling nothing" (315). The tall convict had looked on birth and thought "*And this is all*" (231). Harry looks on death and thinks "*that cant be all of it*" (316).

What he is thinking of, of course, is Rittenmeyer's "monument" to Charlotte, which he assumes will be nothing but a decorous effacement of her and all she did and wanted; a thing as ironic as the one Flem Snopes puts up for Eula in *The Town*. Harry gropes for meaning, seeking an alternative to such decorous effacement, trying to discover

[14] *Mississippi: A Guide to the Magnolia State*, compiled and written by the Federal Writers' Project of the Works Progress Administration (New York: Viking, 1938), 287.

a way to deny or at least forestall oblivion. He rejects the notion that *"memory exists independent of the flesh,"* since *"It wouldn't know what it was it remembered."* And he is right. *"So there's got to be the old meat, the old frail eradicable meat for memory to titillate"* (316). And that "was the second time he almost got it"; there is still no hurry, because "it would return when the time was ready and even stand still to his hand" (316).

His next experience is a travesty of a trial.[15] The tall convict will be given one too. Both of them accept the punishment with equal stoicism, but to say that they each seek punishment, as if through a puritanical desire for expiation, is wrong. They accept their respective fates and then seek to find a meaning. Harry's second temptation comes, yet it is not he, but society, which brushes off Rittenmeyer's attempt to interfere in the trial and absolve Harry. The lynch-hungry mob of onlookers acts in marine terms: "it did roar, in waves . . . the officers of the Court charging into the wave like a football team" (320). Harry is still viewing Rittenmeyer as the "face, the outrageous face: the man who without any warning had had to stand the wrong sort of suffering, the one suffering for which he was not fitted" (318).

Harry is convicted and sentenced to at least fifty years at Parchman, the Mississippi state penitentiary where the tall convict is serving his time. The settlement brings him a further sense of peace that is reflected in the scene. "That afternoon it rained again, a bright silver curtain roaring out of nowhere . . . galloping on vagrom and coltlike . . . bright and harmless" (322). The pacification of the elements, from the black wind to the tail of the hurricane and now to this, is sympathetic. The air comes clean, the palm subsides, "merely murmuring,"

[15] The judge has the face of a "Methodist Sunday School superintendent who on week days was a banker and probably a good banker, a shrewd banker" (317). He resembles Will Varner in Faulkner's next novel: "He looked like a Methodist Sunday School superintendent who on week days conducted a railroad passenger train or vice versa and who owned the church or perhaps the railroad or perhaps both. He was shrewd secret and merry" (*The Hamlet*, 6). Both characters may be based on the Reverend James William Bates, for whom the county seat town in the county adjoining Faulkner's Lafayette was named. The Batesville man was a legend in his own time. He was a Methodist preacher, a cotton farmer, and a railroad conductor who ran the strictest train on the line. Frank Smith, *The Yazoo River* (New York: Rinehart & Co., 1954), 185.

and the bars of the cell grow cool to his touch. Rittenmeyer brings the third temptation: he offers Harry death. In refusing it, Harry reaches full knowledge.

Many people have taken the pessimistic outlook of Schopenhauer's philosophy as a rationale for suicide—McCord, in fact, has made that kind of association in his profane apostrophe (100–101), telling Harry that if he keeps talking "that stuff" someone will hand him a pistol and make him use it. But the philosopher is quite specific in stating that self-destruction is no escape. Rather than "denial of the will, suicide is . . . strong assertion of will. . . . The suicide wills life, and is only dissatisfied with the conditions under which it has presented itself to him." Suicide is, says Schopenhauer, the "masterpiece of Mâyâ,"[16] and as prime an example of the way in which the will to live constantly preys on itself as the struggle for existence between animals and between men.

The thought that had eluded Harry twice before is waiting for him now. At first he believes that Rittenmeyer has brought him the cyanide as a personal gesture, but Rittenmeyer says to Harry's thanks: "I'm not doing it for you. . . . Get that out of your damned head" (323). And everything falls into place: "no flash of comprehension . . . just a simple falling of a jumbled pattern" (323). He realizes that Rittenmeyer had promised Charlotte to take care of Harry if anything happened to her: fix it some way so that Harry does not have to pay. In the scene he imagined between the husband and wife, the intern had not included a promise because a promise would have been too much to ask. But he was wrong, about Charlotte and about Rittenmeyer. He sees suddenly that Rittenmeyer loved his wife, and that the man has performed his promise at the cost of great suffering. He sees through the veil of Maya. Charlotte was able to get a promise from him, too, and though Harry had thought the deed she asked was too great a price to pay, he loved her so much he could not refuse; he performed the abortion. The palm murmurs in a cool night breeze that brings the smell of jasmine (out of the garden of love where they met, the bush they stood beside as they first talked), "blowing on under the dying west

[16] Schopenhauer, *The World as Will and Idea*, I, 514–15.

and the bright star" (324). The bright evening star is Venus. The wild palm outside his cell is the living reminder of his love affair. He sees also a manifestation of normal human life going on, "the light on the concrete hulk, in the poop porthole which he had called the kitchen for weeks now, as if he lived there" (324). He is moving from the contemplation of his own particular sufferings to a general Idea, the suffering—and the love and the life—of mankind. "So it wasn't just memory. Memory was just half of it, it wasn't enough. *But it must be somewhere*, he thought. *There's the waste. Not just me. At least I think I dont mean just me. Hope I dont mean just me. Let it be anyone*" (324).

Great suffering is one means by which a man may attain denial of the will and the subsequent "peace, blessedness, and sublimity" which Schopenhauer associates with it. The philosopher says that "in most cases the will must be broken by great personal suffering before its self-conquest appears." But to produce the proper state, the suffering must be seen not in the particular form in which it afflicts the individual, but under the aspect of the universal: "when he raises his glance from the particular to the universal, when he regards his suffering as merely an example of the whole.... When, finally grief has no definite object, but extends itself over the whole of life, then it is ... a going into itself ... a secret pleasure accompanies this grief, and it is this ... which the most melancholy of all nations has called 'the joy of grief.' " [17]

This is the state which Harry apparently has attained. Yet there is ambiguity and paradox even here. Once again he seems to be pointing in two directions at once, implying one thing but meaning something else. He is talking about the flesh—"*the old wrinkled withered defeated ... the wheezing lungs, the troublesome guts incapable of pleasure ... the old wheezing entrails* [sic]" (324). The images go back to all the evocations of flesh in this novel: the "fumbling flesh" (34) with which Harry had no youthful experience, the contrast between sexless characters in books and real males and females (52), the Falstaff figure "struggling with the mountain of entrails" (91), the acts of

[17] *Ibid.*, 511–12.

Saint Anthony and of Origen (103), and the "bitching." It also should evoke a recollection of the long parenthesis about the "old married" in "Old Man," the "thousand identical coupled faces" or the single survivors on porches and courthouse lawns who seem to have an immortality, "as though with the death of the other having inherited a sort of rejuvenescence ... as though that flesh which the old ceremony or ritual had morally purified and made legally one had actually become so ... and he or she who entered the ground first took all of it ... leaving only the old permanent enduring bone, free and trameless" (254). Harry and Charlotte were not made "legally one" or "morally purified," nor did they have fifty years of married life. The flesh remains, and Harry has fifty years imprisonment in which he must live with it. He has not been good at resisting its temptations.

So Harry is looking at the star which shines over fleshly love, regarding the phallic palm outside his cell, and speaking, as he has all along, in sexually ambiguous terms: "and now it did stand to his hand" (324). Harry's repeated use of this or a similar phrase has been sufficient to prompt two critics to say that he is masturbating in this final scene, which would seriously affect the meaning of Harry's resolution at the end and consequently the meaning of the novel.[18] There is a definite *double entendre* in this phrase; wherever he used it, Faulkner retained the indefinite pronoun that makes for the ambiguity. The passage reaches back to Harry's first groping toward meaning: "it would return; he would find it, hold it, when the time was ready" (312). It recurs again "the second time he almost got it:" "it would return when the time was ready and even stand still to his hand" (316). "To hand" has a perfectly normal meaning, of course: "into posses-

[18] W. T. Jewkes, "Counterpoint in Faulkner's *The Wild Palms*," *Wisconsin Studies in Contemporary Literature*, 2 (Winter 1961), 39–53; Thomas Francis Loughrey, "Values and Love in the Fiction of William Faulkner" (Ph.D. dissertation, Notre Dame, 1962). In *A Farewell to Arms*, the captain teases the priest: "'Priest not with girls...Priest never with girls...Priest every night five against one ... You understand? Priest every night five against one.' He made a gesture and laughed loudly." In the same scene, all in Chapter Two of the novel, the captain makes another sexual joke about potency, using the fingers of his hands to illustrate. Given all the allusions to Hemingway's novel in *The Wild Palms*, and the punning in the title, it is not likely that Faulkner overlooked Hemingway's *double entendre*.

sion" or "in reach" or "into control" among others. The context in which the phrase is used, and the manner in which Faulkner is using it, makes a great difference, however. Hands and palms are among the controlling images of this novel. "If I Forget Thee, Jerusalem," the original title, paraphrases the first half of a verse in the 137th Psalm which ends "let my right hand forget her cunning." The story of the lovers was originally called "The Wild Palms" and even after that title was applied to the novel as a whole, the main plot remained "Wild Palms." Carnality becomes associated with the image through constant juxtaposition: Charlotte likes bitching and making things with her *hands*; she tells Harry the abortion is simple, "You know that now by your own *hand*" (206, italics added). The abortion is described in sexual terms, Charlotte saying, "We've done this lots of ways but not with knives, have we? There. Now your *hand* has stopped. . . . Ride me down, Harry" (221, italics added). All through the novel, both of the lovers have been observed saying one thing and meaning, usually unawares, something else. The contradictions resolve themselves into a pattern: when Charlotte and Harry have been talking about death or stasis in terms of time or the ideality of romantic love, beneath their words or in the acts that followed those words has been sexuality. Charlotte talked of death by water on the train, but they went to the drawing room to consummate the affair. Sexuality, in terms of Charlotte's menstrual periods, brings Harry back into time in the Wisconsin woods. Each raises up some kind of ideal, Charlotte aiming for a perfect love affair as if by art, Harry seeking the contemplative life of idleness (133); but bitching or fornication is always one of the chief activities in the design. They would deny life in order to live in a perpetual noon, yet they repeatedly affirm the continued existence of the will through the flesh. That is what Harry is doing in his final speech. He is not engaged in substitute sex, but there is, inherent in the ambiguous terms of his thoughts, a symbolic elevation of the object of procreation. Transcending his personal suffering and glimpsing the nature of the universe, attaining a denial of the will through knowledge, he nevertheless still expresses the will to live. Schopenhauer says that the "genitals are properly the

173

focus of will ... the life-sustaining principle ensuring endless life to time. In this respect they were worshipped by the Greeks in the *phallus*, and by the Hindus in the *lingam*, which are thus the symbol of the assertion of the will."[19] Harry is surrounded by these life symbols as he approaches a final resolution.

The great overriding irony which works in *The Wild Palms* is the strong sense of contrariety and paradox that runs throughout both stories: things are seldom what they seem; characters are visibly ambiguous as regards sexuality; creation occurs amid chaos and destruction. In this context, there should be no difficulty in accepting Harry's final act as likewise unresolved, as partaking of two distinct alternatives simultaneously. An illuminating parallel can be found in the ending of Thomas Mann's *The Magic Mountain*. Mann, acknowledged a great ironist, invents Hans Castorp, a character as naive and malleable as Harry Wilbourne. In the course of the novel, Mann puts Castorp through a terrific educational experience in which he is exposed to all the contrarieties of life: "adventures of the flesh and in the spirit." [20] He becomes a kind of genius of experience and rises above the lure of death which haunts him throughout his stay at the sanitarium on the "magic mountain." Yet at the novel's end Mann purposely abandons him as he plunges into a battle of the first world war, smiling faintly. It is quite unclear what will happen to Castorp or how his final position may be justified in terms of what he learned. In short, the novel ends upon an ambiguity, and Mann evidently intended it that way.

Faulkner seems to be doing the same thing in a different fashion. Harry has come through intense suffering to a kind of Schopenhauerian denial of the will, as it seems for a time. He is passive, waiting for the knowledge he expects to come, a little like the middle-aged doctor in the first chapter who three times approached the "veil" behind which the enormity of the lover's act was hidden from him. The doctor, we saw, pierced the veil, but fled in horror to the insula-

19 Schopenhauer, *The World as Will and Idea*, I, 426.
20 Thomas Mann, *The Magic Mountain*, trans. H. T. Lowe-Porter (New York: Knopf, 1944), 716.

tion of his barren house. Harry does not flee or retreat or deceive himself. He expresses himself in terms of the flesh and he makes his final statement a Universal Yea. He accepts the "joy of grief," out of Nietzsche, the *amor fati*. He *wills* it. He sees the "palm clashing and murmuring dry and wild and faint in the night but he could face it," that is, he could face the memories which it calls up, "thinking, *Not could, Will. I want to. So it is the old meat after all, no matter how old*" (324).[21] His thoughts return to the specific, "I" and "she." His final words, "*between grief and nothing I will take grief*," have the force not of rejection and not of passive acceptance, but of desire. But the meaning of Harry's act will resolve itself clearly when the tall convict has had *his* last word, which is also the last speech in the novel, and a full discussion of that meaning must wait.

For the moment, however, there is another level of meaning which can be discussed. We have seen how Faulkner threads allusions to Dante's *Divine Comedy* through *The Wild Palms*. Harry and Charlotte are pictured in the first chapter as figurative victims of the seventh circle of the Inferno: for their sins against nature and against art, they suffer on the plain of burning sand (Canto XVII). They pass through the hellish scenes of Chicago life to reach dead end in the frozen hell of the Utah mining camp, which Faulkner specifically calls an Eisenstein Dante (187). Dante and Virgil leave the seventh circle on the back of the monster Geryon, who flies backwards to drop them lower into Hell, while Charlotte and Harry reach the mine by travelling backwards on the little train which has "neither head nor rear" (180).[22] At the end of "Wild Palms," Harry emerges from

21 At one point Harry identified himself with a "middleaged eunuch" (34), but he is neither middle aged nor emasculated. The flesh is there to hold memory, and it may be that Harry has succeeded in Charlotte's dream to create something greater than the "Might-just-as-well-not-have-been" (41). For a similar argument, and a different conclusion, see "Beyond." Cass Edmonds in *Go Down, Moses* also believes that "even suffering and grieving is better than nothing; there is only one thing worse than not being alive, and that's shame." His words condemn the static illusion and the family shame which Ike Mc-Caslin has accepted. William Faulkner, *Go Down, Moses* (New York: Random House, 1942), 186.

22 The passage from Dante goes, "As the bark goes from its station backwards, backwards, so the monster took himself from thence" (Carlyle-Okey-Wicksteed

the Inferno. Just like Dante at the beginning of the second part of his poem, Harry has his eyes on the evening star, Venus; he has reached the Purgatorio,[23] he has moved through despair to hope.

Dante's great poem has many subjects, but one of them, surely, is the same as the principal subject of "Wild Palms." In his essay "Psychology and Poetry," Carl Jung has noted that the *Divine Comedy* is "interwoven with . . . echoes of the initial love experience."[24] Faulkner apparently made a similar perception and he uses elements of Dante to underline the enormity of Harry's initial love experience. But, and curiously in accord with Jung's further observations in the essay, Faulkner does not stop there. He also borrows from Dante slightly different episodes of the *Divine Comedy* for "Old Man." The scene where the irascible steamboat captain transports the convict across the Mississippi and drops him into the coppery bayou landscape (237–52) is a specific example of borrowing,[25] but the very nature of "Old Man," with its anonymous Everyman struggling against the atavistic forces of nightmare in a seriocomic mode, corresponds to the fantastic, horror strewn, and also often comic character of the *Divine Comedy*. (The frightened poet's fainting spells and the convict's nosebleeds should be compared.) Nothing explains the meaning and context of this alternation of a psychological love story and a superhuman nightmare adventure better than Jung's essay. In "Psychology and Poetry" Jung discusses, among other works, *Faust, Thus Spake Zarathustra,* and the *Divine Comedy* in the context of differences between

---

trans.). It is alluded to in "Old Man," as well, where the train the convicts ride travels backwards (69); so does the tall convict's boat (150).

[23] "The fair planet which hearteneth to love was making the whole East to laugh" (*Purg.*, Canto I).

[24] The essay first appeared in English as "Psychology and Poetry," trans. by Eugene Jolas, *transition*, No. 19–20 (June 1930), 23–45. It is perhaps more widely known now under the alternate title "Psychology and Literature" as a chapter in Jung's *Modern Man in Search of a Soul*, trans. W. S. Dell and Cary F. Baynes (first pub. in 1933). The quote appears on page 33 of the *transition* version (which is used here because of the possibility of Faulkner's having read it) discussed below in note 28.

[25] Compare Charon, "with eyes of glowing coal," who in Canto III ferries souls across Acheron, with the captain. Canto IV begins with a "heavy thunder," which calls to mind the single "cannonade of thunder" (157) that marks the convict's arrival on the Father of Waters.

what he calls *psychological* and *visionary* modes of literature. These works, he says, contain a mixture of both modes. They have a realistic, conscious level and a complementary fantastic and subconscious level which serves as virtually undecipherable symbol for the subject of the first level. The *psychological* mode, he writes, "has for material a meaning which moves within the radius of human consciousness, as, for instance, an understanding of life, a shock, the experience of a passion, or human destiny in general." The substance of "psychological artistic creation" comes from "conscious human experience . . . from the psychic foreground of our most intense experiences . . . it is the thing we have always known: passion and its destinies, the destinies and the experience of them by suffering; eternal nature, its beauties and its terrors." [26]

In the *visionary* mode, according to Jung, "everything is reversed." The substance of this experience is "something unknown . . . emerging, as it were, from abysses of pre-historic epochs or from light-worlds and dark-worlds, of super-human nature, a primal experience to which human nature almost threatens to succumb through weakness and incomprehension. Its value and power are based on the fearfulness of the experience which rises, strange and cold, out of timeless depths, a glittering, demonic-grotesque thing, bursting human values and beautiful form, a ghastly-ridiculous skein of the eternal chaos." In this mode, Jung continues, there "are no echoes from the region of human every day life, but dreams, nocturnal fears and ghastly premonitions of psychic darkness come to life." [27]

Jung's categories, even the adjectives he uses to elaborate upon them, perfectly describe the two plots of *The Wild Palms*. "Wild Palms," the main story, the conscious story, is a psychological drama of the tragedy of passionate love and the suffering which follows. "Old Man," the subplot, the counterpoint, flows as an undercurrent, a dark and chaotic superhuman world in which the convict believes a Cosmic Joker toys with his life. "Old Man," as we have seen, is an abstraction that parallels and complements the action of "Wild Palms."

[26] *transition*, 27, 28.
[27] *Ibid.*, 28, 30.

It is not too much to call it the visionary accompaniment to the psychological story that is Faulkner's main concern. Taken together, the two plots reveal the terrific impact of first love experience.

Though the point need not be pushed, there is a chance that Faulkner had, at some time, read Jung's essay.[28] Certainly, given the parallels, Faulkner at least intuited a similar complementary duality out of the works which Jung considered—particularly Dante, and also Nietzsche, as we will see more fully—and he made the effort to put it to use in a different way. In the *Divine Comedy* and *Zarathustra*, Jung implies, the modes are mixed; in *Faust*, Part I is psychological and Part II visionary. Faulkner *alternates* the two "modes" in separate and distinct parts, chapter by chapter. As always in his ambitious experiments with form, he is careful and complex, though the way the book was published—first without its original title and later in texts which separated the tales—caused critics and general readers to miss the significance of his structure for a long time.

[28] Faulkner could have read it in either version at any time prior to writing *The Wild Palms*, of course, since the essay was pretty widely available, but in the early 1930s he was in a good position to come across the June 1930 issue of *transition*. The preceding issue, No. 18, contained a full page advertisement for *The Sound and the Fury*, and both issues carried excerpts from Joyce's "Work in Progress" [*Finnegan's Wake*]. The 1930 issue of *transition* was the last one for two years, and it was the kind of thing literary people would have kept, if only for the Joyce. In 1931 Faulkner visited Charlottesville, to attend the Southern Writers' Meeting; Chapel Hill, where he stayed with the proprietors of the Intimate Bookshop; and New York. Michael Millgate, *The Achievement of William Faulkner* (New York: Random House, 1966), 32–33. The chances of his having seen *transition* and Jung's essay during this trip seem very good.

CHAPTER XI

Conclusion:
Amor Fati Versus
The Will Denied

[S]et free from the miserable striving of the will[,] we keep
the Sabbath of the penal servitude of willing. . . .

SCHOPENHAUER
The World as Will and Idea

   O my brethren, a fresh blustering wind cometh Zarathustra unto all way-weary ones. . . . Even through walls blow-
eth my free breath, and into prisons and imprisoned spirits!

NIETZSCHE
Thus Spake Zarathustra

BOTH STORIES ARE OVER. Harry Wilbourne has brought Charlotte
home to die and has remained to accept a prison term for his part in
her death. The tall convict has surrendered the boat, the woman, and
himself to the authorities. The convict's "attempted escape" that was
no escape suggests that Harry was not fully responsible for the results
of the abortion, as Charlotte believed. Regardless, society and Nature
extract a price in order to balance the books. Like water, the men have
returned to their original level; their adventures have come full circle.
The similarity of the intern's dormitory to the prison bunkhouse emphasizes that for both men the end is a return to the beginning. Their
experiences have been similar, but they each extract a different kind
of knowledge from them. Faulkner confirms the difference by setting
down one more chapter and giving the convict the last speech.

   When Malcolm Cowley corresponded with Faulkner over the selec-

EPIGRAPH: Arthur Schopenhauer, *The World as Will and Idea*, trans. R. B.
Haldane and J. Kemp (London: Routledge and Kegan Paul, 1883), I, 254.
Friedrich Nietzsche, *Thus Spake Zarathustra*, trans. Thomas Common, in *The
Philosophy of Nietzsche* (New York: Modern Library, 1934), 212.

tions for the Viking *Portable Faulkner*, he considered printing all but the final chapter of "Old Man," arguing that the fifth section applied strongly to the novel but seemed superfluous to the story if it were published separately. Faulkner approved, writing, "By all means. The story ends with: 'Here's your boat' etc. Stop it there." [1] His statement does not discount the complex relation of theme, image, structure, plot, and character that connects "Wild Palms" and "Old Man," any more than his preference for removing the fourth section of "The Bear" when it is anthologized separately denies the importance of the remaining four sections to the total texture of the novel *Go Down, Moses*. But what he wrote Cowley does enforce the view that the final episode of "Old Man," and the last chapter of *The Wild Palms*, is crucial to the structure and meaning of the novel.

Faulkner used the term "counterpoint" to describe what he was doing with the alternated plots of *The Wild Palms*. He was fond of another device which may be described by a musical term: the coda, that concluding section of a musical piece which is formally distinct from the rest of the composition. The best example of what might be called a "coda" in Faulkner is the final episode of *Light in August*: the furniture dealer's comic, and bawdily rendered, recounting of his meeting with Byron Bunch and Lena Grove. The interlude with the wild half-Snopes Indian children at the conclusion of *The Town* bears a similar relation to the rest of that novel—comic and different. *Sanctuary* may owe its peculiar ending to the desire for the kind of relief such a form offers. By this, or by less extreme means, Faulkner quite often seeks an altered tone to close his novels: *As I Lay Dying* and *Mosquitoes* both have closing cadences; *Sartoris* and *The Sound and the Fury* and *The Mansion* have the same, though in briefer and more poetic form. The last episode of "Wild Palms" ends with a closing cadence, but then comes the somewhat anticlimactic final chapter of the book. It seems to function as coda and more.

Lest there be any doubt that organized society is corrupt and im-

[1] *The Faulkner-Cowley File*, ed. Malcolm Cowley (New York: Viking, 1966), 55. After getting Faulkner's approval, Cowley changed his mind and printed all five chapters. Cowley's text is a corruption of the first edition; it omits several passages and needlessly revises others.

personal, the opening scene depicts the chicanery of the warden and the governor's emissary as they contrive to save their own political skins at any price. Like the doctors who hide behind professional identities, the "Governor's young man" is just that and no more. He is indifferent and contemptuous toward the people whom he canvasses for votes. He acts not on the basis of humanitarianism or truth, but on the basis of the rules. According to certain papers forwarded to the governor, the tall convict is either dead or free. He cannot be anything else without juggling the whole system. The buck stops with the deputy warden. Since he is ultimately responsible for these so-called facts, he would be the scapegoat, but he has voted the right ticket "three times running through three separate administrations" (327) and, playing by the rules, he has a record that cannot be easily dismissed. They must accommodate him and take enough away from someone else to keep the system in balance. The system works as efficiently and cleanly and impersonally as Nature herself. They promote the deputy into a sinecure, "for meritorious service" (331), thereby reclaiming, in effect, the citation the deputy had suggested for the convict when he was presumed drowned (79–80). To take up the slack and close out the account, the tall convict is given ten additional years of imprisonment. "They are going to have to add ten years to your time," the warden tells him, impersonally (331). The convict has no real choice; he acquiesces: "All right . . . If that's the rule."

Back in his bunk at the prison, the convict is "safe again" (331). Like Harry groping in his memory for the meaning of what has transpired, he tells the rest of his tale, though the others must pump it out of him. He does not know or care whether it has any more meaning than he has extracted already. Responding to the convicts' questions, he finally comes to the part that is crucial for him—there was a woman in it. "He had had a sweetheart. That is, he had gone to church singings and picnics with her—a girl a year or so younger than he, short-legged, with ripe breasts and a heavy mouth and dull eyes like ripe muscadines" (338).[2] It has taken him all this time to realize that "if

[2] Cf. Belle Mitchell (Faulkner, *Sartoris* [New York: Harcourt, Brace, 1929], 183) and Eula Varner (Faulkner, *The Hamlet* [New York: Random House, 1940], 12).

it had not been for her he would not actually have attempted" his absurd crime (338). She married someone else, sending him a card from her honeymoon hotel. But "maybe it wasn't even worth talking about any more," because it was over and "he was safe again" (331). He is glad to be back in his bunk: he lies there, "the cigar burning smoothly and richly in his clean steady hand," calm and peaceful (339). His experiences seem to show him that all life is nothing but a prison. Water held him in its iron grip; women were as dangerous as guns. Taken from this peace against his will, he has returned to it a wiser man. He has participated in symbolic and actual birth. He has responded to the primal lure of sex, which is the basic assertion of the will to live. He has discovered how good it is to create and to earn money. He turns his back on all this; it is not for him. His experiences have taught him what he cannot tolerate and what he cannot do. Alcohol, freedom, and the feminine are anathema to him. When the plump convict casts up the vision of "Ten more years to do without a woman" (339), the tall convict has a word to answer him. One imagines the painful scenes that pass before his mind's eye: his faithless sweetheart, the pregnant hill woman in the boat, the other fellow's wife at the sawmill. One imagines him remembering what he has known, and reconfirmed, about his intolerance for whiskey and about the impossibility of robbing a train. So what he says applies not to any particular woman, but to *women* in the abstract: the female principle: life. As it went in the unbowdlerized typescript: " 'Women, shit,' the tall convict said." [3] It is not even an exclamation.

The ending of *The Wild Palms* does not contrast mere good and bad, and certainly not "primitivism" and "modernism." "Wild Palms" is tragic and "Old Man" is essentially comic, but beneath the surface the same issues and themes are displayed. The force which has held

[3] James B. Meriwether has pointed out to me an interesting analogue in a recent novel by P. G. Wodehouse. After a disillusioning experience and a good ducking at the hands of a female, his character "rose to the surface, spluttering, and for a moment remained spitting out water and regarding his sister with a jaundiced eye as she disappeared. " 'Women!' he said, and not even the philosopher Schopenhauer could have spoken the word with greater bitterness." *Company for Henry* (London: Herbert Jenkins, 1967), 222.

Conclusion: *Amor Fati* versus the Will Denied

Harry captive and swept Charlotte to her death is passion. The force which has carried the tall convict and his companion against their wills down the river is an epochal flood. Passion brings death, ironically, while the destructive flood engenders life. The paradox, however, is apparent and not real. The river was doing what it "liked to do" and what it was meant to do, while the lovers tried to stifle nature in the name of an artificial ideal. The great issue of the novel is life: birth, endurance, death—the recurring cycle of existence and natural order which man thwarts only temporarily and only at his peril. If men had allowed the river to run its course unconfined by frail levees and kept their distance from it, they and their goods would not have perished. If Charlotte and Harry had not desired a love as sterile as the stars, Charlotte would have lived. But if they had not put themselves into jeopardy, if they had not tried to tear their pleasures through the iron gates of life, would the lives they led have been worth it after all?

Schopenhauer's view is that life is miserable as long as man is subject to willing. He swings between pain and boredom in an endless and unsatisfying cycle. The individual dies but new individuals are born to suffer the same fate, to repeat the same disappointments perpetually, so long as will rules. The path to contentment, according to Schopenhauer, is through denial of the will and of life. But Friedrich Nietzsche passed beyond Schopenhauer's pessimism and offered an alternative: it is as natural for man to struggle for mastery of nature (which includes man himself), he says, as it is for nature to assert itself against man. By mastering himself and adapting to his environment, man is able to find joy in life. One must accept the "eternal return" which Schopenhauer regarded so pessimistically; one must invite it, in fact, and through mastery of one life prepare the way for the new mankind to come.

In *The Wild Palms* the circle of eternal return is closed. Harry and the convict have arrived where they started; and, in the words of T. S. Eliot, they know the place for the first time. The tall convict weighs the heavy price of existence against the peace and solitude of his womblike refuge in prison. Holding the cigar which the Warden

183

swapped him for ten additional years of captivity, folded like a foetus between two bunks, he utters the last, Schopenhauerian word on women. Doing so, he illuminates the full meaning of the intern's closing speech and confirms that Harry has taken an alternative attitude toward the difficult round of life. Harry's last speech comes not from Schopenhauer but Nietzsche.

Harry has seen his lover disappear into the awesome facelessness of death. He is tempted by oblivion himself, as well as by a futile escape back into the illusions from which he has—only with great suffering—emerged. He has learned that man cannot be physically free. Both stories point out that the life of the will is a ceaseless struggle rewarded by pain, boredom, and injustice. Suicide offers no escape; it is the quickest means to return to the meaningless round of existence. Looked at from Harry's new point of view, what Rittenmeyer offers him is useless. If Harry were to jump bail he would be fleeing again, and as a fugitive from justice. He has seen the folly of running. Cyanide is no better; he has comprehended the effacement of death. Harry has a clear view of these things because he has learned the true nature and meaning of suffering and grief. He has learned the difference between them. Studying Rittenmeyer's face on the train out of New Orleans, he wondered if the husband's suffering expressed only the "capacity for grief or vanity or self-delusion or perhaps even merely masochism" (55). At the end of the adventure, he imagines Charlotte crying out to Rat: "*Why do you like suffering, when there is so much of it that has to be done, so damned much?*" (223). For Rittenmeyer, suffering is apparently like the suits he wears, the way he behaves, the mask-face he puts on—part of a rigid, artificial code; he finds intrinsic value in it. He behaves like one of those Hemingway characters who, as Faulkner wrote in *Shenandoah*, "made themselves, shaped themselves out of their own clay; their victories and defeats were at the hands of each other, just to prove to themselves or one another how tough they could be." [4] Or, to use Morse Peckham's words, Hemingway and his char-

---

[4] William Faulkner, *Essays, Speeches, and Public Letters*, ed. James B. Meriwether (New York: Random House, 1965), 193.

acters "lived by a code, not because it was a code of right and wrong but simply because it was a code." [5] This perfectly describes Rat Rittenmeyer.

The universe, however, is indifferent to the suffering of the individual. There are only two things that are real: experience and oblivion. But there is also a way to cheat oblivion, and that is what Harry and Charlotte have been trying to do. As Charlotte once said, there must be something beyond the ability "to eat and evacuate and sleep warm so we can get up and eat and evacuate in order to sleep warm again!" (118–19). The tall convict has never had much more than this: he has known chiefly the hill farmer's "niggard fate of hard and unceasing travail not to gain future security ... but just permission to endure and endure to buy air to feel and sun to drink for each's little while" (256). Charlotte wants more—a hope that, in one sense, is wishful, since the romantic code by which she lives is artificial. Like Rat's apparent regard for manly suffering and the tall convict's powerful sense of responsibility to the state, her code brings only self-punishment. The forces that seem to oppose these characters—cosmic jokers and the "They" of bourgeois society—do not exist. There is no one for them to triumph over. Yet there is something one can do to break out of this trap, this mill-race, as Frederick Henry calls it. There is a way to get off the endless wheel of striving, as Schopenhauer conceived it, without accepting that philosopher's life-denying oblivion. In *Absalom, Absalom!* (1936), Judith Sutpen considered the problem in a speech much like one of Harry's. Harry had told himself, "*You are born submerged in anonymous lockstep with the teeming anonymous myriads of your time and generation*" (54). Judith thinks, "You get born and you try this and you dont know why only you keep on trying it and you are born at the same time with a lot of other people, all mixed up with them, like trying to ... move your arms and legs with strings only the same strings are hitched to all the other arms and legs." [6] Life "cant matter ...

[5] Morse Peckham, *Romanticism* (New York: George Braziller, 1965), 31.

[6] William Faulkner, *Absalom, Absalom!* (New York: Random House, 1936), 127.

and yet it must matter"; and then "it's all over and all you have left is a block of stone with scratches on it ... and after a while they dont even remember the name ... and it doesn't matter" (*Abs, Abs*, 127). Judith's solution is to give someone a momento, something that will be passed on. She saves Bon's letter and bequeaths it to the next generation. As Mr. Compson says, she does it "to make that scratch, that undying mark on the blank face of the oblivion to which we are all doomed" (*Abs, Abs*, 129). For the same reason, Cecilia Farmer marks her name and the date into a glass windowpane in *Requiem for a Nun*, to say to eternity: "*Listen, stranger; this was myself: this was I.*" [7] It is an expedient that works. Sutpen, Judith, Rosa Coldfield and many other participants in the fall of the house of Sutpen have made their mark, as the discussions of Quentin and Shreve prove. Even in the iron New England cold, these Southerners live. Cecelia Farmer's presence is also real in the chapter of *Requiem* through which her name runs. It is for the same reason—for this attack upon oblivion—as Faulkner frequently said in essays and interviews, that the artist is impelled to do his work: "Since man is mortal, the only immortality possible for him is to leave something behind him that is immortal since it will always move. This is the artist's way of scribbling 'Kilroy was here' on the wall of the final and irrevocable oblivion through which he must someday pass." [8]

Harry's wishful thinking has included a view of Charlotte's worth: God won't let her perish, he says, because she's too valuable and even the "*one who made everything must fancy some of it enough to want to keep it*" (94). He has learned different. The only chance for permanence either of them has had is to make that mark on the face of oblivion. Where have they done it? Their love affair was doomed to failure, their art was commercial and perverse, their child was killed in the womb. They have, however, marked each other. Charlotte is dead. Only Harry remains. But it is he who is most in-

[7] William Faulkner, *Requiem for a Nun* (New York: Random House, 1951), 262.

[8] *Lion in the Garden: Interviews with William Faulkner, 1926-1962*, ed. James B. Meriwether and Michael Millgate (New York: Random House, 1968), 253. Similar statements occur on pp. 73, 103, 177–78.

Conclusion: *Amor Fati* versus the Will Denied

delibly marked. The Utah cold which left an ineffaceable mark on spirit and memory "like first sex experience or the experience of taking human life" spells out the way in which Charlotte has marked him. She has given him both those experiences. So, as Harry realizes at the end, it is the old flesh after all: his flesh, at least for the time being, holds the memory, the mark. He alone can immortalize Charlotte and their love affair and save her and it from the effacement of the oblivion to which Rat, with his decorous monument, and the world of nature, with its carelessness of the individual, would doom them. He sees what Nietzsche saw, that this is a world "without value, without order, without meaning" and that "only the experience of reality has value, an experience to be achieved by creating illusions so that we may live and by destroying them so we may recover our freedom." [9] Nietzsche wrote that "violating others . . . is the ultimate moral responsibility, for to maintain the tension of human experience, which is to achieve and destroy and re-achieve value, we must violate others—as we violate ourselves." [10]

Harry has seen the illusions which he and Charlotte created shattered and rebuilt and shattered and rebuilt again and again. The tall convict has had a similar experience, but he is not sure his adventures are even worth the telling. Harry discovers that *all* value lies in his memories of the months with Charlotte. He wants to preserve those memories, which he can do only by choosing to live; only the living flesh holds memory, only the person who has been moved and marked, violated, in Nietzsche's phrase, carries the past and keeps it alive.

[9] Peckham, *Romanticism*, 33. Professor Peckham first pointed out to me the Nietzschean alternative in Harry's act. The imagery and numerous statements out of the third book of *Thus Spake Zarathustra* suggest that Faulkner is paraphrasing Nietzsche several places in *The Wild Palms*: "On what bridge does the present pass to the future"; ". . . the charge, the sword of judgment, *the great noon:* much shall be revealed there"; "man is a bridge and not a goal—rejoicing over his noontides and evenings, as advances to new rosy dawns"; "is not everything *at present in flux?* Have not all railings and gangways fallen into the water?" [Nietzsche's italics]. *The Wild Palms* contains a number of important noontides and jonquil or roseate dawns. The bridge the convicts cross on the truck is under water, the one Harry and Charlotte cross leaving New Orleans is in the midst of watery chaos. At turning points, both Harry and the convict look up at bridges painted by dawn light.

[10] Peckham, *Romanticism*, 33.

So Harry rejects Schopenhauer's alternatives—either to plunge into the meaningless illusion naively and repeat the round of suffering or to pierce the veil of Maya to primal reality and accept oblivion. He discovers that there is a fierce joy to life. In his final scene, the wind blows into Harry's cell. It is like Zarathustra's "fresh roaring wind" coming to "prisons and imprisoned spirits." Referring to his hand and evoking the phallus—the specific fleshly parts that have been the means through which Charlotte has marked him: sex and the taking of life—Harry proves that he has learned the lesson of Zarathustra: "willing emancipateth; for willing is creating." He has been taught to redeem his past, "and every 'It was' to transform, until the Will saith: 'But so did I will it! So shall I will it—' " [11] *"Not could. Will. I want to ...if I become not then all of remembering will cease to be.—Yes,* he thought, *between grief and nothing I will take grief"* (324).

William Faulkner had come a long way from the brilliantly depicted but unredeemed wasteland worlds of *The Sound and the Fury* (1929), *As I Lay Dying* (1930), and *Sanctuary* (1931)[12] with which he had begun his greatest decade. In subsequent novels up to 1939, Faulkner's characters make tragic but often successful gestures in the face of oblivion and mortality. In *Light in August* (1932), Joe Christmas achieves apotheosis by the ineffaceable mark he leaves on the men who participate in his death—"They are not to lose it" [13]— and perhaps redeems Gail Hightower from a life of static futility, while Byron Bunch enrolls himself in destiny by accepting the role of Nature's companion and following the fecund Lena Grove. In *Pylon* (1935), most of the gestures seem futile, but the aviators have marked the reporter and achieved thereby a kind of immortality; the incomplete story which he writes but does not file is reconstructed from scraps by a copyboy who, deeply if naively moved, believes he has found "not only news but the beginning of literature." [14] In

[11] *Thus Spake Zarathustra*, 204, 212.
[12] For a discussion of *Sanctuary*'s relevance to this context, see Thomas L. McHaney, "*Sanctuary* and Frazer's Slain Kings," *Mississippi Quarterly*, 24 (Summer 1971), 223–45.
[13] William Faulkner, *Light in August* (New York: Smith and Haas, 1932), 440.
[14] William Faulkner, *Pylon* (New York: Smith and Haas, 1935), 314.

Conclusion: *Amor Fati* versus the Will Denied

Absalom, Absalom! (1936), Sutpen fails to establish his envisioned kingdom on earth and create a legitimate line, but Judith saves Bon's letter and the story of Sutpen lives; not only that, but, also, ironically, so does his illegitimate progeny: "Of course you can't catch him and you don't even always see him and you never will be able to use him," Shreve says. "But you've got him there still. You still hear him at night sometimes. Don't you?" "I think in time," he concludes, "the Jim Bonds are going to conquer the western hemisphere." [15] And in *The Unvanquished* (1938), by repudiating the heritage of violence that is a kind of curse on his family, Bayard Sartoris wins a different laurel from that which the goddess usually bestows. For most of the characters in the important early novels, the world has been a place devoid of meaning and they have not been able to break through and create a viable illusion of their own, but as the decade of the thirties progressed, Faulkner seemed to find ways for his characters to grasp a meaning of their own, however tentative, and to dignify man. They achieved this by virtue of their own conceptions and acts, though there was always the real presence of that which, Faulkner said later, Hemingway's novels lacked: "something somewhere which made them all," [16] a real physical nature that overpowered those who tried to ignore it in their plans.

It was in 1946 in the appendix to the *Portable Faulkner* that the author of *The Wild Palms* set down beneath the name of Dilsey the words "They endured." That phrase and subsequent statements up to and beyond the Nobel Prize address have been interpreted to mean that Faulkner put a premium upon the human ability to bear well the grief and suffering of a difficult existence. But man, he indicated many times, will not only endure life's hardships, he will prevail over them and over his own folly to ennoble his very existence. It was not a cynical playing to the crowd or wishful thinking that inspired Faulkner to these statements about man's potential. He found in history, in himself, and in many of his characters the human qualities that proved his belief. Mink Snopes becomes the hero of the Snopes trilogy and

[15] *Absalom, Absalom!*, 378.
[16] *Essays, Speeches, and Public Letters*, 193.

189

achieves transfiguration as he dies because Faulkner discovered in the seed he had planted in *The Hamlet* a man who could patiently bear unremitting hardship and finally go beyond the passive acceptance of his lot in life. Faulkner explained the human phenomenon of transcendence best in terms of the artist's life in the preface to *The Faulkner Reader* (1954). When he writes, Faulkner said, the artist is "saying No to death for himself by means of the hearts which he has hoped to uplift, or even by means of the mere base glands which he has disturbed to that extent where they can say No to death . . . realizing . . . *At least we are not vegetables because the hearts and glands capable of partaking in this excitement are not those of vegetables, and will, must, endure.*" [17]

In *The Wild Palms*, Harry Wilbourne's act and the philosophical implications behind it seem to be Faulkner's first full expression of this idea. It seems appropriate that he found the characters and events he needed to dramatize his philosophy in a novel which has so much biographical significance for him and for his artistry. It is a needless oversimplification to say that Faulkner simply borrowed a "philosophy" from Schopenhauer and Nietzsche to put into the mouths or behind the actions of his characters, but the evidence that he deliberately alluded to them both is strong. The situation with his use of Bergson's concept of Time or Freud's theories of consciousness and dreams is similar; his published works and statements provide indisputable evidence of influence, though they do not point directly to specific sources. But like the work of Freud and Bergson, the ideas of Schopenhauer and Nietzsche were very much in the air when Faulkner was making himself into a literary artist. Translations, interpretations, and summaries were widely available, even in popular American magazines, and there was considerable poetry and fiction which would have brought all four influences—and many more of the ideas and literary practices that constituted modernism in the arts—to his attention. D. H. Lawrence and T. E. Lawrence; Hardy; Proust; Thomas Mann; Joyce and Eliot; and O'Neill come immedi-

[17] *Ibid.*, 181–82.

ately to mind and there were more.[18] These novelists and poets who used popular psychological and philosophical concepts may have provided Faulkner with images and themes and phrases for ideas already in his mind; they may have sent him, as is quite likely, to the originals. But early in his career the ideas he could have gotten from Schopenhauer and Nietzsche particularly may have been difficult, given his view of the human lives around him, to dramatize honestly in his fiction. Still, *The Wild Palms* is not the first place to look in Faulkner's fiction for a conception of existence that is compatible with Bergson or Freud or Schopenhauer or Nietzsche. One may go to *The Sound and the Fury* for fictional images of Bergsonian time and Nietzschean *amor fati* in a world as sad as Schopenhauer's. *Light in August* and *Absalom, Absalom!* portray life in themes, images, and symbols which are even more in accord with the philosophers mentioned above. In "Sutpen's Garden," H. L. Weatherby writes that Quentin, in *Absalom, Absalom!* "seems to have discovered something very much like Schopenhauer's irreconcilable struggle between Will and Idea, which is, of course, the sort of thing his father keeps harping on." Mr. Compson demonstrates the impossibility, in Schopenhauer's world, of the mind imposing order upon the mindless flux of which it is a mere part, the life force which has created the individual himself. "There is no peace for Schopenhauer's Will, for it is by nature hostile to the static form which it creates. Consequently there is no peace for man as long as he remains alive, because the very nature of life is self-contradictory." Quentin, Weatherby goes on to say, is not alone among Faulkner's characters as victim of the World as Will; he contrasts Ike McCaslin and Lucas Beauchamp and, un-

---

[18] See Patrick Bridgwater, *Nietzsche in Anglosaxony: A Study of Nietzsche's Impact on English and American Literature* (Leicester, England: Leicester University Press, 1972); "Nietzsche and the Will to Power," 104–11 in Jeffrey Meyers' *The Wounded Spirit: A Study of Seven Pillars of Wisdom* (London: Martin Brian and O'Keeffe, 1973); dissertations on Faulkner and Bergson by Shirley Callen, "Bergsonian Dynamism in the Writings of William Faulkner" (Tulane, 1962), and Susan Parr, " 'And By Bergson, Obviously,' Faulkner's *The Sound and the Fury, As I Lay Dying,* and *Absalom, Absalom!* from a Bergsonian Perspective" (University of Wisconsin, 1972).

awares, provides an analogue to Harry Wilbourne and the tall convict. Weatherby says rightly that Ike "gives up both women and the land in a kind of Schopenhauerian denial of the will to live," but he thinks that Lucas's story is merely a "comic version of the whole dark McCaslin drama." Lucas, however, is like Harry Wilbourne; he chooses life, with all its hardship and folly. Unlike Ike, Lucas never has any illusory sense of his "freedom," for no man is free, as Cass tries to tell Ike; there are irrevocable responsibilities and an interdependence that reaches backward and forward in time. Man can meet his responsibilities; he can bear his trials and even transcend them; he can, if he will, make the world a little better than he found it. Weatherby's insights about the Schopenhauerian parallels he finds in Faulkner go to waste as he tries to interpret *Absalom, Absalom!* and Faulkner in purely Christian terms, concluding that Faulkner might have written a better novel if he had understood Christianity and had allowed the "aristocratic lives" of his characters to stand as "sacraments of, indexes to, the grace, order, and beauty of God." [19]

While he did not exactly deny God—which he conceived in terms of Bergson's creative will—Faulkner believed in man, as he repeatedly showed us. He was a great and an honest artist, and the images of man he often found in his world did not at first make it easy for him to create a fictional portrait that measured up to his belief. He approached the problem again and again, however; and like Dante and Milton and Shakespeare, like Hawthorne and Melville, indeed like most of us, he was quite fascinated at first with man's sad failures to meet his potential for love and sacrifice and creativity and endurance. A recent critic hit close to the mark when he wrote that *Absalom, Absalom!*, like *The Sound and the Fury*, "asserts that the old, mindless, sentient, undreaming meat endures. Yet both novels are composed of and dedicated to the *mind's* search for purpose, meaning,

[19] H. L. Weatherby, "Sutpen's Garden," *Georgia Review*, 21 (Fall 1967), 360, 369. Without expressing an opinion or claiming that Faulkner knew Schopenhauer, H. M. Campbell and Ruel Foster note that Faulkner displays affinities with Schopenhauer by his emphasis upon the primacy of the will and the unconscious life. *William Faulkner: A Critical Appraisal* (Norman, Oklahoma: University of Oklahoma Press, 1951), 42.

Conclusion: *Amor Fati* versus the Will Denied

and truth; how then, one may ask, is the *body's* endurance relevant to that search?" [20] The answer is simple; it is in *The Wild Palms*: Harry Wilbourne discovers that there is no mind/body or spirit/ body duality; the mind and the memory, which have recorded and save all that is worth saving, exist only in the "old meat after all." Death is oblivion and effacement—unless you have touched and marked some other human meat and memory and made it more than vegetable. Memories contain all the immortality that we know.

Harry Wilbourne is not the likeliest hero in fiction (but neither was Shakespeare's young prince of the same first name), yet he makes a choice Faulkner approved: he takes life over death. By contrast, the convict is overwhelmed when he is exposed to the enormity of existence and he retreats into will-lessness. He is an attractive character throughout his comic adventures, but we are not supposed to approve his acceptance of defeat any more than we are to congratulate Ike McCaslin upon the occasion of his own repudiation. Nietzsche put it quite neatly in a short episode of *Thus Spake Zarathustra* entitled "The Shadow." Zarathustra's shadow catches him and complains that, with Zarathustra, he has "wandered about in the remotest, coldest worlds... pushed into all the forbidden, all the worst and furthest... broken up whatever my heart revered; all boundary-stones and statues have I overthrown.... Into the coldest water did I plunge with head and heart." But Truth, says Shadow, kicked him in the face, and now what is left is a "heart weary and flippant; an unstable will." Sadly, Zarathustra replies:

Thou hast had a bad day: see that a still worse evening dost not over-take thee!

To such unsettled ones as thou, seemeth at last even a prisoner blessed. Didst thou ever see how captured criminals sleep? They sleep quietly, they enjoy their new security.

Beware lest in the end a narrow faith capture thee, a hard, rigorous delusion! For now everything that is narrow and fixed seduceth and tempteth thee.[21]

[20] Duncan Aswell, "The Puzzling Design of *Absalom, Absalom!*," *Kenyon Review*, 30 (1968), 84.
[21] *Thus Spake Zarathustra*, 272-75.

In his narrow bunk, the convict, Harry's shadow in this contrapuntal novel, has embraced a narrow faith, while Harry, like Zarathustra, accepts the joy of grief and becomes the master of his world. The convict says No to life; Harry says No to death. No one, least of all William Faulkner, would say that Harry's decision is simple, but, where the alternative to existence is oblivion, it is the only decision a man who would be a man can make.

APPENDIX

Time and Money
in
The Wild Palms

CHRONOLOGY OF "WILD PALMS"

Date	Event	Relevant Quote or Conjecture	Page
[March 20] 1910	Harry born	"Harry's birth in 1910" [For date, see below].	32
1912	Harry orphaned	His "father died two years" after will "dated two days after Harry's birth."	32
post–1912	Charlotte born	In 1937 she is "under twenty-five."	38
[late June] 1935	Harry comes to New Orleans to intern	After graduation, he went "straight to" N.O.; that was twenty months from time of his twenty-seventh birthday, which is therefore late March.	33 84, 85 283
[March 20] 1937	H. meets C.	His birthday. "I'm twenty-seven years old."	39
[March 22] 1937	H. visits the Rittenmeyers	"Two evenings later he went to dinner."	42
[between March 22 and May 1]	5 meetings in town by lovers	"During the next six weeks they met five times more."	43
[April 9] 1937	C. tells Rat about meetings	"At the third of these she said . . . 'I have told Rat.' "	43
[May 1] 1937	Go to cheap hotel; H. finds cash; C. calls him	"The fifth time they did not lunch. They went to a hotel." It is a Saturday [May 1 fell on a Saturday in 1937].	44 51

195

Appendix

[May 2] 1937	H. cuts up wallet	At "four o'clock the next morning."	53
[May 3] 1937	H., C. leave for Chicago	On the "next day at noon."	53
[May 5] 1937	Arrive Chicago	Assuming more than 36 hours by train from N.O. to Chicago in 1937.	
[May 7] 1937	In Chicago hotel	"On the second morning in the Chicago hotel. . ."	81
	C. finds studio apartment; they move in	" 'I've found it.' "	82
		" 'I told the man we would move in today.' "	83
[May 8–13] 1937	H. seeks job	"During the next six days."	84
[May 13] 1937	H. gets position making Wasserman tests; C. calculates the money will last till September	Harry "found a job."	85
		"The figures were cold."	85
[May 16] 1937	C. sculpting	It was "three days later."	86
[May 17] 1937	C. sells figures	On "the afternoon after that."	87
[May 17–June 21] 1937	C. is working; summer almost on them; sales stop	During "the next five weeks."	88
		The "summer season was on now."	89
[August 12] 1937	Makes figures again	"In less than a month . . . her at the bench again."	90
[August 20] 1937	Puppet business ends; Harry loses job	It "was August now."	92
		He "did not tell her about the job for another two weeks."	93
[September 1] 1937	H. tells C. about job; they haven't funds to stay in Chicago	By "the day it would be due there would not be enough to pay the quarter's rent on the first day of September . . . 'you have paid next quarter's rent already.' "	
			94–95

196

Appendix

197

Appendix

[January 16] 1938	H. says his eclipse went 8 months, but the affair had begun mid-March, so it was a total of 9 months [March 20–December 23, 1937]	It " 'began that night in New Orleans when I told her I had twelve hundred dollars and it lasted until ... she told me the store would keep her on' " [May 1–December 23, 1937].	137
[February 1] 1938	Arrive mining camp	" 'Why start out in February to live in a mine shaft in Utah' " [ore train comes in once a month, probably on first, which is also proper time for a job to begin; they have thus spent Jan. 16–Jan. 31 getting to Utah, waiting for train to site of mine, etc.]. " 'I have to make a trip every thirty days ...' Hogben said."	131 179 202
	Bill Buckner is about one month pregnant	" 'Bill turns up a month gone.' "	190
[February 27] 1938	Bill 2 months pregnant; Harry performs abortion	"They had been there a month, it was almost March now."	193
[March 2] 1938	Buckners depart on ore train [30 days since previous trip]	"Three days later."	195
	6 weeks have gone by since H. and C. last made love [*i.e.*, from Chicago]	" 'Six weeks.' "	197
	On this night C. allows douche bag to freeze; now or any time from now she conceives.	" 'That first night alone.' "	205
[March 16] 1938		" 'The toy train hasn't been back since ... two weeks ago.' "	198
[April 1] 1938	Train reappears; Poles leave	Two "weeks later the train did return."	198

Appendix

[April 24] 1938	Buckners' postcard comes [it is 3 weeks old]	One "day about a week before the ore train was due."	204
	C. 16 days late on first period following conception	" 'Sixteen days.' "	205
[May 1] 1938	They leave mine on ore train	"The next week passed."	206
		"Then the ore train came."	209
[May 4] 1938	Leave snow behind	They "rode two nights and a day."	209
[May 6] 1938	Reach San Antonio	" 'My period would come now, tomorrow' " [therefore this is a date roughly 12 or 13 days beyond that point at which she was 16 days late (April 24)].	209
[May 11] 1938	Abortion pills have failed; C. now in her 3rd month of pregnancy [after 2nd period]	After "five days."	216
[May 20] 1938	13 days before 3rd period, when she will be in 4th month and H. will be safe.	" 'She will be in the fourth month soon.' "	217
		It was "thirteen days away" [due ca. June 2].	218
[late May] 1938	H. performs the abortion	[He promised to do it *before* June 2.]	218
	Arrive New Orleans	It was "not yet June" [Though Harry imagines C. saying the abortion was "*a month ago*" (224), he is demonstrably wrong about the passage of time; may be his error, and abortion only ca. a week ago.]	221
[late May]	Go to beach	It was " 'not five months ago' " since they left Chicago [mid-Jan.–late May].	226

199

Appendix

Date	Event	Relevant Quote or Conjecture	Page
		A "full year and better" since their departure from New Orleans [May 3–late May].	221
[late May–early June] 1938	4 days at beach; 1-Rent cottage; 2-Milk truck stops; 3-Doctor's wife sends gumbo; 4-H. comes for doctor; C. dies; first day in jail Rat's first visit	That was "four days ago." "Two mornings ago." It was "made that morning." It was "after midnight." Then "dawn began."	5 8 5 3 307 311
[July] 1938	H. awaits trial	"June . . . became July." The "moon began and waxed nightly."	313 314
[August] 1938	Hurricane's tail hits coast H.'s trial; 22 minutes to get a jury; Rat's 2nd attempt; less than 2 minutes to reach a verdict Rat's 3rd attempt	"That afternoon."	315 317– 321 322

CHRONOLOGY OF "OLD MAN"

Date	Event	Relevant Quote or Conjecture	Page
1902	Tall convict born	In 1927 he is "twenty-five."	249
1920	Commits crime Imprisoned	" 'I was eighteen then.' " He had "arrived shortly after his nineteenth birthday." He had been in "for seven years now."	249 24 72
late April, 1927	Plump convict begins reading Memphis paper flood news	It was "toward the end of April."	28
[May 1] 1927	Headlines 2 in. tall	"Presently it was May." "May, in the flood year 1927."	29 23

200

Appendix

201

Appendix

202

Appendix

Appendix

HARRY'S ACCOUNTING OF MONEY

Income	Expenditure	Balance & Date
$2000 from father's estate, plus $2.00 weekly from sister.	Four years medical education plus train ticket to New Orleans.	
		$1.36 upon arrival in New Orleans (33).
Intern's salary, unspecified.	Room & board. One pack of cigarettes per week. $2.00 per week to repay sister, a sum that is diverted to his weekly meetings with Charlotte for six weeks.	
		$0.00, ca. May 1, 1937. He doesn't even have money for a taxi (50).
$1278.00 found in wallet.	Two tickets to Chicago, including drawing room. Apartment rent and food for summer quarter in Chicago.	
Salary during briefly held hospital job. $188 from Charlotte's figurines.		
		$182.00, late August, 1937 (94). Non-negotiable resources include $300 cashier's check from Rat Rittenmeyer and $125 in savings held by Charlotte, which she invests in photographic venture and evidently loses. $148.00, early September, 1937 (97).

204

Appendix

	Food, drink, taxi fare for Charlotte's "black" celebration.	
0.00		
		$122.00 (97), late September.
	More taxi fare for trip to suburbs and back that same night.	
		$100 plus.
	$100 worth of food for trip to woods; remainder spent on bottle of whiskey, set of paints and drawing pad.	
		$0.00 Labor Day, 1937 (99,102).
One box of food, a gift from Bradley.	Daily eating.	
		Food becomes the equivalent of cash. On November 12, 1937, they have six days of food left (114,116). $25.00 plus "nine dollars and twenty cents' worth of food" (139), late November, 1937.
$25.00 check from McCord, for sale of remainder of Charlotte's figurines.		
Money from Harry's writing and Charlotte's window decorating.	Living expenses. Purchase of typewriter. Christmas presents for Charlotte's children.	
		$185, early February, 1938 (191).
Food from mine commissary, in lieu of payment for abortion.	Daily eating.	
		$185, plus $75 worth of food, ca. March 15, 1938 (198).
$21 cash, realized from sale of remainder of food taken out of commissary.		
		$206 ($185 plus $21), ca. May 1 (209).

Appendix

Cost of travel from Utah
to San Antonio, Texas.

$152, late May (209).

Taxi fare to whore
house, $5.00 for fake
abortion pills, two pints
of whiskey to augment
pills; living expenses in
San Antonio. Travel to
New Orleans.

$48, late May (225).

Purchase of beach chair,
taxi fare to Rat's house
and train station; train
fare to Pascagoula, Miss.

$30, upon arrival at
realtor's office (7).

$10 rent for beach cabin,
paid in advance.

$20.

Purchase of fish, milk.
$5 to doctor.

Less than $15 (15).

Index

Ahenobarbus. *See* Nero
Aiken, Conrad, appraises *The Wild Palms*, xx
Anderson, Sherwood, works of: *Dark Laughter*, 3–24 *passim*, 34, 74, 81, 83, 84; *Horses and Men*, 18; *Letters of Sherwood Anderson*, 5, 10; "A Meeting South," 5; "Seeds," 122; *Sherwood Anderson's Memoirs*, 9, 11, 19; "They Come Bearing Gifts," 17–18; *The Triumph of the Egg*, 11, 122
Arthurian romance, as prototype for *The Wild Palms*, 52

Babylon, 48; Jewish captivity in, 40, 75, 109
Baird, Helen, 21–24, 45
Baird, Pete, 22*n*
Bates, James W., as basis for Faulkner's characters, 169
Baynes, Cary F., 176
Bayreuth, 120
Beck, Warren, appraises *The Wild Palms*, xx–xxi
Bergson, Henri, xvii, xix, 190, 191
Biblical references in *The Wild Palms*: Abraham, 142; Adam, 91, 93, 134; Adam and Eve, 142; deluge, 142; Dives and Lazarus, 82; Genesis, 134, 142; Hebrews, 109; Isaiah, xiii, 109; Kings, 93; Luke, 82; Matthew, 58, 78, 82; Psalms, xiii, xiv, 36, 40, 119; Revelation, 48, 93; Sermon on the Mount, 78; whore of Babylon, 92–93
Boni and Liveright, 4
Brothers Karamazov, The, xiv, 77–78
Burrow, Trigant, 56*n*, 122

Carter, Hodding, 45
Cerberus, compared to Charlotte's dog, 81
Claflin, Tennessee, 10
Cowley, Malcolm, as Faulkner's editor, xiv, 89, 179–80

Cyrano de Bergerac, symbolic use of in *The Wild Palms*, 76–77, 114

Dante, 35, 63, 72, 82, 87, 127–28, 178, 192
Demeter, compared to Charlotte, 50*n*
Demille, Cecil B., reference to altered by Faulkner, 127–28*n*
Divine Comedy, The, xvi–xvii, 34, 178
  Inferno, 52, 53
    Canto III, 176
    Canto IV, 116, 176
    Canto V, 144
    Canto XII, 65
    Canto XVII, 175–76
  Purgatorio
    Canto I, 176
Doherty, Meta, 25

Eisenstein, Sergei, 35, 127–28*n*
Eliot, T. S., 114, 183, 190
Egeria, as fertility symbol, 112, 115
Emerson, Ralph Waldo
  "Illusions," 30*n*
  "Maia," 30*n*, 85*n*
  "Waldeinsamkeit," 85
Epicurus, philosophy of, 129

Falstaff, Sir John, as symbol in *The Wild Palms*, 76, 118, 171
Faulkner, William, works of: *Absalom, Absalom!*, 32, 33, 51, 68, 96, 105, 107, 185–86, 189, 191, 192; "Ad Astra," 120, 152; "Address upon Receiving the Nobel Prize," xx; "Afternoon of a Cow," 21; *As I Lay Dying*, xvii, 38, 82, 96, 105, 133, 154, 180, 188; *Banjo on My Knee* (film), 153; "The Bear," xiv; "The Beggar," 68, 103; "Beyond," 105; "Carcassonne," 103, 116; *Collected Stories*, 116, 118, 120, 152; *Country Lawyer* (film), 51; "Doctor Martino," 80; "Elmer," xvi, xvii, 22, 43; *Essays, Speeches and Public Letters*, 3, 9, 14, 18, 23, 184, 189; *The Faulkner Reader*, 23, 190;

Index

"Flags in the Dust," 59; *Go Down, Moses*, xiv, 175, 191–92, 193; "Golden Land," 118; *The Hamlet*, xiv, 128, 130, 155, 165, 169, 181, 190; "Honor," 32; *Intruder in the Dust*, 59; *Light in August*, 51, 96, 133, 165, 180, 188, 191; *Lion in the Garden: Interviews with William Faulkner, 1926–1962*, 21, 37, 56, 84, 88, 94–95, 154, 186; *Louisiana Lou* (film), 153–54; *The Mansion*, 61, 84, 133, 180; "Mirrors of Chartres Street," 96; *Miss Zilphia Gant*, 51; *Mosquitoes*, xvi, 3–24 *passim*, 45, 49, 51, 144, 156, 167, 180; "A Note on Sherwood Anderson," 3, 5, 18; *New Orleans Sketches*, 68, 96, 103; "Old Man," xiv, xv, 123, 178–80; "An Odor of Verbena," 20, 43, 157; *Pylon*, 21, 32, 51, 94, 188; *The Portable Faulkner*, xiv, 179–80, 189; *Requiem for a Nun*, 21, 88, 186; review of Hemingway's *The Old Man and the Sea*, 14; *The Reivers*, 133; *Sanctuary*, 19, 23, 38, 96, 133, 188; *Sartoris*, 9, 23, 51, 55, 59, 154, 158, 180, 181; "Shall Not Perish," 154; "Sherwood Anderson," 18–19; *Sherwood Anderson & Other Famous Creoles*, 5; *Soldiers' Pay*, xvii, 4, 51; *The Sound and the Fury*, xvii, 25, 33, 36, 38, 43, 69, 96, 105, 178, 180, 188, 191, 192; "Spotted Horses," xiv; "The Tall Men," 154; *Today We Live* (film), 68; *The Town*, 133, 168, 180; "Two Soldiers," 154; *The Unvanquished*, 9, 12, 20, 43, 81, 125, 157, 165, 189; *William Faulkner: Three Famous Short Novels*, xv; *The Wild Palms*, xiii–xv, 37, 40, 73, 127–28

Feaster, John, uses psychoanalytic approach to "Old Man," 122, 123, 138–40, 148

Frazer, Sir James G., *The Golden Bough*, in *The Wild Palms*, 112–15, 165

Freudianism in *The Wild Palms*, 28, 43, 56*n*, 122, 190, 191

Hamlet, xviii, 124

Hardy, Thomas, 190
Hawthorne, Nathaniel, 192
Heine, Heinrich, 85
Hemingway, Ernest, works of: *Death in the Afternoon*, 17; *A Farewell to Arms*, xvi, 3–24 *passim*, 52, 55, 68, 161–62, 172; "Hills Like White Elephants," 13; *In Our Time*, 4; *Men Without Women*, 13; *The Old Man and the Sea*, 14, 16; "The Short Happy Life of Francis Macomber," 12, 20; "The Snows of Kilimanjaro," 12, 81; *The Sun Also Rises*, 81; *This Spanish Earth* (film), 20; *To Have and To Have Not*, 20; *The Torrents of Spring*, 3, 4, 8, 19
Hermaphroditus and Salmacis, 146
Hollywood, Calif., 20, 51, 52, 54, 127–28
Homer, xvii, 82

If I Forget Thee, Jerusalem, as original title of *The Wild Palms*, xiii, xv, 4, 36, 37, 40, 85, 93, 173
Impressionism, xvii

Joyce, James, xx, 178*n*, 190
Jung, Carl G., xvii, 176–78
Jupiter, 112–13, 115

Lawrence, D. H., 190
Lawrence, T. E., 190
Lilith, 93, 94
Liveright, Horace, 5, 19

Macbeth, 26*n*
Mann, Thomas, 29–30, 31, 56, 101, 129, 190
Masters, Edgar Lee, 10, 11
Maya, veil of, 25–36, 41, 85*n*
Melville, Herman, 41*n*, 192
Meriwether, James B., xiii, xx, 21, 37, 182
Millgate, Michael, 20, 21, 37
Milton, John, 192
Mitchell, Tennessee, 3–24 *passim*, 56, 122
Moorhead, Miss., 62
Mound's Landing, Miss., 45*n*, 62*n*

Nero (Ahenobarbus), 48, 75, 93

208

Index